adobe
photoshop elements
and
adobe
premiere elements

Visual QuickProject Guide Collection

by Nolan Hester, Katherine Ulrich, and Jan Ozer

Peachpit
Press

Adobe Photoshop Elements and Adobe Premiere Elements
Visual QuickProject Guide Collection

Nolan Hester, Katherine Ulrich, and Jan Ozer

Peachpit Press
1249 Eighth Street
Berkeley, CA 94710
510/524-2178
800/283-9444
510/524-2221 (fax)

Find us on the Web at: www.peachpit.com
To report errors, please send a note to errata@peachpit.com

Peachpit Press is a division of Pearson Education

Note: This edition is a collection of these three books, also published by Peachpit Press:

Retouching Photos in Photoshop Elements 4: Visual QuickProject Guide (ISBN 0-321-41248-6)
Copyright © 2006 by Nolan Hester

Creating a Photo Album in Photoshop Elements for Windows: Visual QuickProject Guide (ISBN 0-321-27081-9)
Copyright © 2005 by Katherine Ulrich

Making a Movie in Premiere Elements: Visual QuickProject Guide (ISBN 0-321-32120-0)
Copyright © 2005 by Doceo Publishing

ISBN 0-321-37464-9

9 8 7 6 5 4 3 2 1

Printed and bound in the United States of America

A Note About This Collection

Thank you for purchasing the Adobe Photoshop Elements and Adobe Premiere Elements Visual QuickProject Guide Collection. By combining three books into one, you save money and learn just what you need to get the job done.

Retouching Photos in Photoshop Elements 4: Visual QuickProject Guide is the first book in this combined volume, with the index for the book following immediately after the text. This is followed by Creating a Photo Album in Photoshop Elements for Windows: Visual QuickProject Guide and Making a Movie in Premiere Elements: Visual QuickProject Guide, with their respective indexes following immediately after each book, as well.

Full-color projects
from the folks
who bring you
Visual QuickStart
Guides...

 Visual QuickProject

Retouching Photos in
Photoshop Elements 4

NOLAN HESTER

retouching photos
in photoshop
elements 4

Visual QuickProject Guide

by Nolan Hester

Peachpit Press

Visual QuickProject Guide
Retouching Photos in Photoshop Elements 4
Nolan Hester

Peachpit Press

1249 Eighth Street
Berkeley, CA 94710
510/524-2178
800/283-9444
510/524-2221 (fax)

Find us on the Web at: www.peachpit.com
To report errors, please send a note to errata@peachpit.com
Peachpit Press is a division of Pearson Education

Editor: Nancy Davis
Production Coordinator: David Van Ness
Compositor: David Van Ness
Proofreader: Tracy D. O'Connell
Indexer: Emily Glossbrenner
Cover design: Peachpit Press, Aren Howell
Interior design: Elizabeth Castro
Interior photos: Nolan Hester (except as noted in Special Thanks on page iv)
Cover photo credit: Photodisc

ISBN 0-321-41248-6

Printed and bound in the United States of America

This one's for Laika, a true-eyed soul.

Special Thanks to...

Nancy Davis, my beyond-the-call editor, wise counsel, and friend.

David Van Ness for his deft layouts and calm amid my bookmaking storms.

Nancy Aldrich-Ruenzel, Peachpit's publisher, for making this work-from-home life possible.

And, as always, Mary.

Finally, my thanks to the friends who so kindly let me use their great photos: Ray Montoya (page 3), and Amy and Kelly Oliver (pages 65–66). My heart-felt appreciation also goes to everyone who appears in these photos: the entire Engel clan, Bruce Hammel, Nancy Harbert, Kerry Harder, plus Joshua, Jacob, and Soli. Thanks as well to the beauty of the Colorado Plateau, eastern France, New England, and to New Orleans— may she rise again.

contents

contents

introduction

The Visual QuickProject Guide that you hold in your hands offers a unique way to learn about new technologies. Instead of drowning you in theoretical possibilities and lengthy explanations, this Visual QuickProject Guide uses big, color illustrations coupled with clear, concise step-by-step instructions to show you how to complete each photo retouching project in less than an hour.

In this book you'll be retouching your photos using Adobe Photoshop Elements 4, one of the most powerful, yet easy to use image editing programs available. Each chapter walks you through fixing some of the most common—and often bedeviling—problems you'll encounter when working on your photos. By the end of the book, you'll not only know how to deal with these problems, you'll also understand which tools work best in each situation and how to work quickly and efficiently.

Aside from Adobe Photoshop Elements 4, your Windows computer must be running Microsoft Windows XP Professional or Home Edition with Service Pack 2.

Adobe has improved Photoshop Elements 4 with lots of little tweaks. Major new features are highlighted with NEW. Examples include the Magic Selection Brush (page 54) and the Magic Extractor Tool (page 101).

You'll find all the example files used in the book—including before and after versions of the photos—at this book's companion site http://www.waywest. net/psevqj/. The site also includes corrections for any mistakes that might be found after the book was printed.

you'll create

These two pages represent just some of the photo problems you'll learn how to solve.

Use Elements to quickly fix red eye, a common problem when photographing people with a flash at night or in a darkened room. (See page 19.)

The Auto button, found in the Quick Fix mode, lets you quickly rebalance an over- or under exposed photo. (See page 28.)

The Standard Edit mode's various tools gives you far more precise control over a photo's shadows and highlights. (See page 54.)

Easily restore distorted skin tones by adjusting Saturation, Hue, Temperature, and Lightness. (See page 69.)

Rescue torn or faded heirloom photos with some of the advanced tools in Elements. (See page 85.)

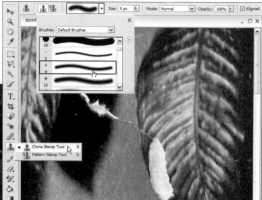

Stitch together a series of side-by-side photos to create wonderfully detailed panoramas that look great as large prints. (See page 111.)

introduction

how this book works

The title explains what is covered in that section.

Significant new features in Photoshop Elements 4 are highlighted with **NEW** to alert users of earlier versions of Photoshop Elements.

extract & defringe objects

NEW In the previous section, we carefully removed just the wires while preserving the blue sky. But suppose, we wanted to remove all the sky and work only with the remaining sign and building? The new Magic Extractor is perfect for that sort of task, especially since it includes a Defringe option to automatically remove the boundary fringe of pixels often mistakenly selected with an object. (See extra bits on page 115.)

Numbered steps lead you through the sequence of actions, showing only the details you really need.

1 Open a photo from which you want to extract a particular area. In our example, we'll start by opening the same wire-free photo we created on pages 98–100. Choose Image > Magic Extractor and the image appears within the Magic Extractor dialog box.

2 The Foreground Brush Tool will be selected by default with a Brush Size of 20 pixels.

Screenshots focus on what part of Elements you'll be using for the particular project step.

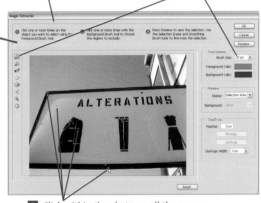

3 Click within the photo on all the areas you want to add to your selection. Each of the areas will be marked by a red dot.

Names of Elements tools, palettes, and any crucial concepts are shown in orange.

repair & transform photos

101

The extra bits section at the end of each chapter contains additional tips and tricks that you might need to know. Read them in tandem with the particular page you're working on.

fix skin tone with mask

extra bits

set color management p. 62

- The Always Optimize Colors for Computer Screens choice makes the most sense when you're creating onscreen slide shows, photos for emailing, posting on the Web, and even ordering prints online. If, however, you always create photos for your own local (desktop) printer then choose Always Optimize for Printing.

adjust with variations p. 65

- It's common to bounce between the Midtones and Saturation choices in the Color Variations dialog box.
- If you have a faded print or slide try boosting the saturation in the Variations dialog box.

fix hue with layer p. 67

- You can readjust the hue/saturation any time by double-clicking the adjustment layer.
- If you want more control, click in the number text window and use the ↑ or ↓ keys to change the number one digit at a time. Use Shift↑ or Shift↓ to move in 10-digit steps.

fix skin tone p. 69

- Feel free to try the new Enhance > Adjust Color > Adjust Color for Skin Tone feature on page 32. In this example, that feature fixed the skin tones—but skewed the color of the flowers.
- With a mask, you can adjust the color and exposure. Depending on which layer you select, you can apply color/lighting changes to the Background or Background copy.
- Depending on the photo, it may be quicker to create the layer mask using the Magic Selection Brush Tool (see page 54–55).

remove color noise p. 74

- The remove color noise feature also can be a lifesaver if you're using a low-resolution camera phone. Faces in particular can wind up looking splotchy.

warm or cool colors p. 76

- While you could apply a warming or cooling filter to the photo's Background layer, the adjustment layer preserves your original pixels.
- Whether you're warming or cooling a photo, feel free to readjust the Density slider from the standard 25 percent. For a realistic effect, keep it below 40 percent.

The heading for each group of tips matches the section title. (The colors are just for decoration and have no hidden meaning.)

Next to the heading there's a page number that also shows which section the tips belong to.

80   adjust colors

the next step

This Visual QuickProject Guide focuses on fixing common exposure problems, repairing damaged photos, a few cool transformation tricks, and then sharing the results with friends and family. It does not dive deep into all the amazing tools and filters packed into Elements. If you want to learn more about them, try Photoshop Elements 4 for Windows: Visual QuickStart Guide, by Craig Hoeschen.

CRAIG HOESCHEN

VISUAL QUICKSTART GUIDE

PHOTOSHOP ELEMENTS
FOR WINDOWS

4

Teach yourself Photoshop Elements the quick and easy This Visual QuickStart *e uses pictures rather than hy explanations. You'll be nd running in no time!*

Creative Techniques

Figure 12.77 This final composite image was created from two separate images.

Figure 12.78 Here, I used a picture of a boy and a photograph of space to create an otherworldly image.

Figure 12.79 Use the Background Eraser tool (or any other selection tool) to isolate your source image.

Creating whimsical composite images

In many cases, as in the previous example, you composite images to improve them in a way that isn't obvious to the viewer. You don't want to draw attention to your work; you just want to improve the image (as in the ship and sky example). But sometimes you want your audience to wonder how you created that cool special effect. This composite for an elementary school astronomy fair poster is an image that looks pretty realistic, if a little fantastical (**Figure 12.77**). (See the color plate section of this book for a full-color view of this task.)

To combine images:

1. Open two images that you want to composite (**Figure 12.78**).

2. Use the selection tools and/or eraser tools to isolate part of the source image. In this case, we'll use the Background Eraser tool to erase the background from the boy, leaving the area around him transparent (**Figure 12.79**). This way, he'll insert nicely into the target image, with no messy halos or edges around his body.

3. Copy the area of the source image that you want to composite.

continues on next page

COMPOSITING IMAGES

391

The Visual QuickStart Guide teaches you step-by-step how to use every aspect of Elements. Its 400-plus pages are packed with clear examples and helpful tips. Like all the books in Peachpit's Visual QuickStart Guide series, it also works as a reference guide when you just need to learn (or remember) the steps for completing a task.

1. getting ready

Part of what makes taking digital photos so much fun is that you can immediately see if you got the shot. Using Adobe Photoshop Elements, you're about to discover the other part of the digital fun: It's easy to make good shots great. You'll learn how to tweak your photos so that they pop off the screen and page. You'll fix not-quite-perfect shots faster than any darkroom technician. And you'll double your skills to create eye-catching photos to share with your family and friends This chapter's quick overview will get you going. Later chapters will cover all the details you'll need to know.

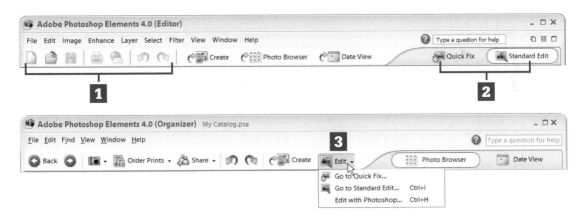

Here are, for example, the shortcuts bars for the Elements Editor (top) and Organizer (bottom). Beyond icons for such basic functions as opening, saving, printing, and undoing mistakes **1**, the Editor's shortcuts bar gives you a quick way to switch between Elements' Quick Fix and Standard Edit modes **2**. The Organizer's shortcuts bar includes buttons for navigating through your photos, ordering prints, sharing them, adding and removing organizing tags, creating multimedia items, and most importantly, switching back to the Editor's Quick Fix and Standard Edit modes **3**.

Welcome screen

When you first launch Elements from your desktop, the Welcome screen appears by default. (See extra bits on page 15.)

You can choose whether to work in the Quick Fix or Standard Edit mode of the Elements Editor. If you prefer, you can launch the Organizer, which offers an easy way to view all your photos and decide which ones need editing. (For more information on the Elements Editor, see the next page; for the Organizer, see page 4.)

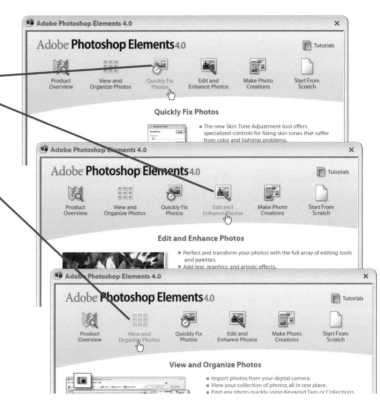

If you are upgrading to Photoshop Elements 4 from version 3, you'll be asked if you want to convert your existing catalog of images. Click OK to begin the conversion, which can take several minutes depending on how many images you've previously catalogued using Elements.

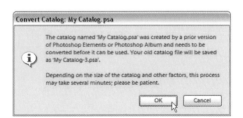

Elements Editor

The Elements Editor offers two modes: Quick Fix and Standard Edit. Quick Fix lets you make simple corrections for the most common photo problems. When you need more control—fine-tuning a particular aspect or changing a selected part of the photo—use Standard Edit.

In both edit modes, the Toolbox runs down the left side of the main window with the related Options Bar across the top of the window. Your choices in the Options Bar change depending on which tool you select.

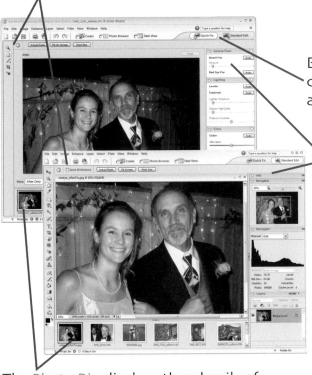

By clicking either tab, you can jump between Quick Fix and Standard Edit.

In Quick Fix, the Palette Bin offers a few simple sliders to fix photos; the Standard Edit palette is packed with controls for more complex fixes. The Quick Fix palette is locked in place, but you can reposition every pane in the Standard Edit palette. (See arrange work space on page 6.)

The Photo Bin displays thumbnails of every photo open at the moment, and puts a blue border around the photo being displayed in the main window. Click another thumbnail to see that photo in the main window.

Elements Organizer

The Organizer gives you a way to quickly find, sort, and label all your photos. Its Photo Browser tab includes the Organizer Bin, which you can use to apply category/subject Tags to individual photos.

Click the drop-down menu to edit a selected photo in the Editor's Quick Fix or Standard Edit mode.

Click the Date View tab to find photos by when they were shot. (See next page.)

The main window displays all your photos or just those matching your search criteria (in this example, the New Orleans tag).

Click the drop-down menu to sort photos with newest first, oldest first, or group by import batch.

Move the slider to change the size of photos in the main window. Click the left button to shrink them as much as possible, the right button to zoom in on just one photo, or the far-right button to trigger a full-screen slide show of all photos in the main window.

Use the Tags tab and its tools to create and apply category/subject labels to photos.

Check boxes to find photos marked with that tag. Check multiple boxes to find photos marked with all those tags.

getting ready

The main Date View window uses thumbnail images to mark days when photos were shot. Use the buttons to move forward or back.

Click to select any day in the main window, or use the forward and back buttons to select another day.

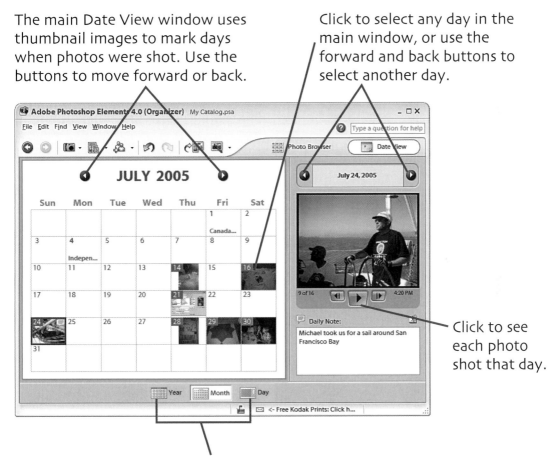

Click to see each photo shot that day.

Use the Year, Month, and Day buttons to widen or narrow your search for photos.

arrange work space

Digital cameras make it so easy to take lots of photos, you'll find yourself using Elements a lot. Make yourself at home—and work more efficiently—by arranging the Editor and Organizer work spaces just as you like. If you're using a laptop with a small screen, you'll find it helpful to collapse the Palette, Photo, and Organizer bins.

In either Quick Fix or Standard Edit mode, you can gain some screen real estate by collapsing the Photo Bin. Click the thin arrow-bar separating the main window from the Photo Bin below. Then, expand your photo to fill the larger main window by choosing Ctrl O. To expand the Palette Bin back to its full size, click the bar again.

Here's another way to collapse or expand any of the bins: click the green arrow at the bottom of the bin. To restore the bin to its full size, just click the arrow again.

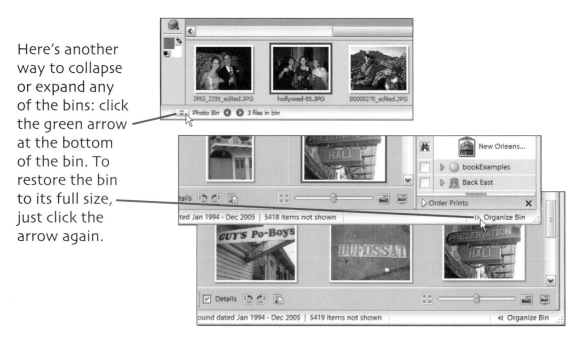

getting ready

Collapsing the Palette Bin or Organizer Bin creates lots of elbow room. As with the Photo Bin, click the thin arrow-bar separating the main window from the bin on the right.

You can then use Ctrl O to expand your photo to fill the expanded main window.

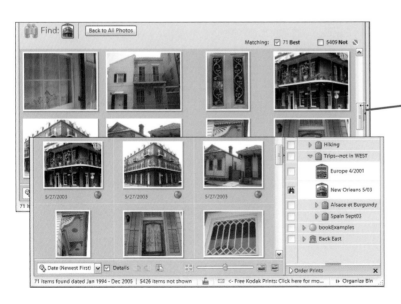

Click the thin arrow-bar again to restore any bin.

getting ready

arrange work space (cont.)

If you only need one or two palettes for the moment, why let the Palette Bin hog your screen? Instead, click the needed palette's top tab, and drag it to a new spot on top of the photo.

Now, collapse the Palette Bin as explained on page 7, and drag it to a new spot.

Then, expand your photo to take advantage of the extra space, using Ctrl O.

Finally, you can hide or reveal the details of any pane in the Editor, or tag in the Organizer, by clicking its triangular arrow.

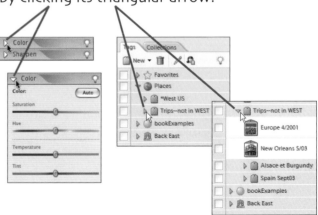

set & calibrate monitor

Most likely your monitor is already set to display colors at its highest quality, but it's best to make sure. Calibration is only possible if you're using a traditional monitor with a cathode ray tube (CRT). It's not practical for an LCD monitor (all laptops or any thin-flat external monitor) because the LCD's apparent brightness changes with your angle of view. (See extra bits on page 15 for a workaround.)

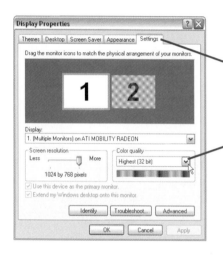

Choose Start > Control Panel > Display, and then click the Settings tab.

Make sure the Color quality panel is set to Highest (32 bit) or True Color (24 bit) and click OK to close.

To calibrate the monitor, choose Start > Control Panel > Adobe Gamma.

If Adobe Gamma is not a choice, do this instead: navigate here on your C hard drive (that's your main drive): ~\C:\Program Files\Common Files\Adobe\Calibration\ and double-click Adobe Gamma.

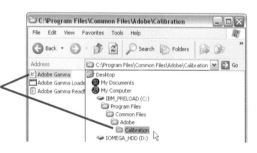

When the Adobe Gamma dialog box appears, choose Step By Step (Wizard), click Next, and follow the instructions.

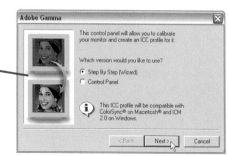

getting ready

get from Organizer

Thanks to its thumbnail images, the Organizer is often the easiest place to find a photo. So it's not surprising that you'll often find yourself wanting to open photos within the Organizer and then switch to the Editor to work on them. (see extra bits on page 16.)

1 If you're in the Editor, click Photo Browser in the Shortcuts bar.

2 If the Organizer is already running, it will appear immediately, otherwise a progress bar will appear while it launches.

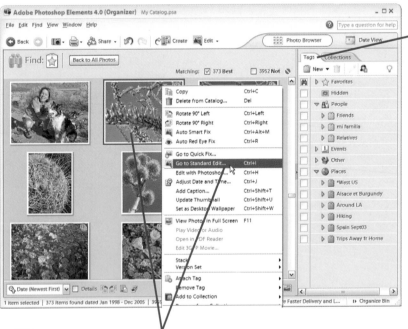

3 You can then use your Tags, or any of the Organizer's many sort tools, to find the photo you want to fix.

4 Once you find the photo, right-click it and choose either Go to Quick Fix or Go to Standard Edit from the drop-down menu. The photo will then appear in the Elements Editor for retouching.

getting ready

get from camera

Make sure your camera or loaded card-reader is connected. (If the Adobe Photo Downloader tries to take over the process, see extra bits on page 16.)

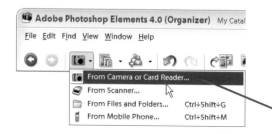

1 Switch from the Elements Editor to its Organizer by clicking the Photo Browser button in the shortcuts bar. When the Organizer appears, click the camera button in the shortcuts bar and choose From Camera or Card Reader in the drop-down menu.

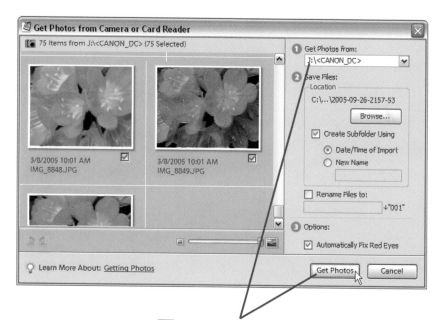

2 Select your camera or card in the Get Photos from drop-down menu and click Get Photos.

get from camera (cont.)

3 The photos will be copied to your computer and a task bar will track their progress.

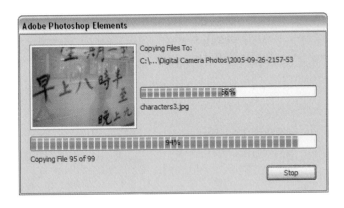

4 Elements will then automatically scan the photos you're importing for instances of red-eye. Just be aware that the dialog box will say it's fixing cases of red-eye even when, as with this landscape photo, there aren't any people.

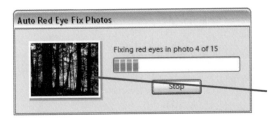

If you want to know if any eyes were fixed, look at this dialog box, which appears after all the photos are imported. Click OK and the photos will appear in the Organizer, where you can open them for retouching in the Editor. (See the third step in get from Organizer on page 10.) (See extra bits on page 16.)

get from scanner

No doubt you have photos not shot with a digital camera that you'd like to fix. A scanner makes it simple to move prints onto your computer. If you've already used a program included with the scanner to import photos, then just follow the steps in get from Organizer on page 10.

1 To import scanner images directly into Elements, switch from the Editor to the Organizer by clicking the Photo Browser button in the shortcuts bar.

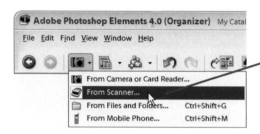

2 When the Organizer appears, click the camera button in the shortcuts bar and choose From Scanner in the drop-down menu. A progress bar will track the scanning. When the import is completed done, the photos will appear in the Organizer, where you can open them for retouching in the Editor. (See the third step in get from Organizer on page 10.)

reformat photos

Most digital cameras save photos as JPEG (or JPG) files because they're compact yet they capture lots of detail. Unfortunately, every time you resave a JPG file, which you'll do as you edit and re-edit, it throws away data. By saving your newly imported photos as TIFF files, you can retouch without losing crucial detail. Later, if you want to send out an email or Web version, Elements can automatically convert the TIFF. (See extra bits on page 16; share photos on page 117.)

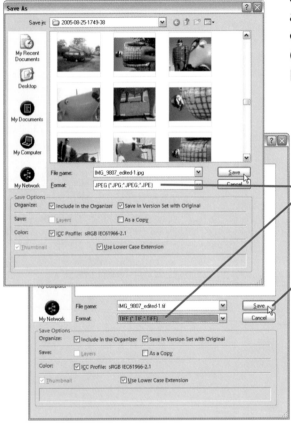

1 Open the photo you want to reformat in the Editor and choose File > Save As. Click the Format drop-down menu to select TIFF, and then click Save.

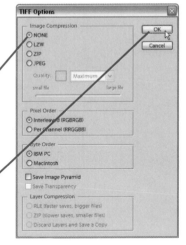

2 In the TIFF Options dialog box, leave the compression set to NONE. Most recent image applications will be able to open the file whether the Byte Order is set to IBM PC or Macintosh, so the choice is yours. Leave everything else as it is and click OK. Now we're ready to start editing in the next chapter!

extra bits

Welcome screen p. 2

- If you want to bypass the Welcome screen and start up directly in the Editor view, click the drop-down menu in the bottom-left and select Editor. Uncheck the Show at Startup box, also at the bottom-left of the Welcome screen.

Elements Editor p. 3

- Clicking the Photo Browser button in the shortcuts bar lets you jump to the Elements Organizer. The Photo Browser, by the way, is not the same thing as the now-retired File Browser found in Elements 3.

set & calibrate monitor p. 9

- Many monitors now are self-calibrating, which makes this step unnecessary. Check your display's manual to make sure.

- If you're using an LCD monitor, open a photo file that has an even range of colors and tones, from bright to dark. Adjust the LCD's angle to minimize any glare or distortion in the image. (In contrast, if you crank the LCD nearly flat you'll see how it distorts the color of the image.) Similarly, work away from bright sun or windows when you're retouching your photos, since that will skew your perception of the image.

- If you're lucky enough to have a CRT and an LCD monitor, run the Elements Editor on the CRT screen for the best results.

extra bits

get from Organizer p. 10

- If you make a point of opening all your photos from within the Organizer, it will automatically keep track of your photos—no matter where they reside on your hard drive.

get from camera p. 11

- When you're getting photos, you may have to battle the Adobe Photo Downloader, which auto-launches whenever you connect a camera or load a flash card. For me, it adds an unwanted step. To disable it, open the Organizer preferences (Edit > Preferences > Camera or Card Reader) and uncheck Use Adobe Photo Down-loader.

- When Elements offers to erase your card after importing photos, click No to avoid accidentally erasing any photos. Reformat the card with your camera, not the computer.

- If you find the new auto red-eye fix feature a bother, you can turn it off by unchecking the box in the Options pane of the Get Photos dialog box.

reformat photos p. 14

- If you're lucky enough to have a newer, high-end digital camera that saves photos in the RAW format, use RAW since it's even better than using TIFF files.

- Be sure to check Include in the Organizer. The photo will be stored with all the other versions of the photo, no matter what their formats.

- Yes, it's tempting, but resist renaming all your images from their arbitrary numbers to some-thing you'll recognize. The whole point of date-and-keyword programs like the Organizer is to make it easy to find your photos, no matter what they're named.

getting ready

2. make quick fixes

The Quick Fix mode helps you correct the most common—and easiest to solve—problems found in photos. Like the Quick Fix pane itself, this chapter starts with general items like rotating and red-eye, then makes lighting and color adjustments, and ends with sharpening. Always work in that order. If you apply sharpening first, for example, your results will not look as good.

Before any fixes, the top-left photo suffers from the usual problems: red-eye, too-dark shadows, overly bright highlights, and a slight color cast.

The lower-right version shows the fixes explained in this chapter. And the fixes really are quick: it only took two minutes to apply them all.

rotate photo

Digital cameras have become so good at sensing when you're shooting a vertical image that you rarely need to manually rotate photos. Still, there's always the exception. Photos can be rotated in Quick Fix mode or Standard Edit mode, though the buttons are available only in Quick Fix. (See extra bits on page 35.)

1 In the Organizer, select the photo you want to rotate, then open it with the Editor by right-clicking the photo and choosing Go to Quick Fix or Go to Standard Edit in the drop-down menu. (Ctrl I takes you directly to the Standard Edit mode.)

2 Click the rotate left or right button just below the main photo window.

3 A progress bar will appear briefly before the photo rotates 90 degrees. Repeat if necessary to properly orient the image.

4 If you change your mind, click Reset and the image will return to its original orientation. Be sure to save your changes (Ctrl S).

make quick fixes

fix flash red eye

Take a flash shot of people in a darkened room and almost inevitably the centers of their eyes will appear blood red. Fortunately, this is easy to fix, especially with the new Auto Red Eye Fix. The red eye tool and technique work the same whether you're in Quick Fix mode or Standard Edit mode. (See extra bits on page 35.)

1 Open the photo you want to fix and set the drop-down menu in the main window to Before and After (Portrait).

2 Select the Zoom tool in the Toolbox.

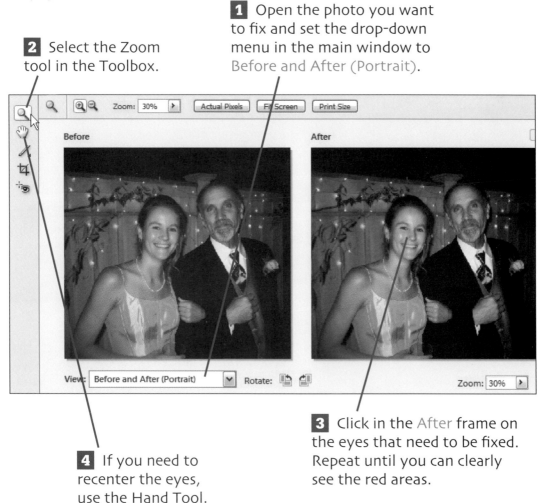

4 If you need to recenter the eyes, use the Hand Tool.

3 Click in the After frame on the eyes that need to be fixed. Repeat until you can clearly see the red areas.

fix flash red eye (cont.)

5 Click the Toolbox's Red Eye Removal tool.

6 NEW Start by clicking Auto, which works amazingly well and just may save you from doing the rest of these steps. Two progress bars will appear briefly as the photo is scanned. If you're not happy with the results of the auto fix, click Reset and see the next step.

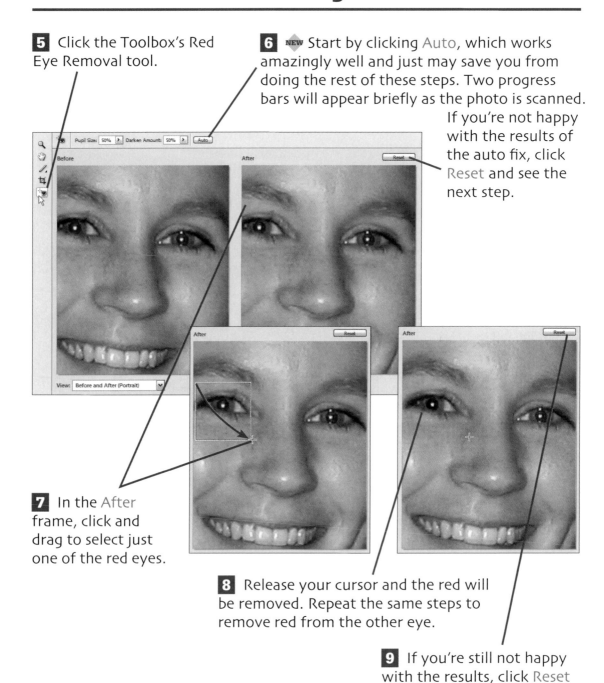

7 In the After frame, click and drag to select just one of the red eyes.

8 Release your cursor and the red will be removed. Repeat the same steps to remove red from the other eye.

9 If you're still not happy with the results, click Reset and see the next step.

make quick fixes

10 The red eye tool sometimes needs a little help finding and removing all the red. By default, the red eye tool is set at 50-50 in the Options Bar, so it darkens exactly half of the pupil's size by half its original darkness (the photo equivalent of an F-stop).

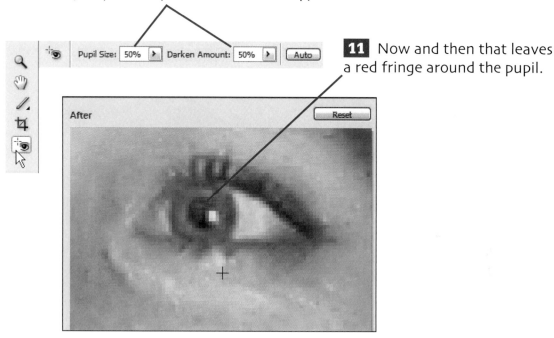

11 Now and then that leaves a red fringe around the pupil.

12 To fix it, click the Pupil Size drop-down menu in the tool's Options Bar and move the slider a little to the right.

13 If you find the tool is turning red eyes pinkish-gray instead of black, drag the Darken Amount slider to the right.

14 When you have finished reapplying the red eye fix, reset the tool, and it will return to the 50-50 default.

make quick fixes

crop photo

Make a rough crop of your photos before you dive into fixing any exposure or color problems. After you've fixed everything else, you can then come back and make a second, final crop to put the borders exactly where you want them. (See extra bits on page 35.)

Open the photo you want to crop in either Quick Fix mode or Standard Edit mode.

The Crop Tool works the same in either mode, though its location in the Toolbox changes.

If you're in Quick Fix mode, use the View drop-down menu to switch to any view other than Before Only, which won't let you crop.

make quick fixes

If you'll eventually want prints of the photo, choose a crop ratio from the Aspect Ratio drop-down menu. In the example, we've chosen 4 x 6 in since that's the most popular print size. (For more on print sizes, see page 118.)

1 Click and drag in the main window, where your aspect ratio will be used as you position the crop box.

2 Release the cursor and, if necessary, click the Hand Tool if you need to reposition the overall position of the crop. (To switch back, click the Crop Tool again.)

3 To resize a particular side, click and drag any corner of the crop box.

5 If you don't like the results, click Reset.

4 To apply the crop, double-click the photo or click the check mark.

use Smart Fix

Smart Fix essentially lets you retouch a photo with a single click. If you don't like the effect, which applies a combination of lighting and color fixes, you can adjust the amount with the slider. If you need more control, see the fix lighting and fix colors sections on pages 28 and 31. (See extra bits on page 35.)

1 Open the photo you want to fix in Quick Fix mode and set the main window's drop-down menu to Before and After (and choose between Portrait or Landscape). Choose the one that best shows the main part of your photo, repositioning if necessary with the Hand and Zoom tools.

2 If the General Fixes pane isn't already show-ing in the Palette Bin, click its triangle.

3 Click Auto to apply the Smart Fix.

Before

After

4 In the example, Smart Fix lightened the black dress a tad too much, making it look gray. We'll click Reset to cancel the effect.

use Smart Fix (cont.)

5 Drag the Amount slider to find the best balance between lightening the dark areas without washing out the light areas.

6 Once you find the right spot for the slider, click the ✔ to apply the effect or press ⏎Enter.

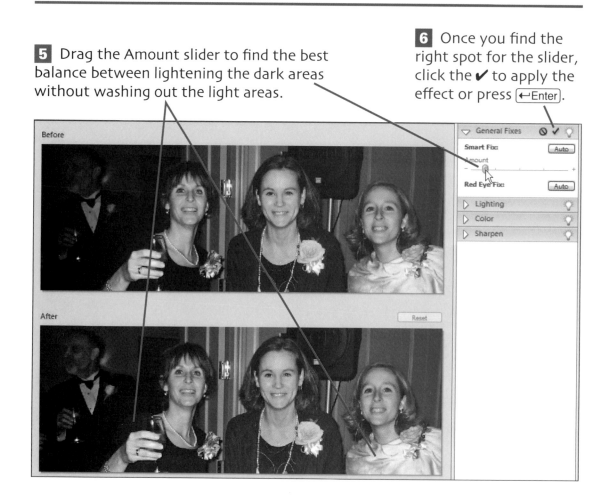

make quick fixes

match the light

Here's a quick bit of background before using the Quick Fix Lighting pane, which controls levels and contrast, two key aspects of your photo's exposure. Levels refer to a photo's overall mix of tones, from light (highlights) to midtones to dark (shadows). Contrast refers to the amount of difference between a photo's lightest and darkest tones.

In the stork photo on the left, there's so little contrast that it's all gray midtones with virtually no highlights or shadows.

The street-scene photo on the right has great contrast, but a skewed mix of lighting levels. Its shadows are too dark to show any detail, while the sun reflecting off the windows is so bright that the highlights are completely washed out.

In general, you want the mix of levels to match the light you saw when you took the shot. That mix, of course, varies from scene to scene. Night scenes naturally have more shadows, mid-day desert scenes more highlights. The Lighting pane cannot work miracles by resurrecting badly exposed photos like these two. But if you start with a halfway decent exposure, the Lighting pane can take your photo the rest of the way.

make quick fixes

fix lighting

When using the Quick Fix Lighting pane, the Levels Auto button will adjust a photo's levels and color. The Contrast Auto button affects only the contrast and leaves the colors unchanged. Feel free to experiment: The difference can be subtle or dramatic, depending on your photo. But if you're happy with the colors, use Contrast Auto, as in the example below.

1 Open the photo you want to fix in Quick Fix mode and set the main window's drop-down menu to Before and After (and choose between Portrait or Landscape). Choose the one that best shows the main part of your photo, repositioning if necessary with the Hand and Zoom tools.

2 If the Lighting pane isn't already showing in the Palette Bin, click its triangle.

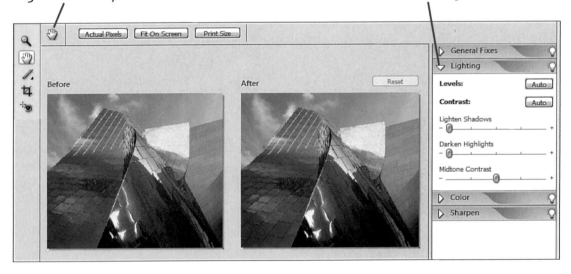

make quick fixes

3 Click Auto to fix the contrast.

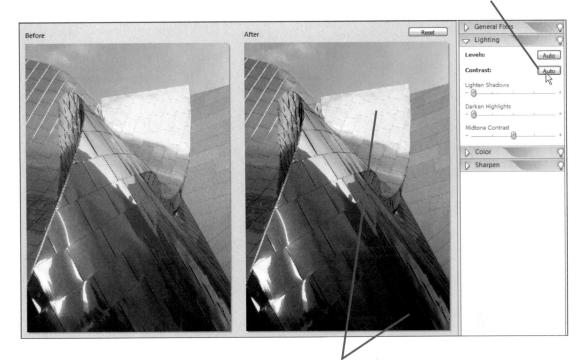

4 In the example, the Quick Fix does a pretty good job reducing the glare off Disney Hall's stainless steel while preserving shadow details. But we can do better.

make quick fixes

fix lighting (cont.)

5 By first dragging the Darken Highlights slider a tiny bit to the right, we take out the last bit of glare.

6 Now Lighten Shadows a bit by dragging that slider to the right. (In both cases, dragging to the right increases the effect; to the left reduces it.)

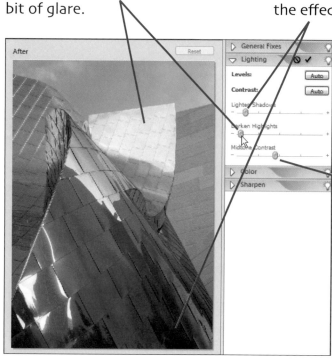

7 By moving the Midtone Contrast slider ever so slightly to the left, the steel's midtones lose any harshness. (This slider normally sits at the middle tick mark.)

8 That's much better than the original image, so apply the change by clicking the ✔ or pressing [←Enter].

fix colors

You'll find that Quick Fix does a fairly good job of adjusting colors. It does this by applying a neutral color cast to the photo's midtones, which is especially helpful if your photo looks too cool (blueish) or too warm (reddish). (See extra bits on page 36.)

1 Open the photo you want to fix in Quick Fix mode and set the main window's drop-down menu to Before and After (and choose between Portrait or Landscape). Choose the one that best shows the main part of your photo, repositioning if necessary with the Hand and Zoom tools.

2 If the Color pane isn't already showing in the Palette Bin, click its triangle.

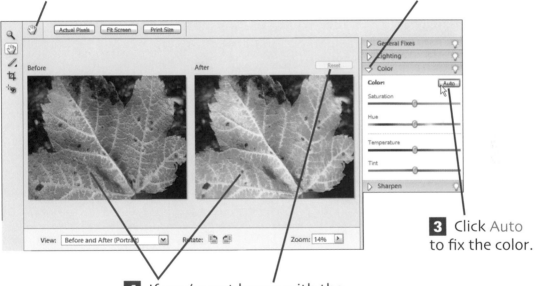

3 Click Auto to fix the color.

4 If you're not happy with the results, click Reset to cancel the effect and see adjust colors on page 61 for a method that offers finer control over colors.

fix skin tones

NEW In Photoshop Elements 4 Adobe has greatly improved how well it adjusts skin tones to make them appear more natural by removing any blue or red tinge from the photo's overall color cast. Amazingly accurate, it takes the guess work out of what had been a frustratingly subtle adjustment.

1 Open the photo you want to fix in Standard Edit mode (Ctrl I) and set the main window's drop-down menu to Before and After (and choose between Portrait or Landscape). Position the photo so that you have a close view of a facial area.

2 From the Enhance menu, choose Adjust Color > Adjust Color for Skin Tone.

3 When the Adjust Color for Skin Tone dialog box appears, use the eye-dropper-shaped cursor to click a representative area of skin (neither flashed nor shadowed).

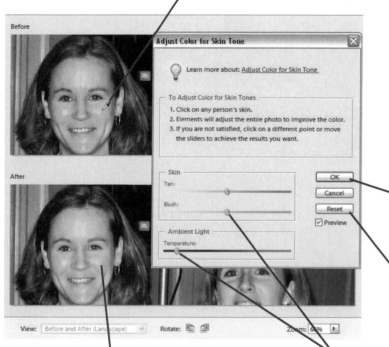

6 If you're happy with the results, click OK and save your changes (Ctrl S). If you want to start fresh with a different skin sample, click Reset.

4 Compare the photo's sometimes-subtle overall color shift in the After window to the Before window.

5 If necessary, use the Skin and Ambient Light sliders to further adjust the color.

make quick fixes

sharpen automatically

It's common for digital photos to lose a bit of sharpness as you work on them. The Sharpen pane helps fix that by increasing the contrast along the edges of objects. But be careful. Too much sharpening will make the photo look fake, as if the foreground objects are pasted onto the background.

1 Open the photo you want to sharpen in Quick Fix mode and set the main window's drop-down menu to Before and After (and choose between Portrait or Landscape). Avoid zooming in very much because you won't be able to accurately judge the effect of the sharpening.

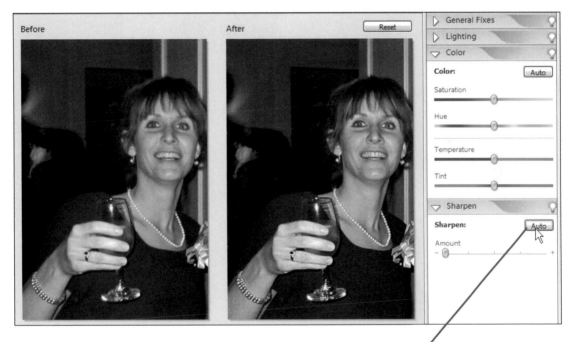

2 If the Sharpen Pane isn't already showing in the Palette Bin, click its triangle. Click Auto to apply the sharpening. The effect should be subtle, adding just a bit of crispness.

sharpen automatically (cont.)

3 You can zoom in to see the effect at the pixel-by-pixel level.

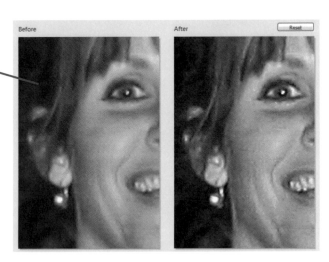

4 By dragging the slider all the way to the right, you can clearly see the speckly distortion created by over sharpening.

5 To cancel, click Reset or the ⊘.

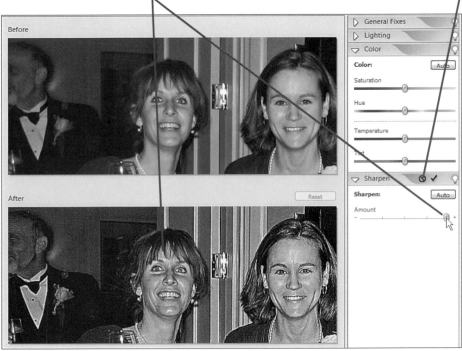

make quick fixes

extra bits

rotate photo p. 18

- To rotate images within Standard Edit mode, choose Image > Rotate and make a choice from the drop-down menu.

- Beyond the standard 90° and 180° button choices, you also can rotate a photo by just a few degrees—extremely handy if the horizon in your landscape shot is a bit crooked. From Quick Fix or Standard Edit modes, choose Image > Rotate > Custom and when the Rotate Canvas dialog box appears, enter a number in the Angle window and click OK.

fix flash red eye p. 19

- More and more digital cameras now have a red-eye reduction flash, which uses a blinking light to shrink the subject's pupil before firing the main flash. You also can reduce red eye by taking pictures at a slight angle to your subject's eyes.

- If you have Elements set to automatically fix red-eye as you import photos (see pages 11–12), then you generally won't need to manually fix red-eye in new photos. But you may still need the feature for any pre-version 4 flash photos in your Elements catalog.

- The red eye tool does not work as consistently if you select both eyes together.

crop photo p. 22

- If possible, it's best to crop your image before shooting by moving closer to your subject. The more you crop after you take the picture, the harder it becomes to produce a big print that's still sharp because, in effect, you're throwing away pixels.

- To cancel the crop before you apply it, click the Options Bar's ⊘ or press Esc.

use Smart Fix p. 24

- While you could use Smart Fix in Standard Edit mode by choosing Enhance from the menu bar, in this case using Quick Fix mode is better since you can compare Before and After views, as well as use the slider adjustment.

- Don't zoom in so close on your Before and After views that you can't see the overall effect of the Smart Fix.

- Clicking Auto repeatedly will only muddy the photo; hit Reset and start fresh.

extra bits

fix colors p. 31

- While the Color pane includes four sliders, they are too sensitive for subtle adjustments, such as skin tones. (For that, use the new fix skin tones feature on page 32.). But the color sliders can be fun for creating surreal colors in non-people photos. For finer control over colors other than skin tones, see adjust colors on page 61.

3. correct exposures

Standard Edit mode offers far more control than Quick Fix mode for correcting a photo's exposure problems. By combining the Levels dialog box, adjustment layers, and a few items from the Toolbox, you can fix even the most challenging exposures.

undo multiple changes

When working in Quick Fix mode, the standard undo command ($Ctrl$$Z$) is all you need. But as you edit your photos in Standard Edit mode you'll quickly learn to appreciate the Undo History palette. As long as you haven't yet saved your edits, the palette lets you step back through all your changes. That frees you to plunge into photo editing's necessary trial-and-error process without fear.

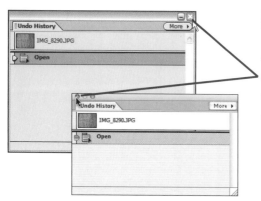

1 In the menu bar, choose Window > Undo History and the Undo History palette will appear in the Palette Bin. If it appears instead as a free-floating palette, click the red button (in the upper right) and it will close and reappear within the Palette Bin.

2 As you make changes to the photo, the Undo History palette tracks the steps.

3 To undo a step or multiple steps, click and drag the palette marker.

4 The photo will immediately reflect the undo—this is useful for comparing the before and after states of a multi-step fix.

correct exposures

lighten shadows

This technique works best in Standard Edit mode, where it's easier to control. We'll start here with the shadows, then fix the highlights on the next page, and if necessary, finish by tweaking the midtone contrast on page 42. (See extra bits on page 59.)

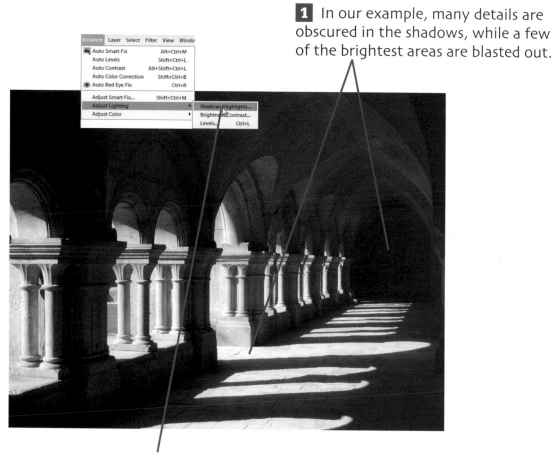

1 In our example, many details are obscured in the shadows, while a few of the brightest areas are blasted out.

2 In Standard Edit mode, open the photo you want to fix and choose Enhance > Adjust Lighting > Shadows/Highlights.

lighten shadows (cont.)

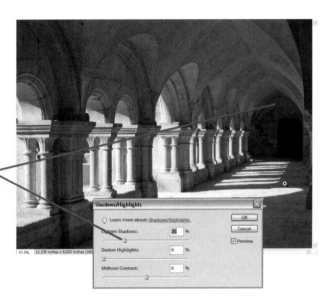

3 When the Shadows/Highlights dialog box opens, it immediately lightens the shadows by the default value of 25 percent. That's too much for this example.

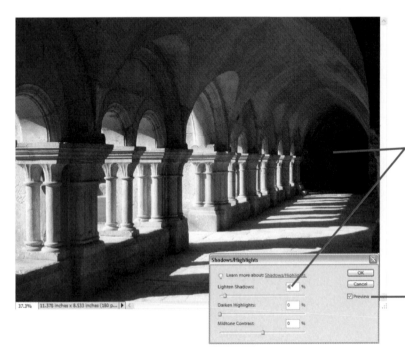

4 Move the Lighten Shadows slider left to 6, which in this case, opens up the shadows without wiping out the dramatic lighting.

5 Use the Preview checkbox to gauge what looks best. Next, we'll fix those highlights.

correct exposures

darken highlights

Sometimes you only need to fix the "hotspots" or highlights in a photo. But if you also need to lighten the photo's shadows, do that first, as explained in lighten shadows on pages 39–40.

1 In Standard Edit mode, open the photo you want to fix and choose Enhance > Adjust Lighting > Shadows/Highlights.

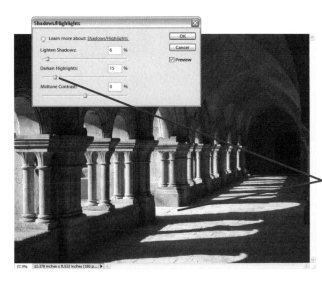

2 When the Shadows/Highlights dialog box opens, the Darken Highlights slider will be at the far left, set at 0. Drag it to the right until the very brightest areas just start to show some detail (in our example, about 15).

3 Be careful not to overcorrect the highlights. In the example, with the slider set to 100, the brightest areas show plenty of detail, but other areas look artificially lit.

We'll finish by adjusting the midtone contrast on the next page.

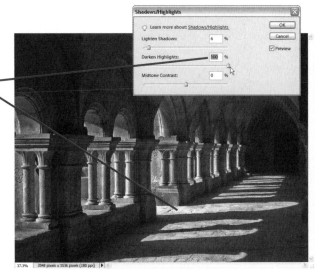

correct exposures

adjust midtones

Even when your photo has a good range of shadows and highlights, it may need a bit more "pop." You can get exactly that by adjusting the brightness of the midtones—without affecting the shadows or highlights.

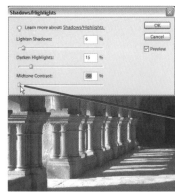

Adjusting the midtone contrast too far in either direction can wreck all your previous fixes in the shadows and highlights.

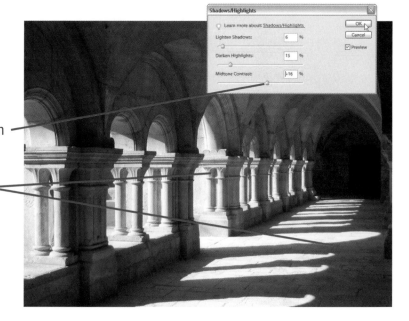

In our example, we've increased the midtone contrast to +16, which preserves the natural-ness of the scene in both the darker and lighter midtones.

Save your fixes and you're done.

correct exposures

read the histogram

As we saw on the previous pages, you can make most basic exposure adjustments with just the Shadows/Highlights dialog box. But if you learn how to read the Photoshop Elements histogram, you'll have a better sense of what's wrong with a problem exposure—and how to fix it. Open the histogram by choosing Window > Histogram and it will appear in the Palette Bin. It might look a bit strange, but it's actually pretty easy to understand. Take a look at the histograms for the next four photos. (See extra bits on page 59.)

From left to right, the histogram shows the range of tones from pure black to pure white.

The top-to-bottom axis shows how much of each tone the photo contains.

This shot of a Utah canyon has few shadows, so it's not surprising that the histogram is weighted toward the right (brighter) side. But notice how the histogram stops short of reaching the far-left side. That means the photo lacks any pure black. On page 50, we'll slightly boost the contrast to improve its tonal range.

read the histogram (cont.)

Dominated by shadows, the histogram for this photo of a French cloister is almost the opposite of the canyon's.

At the far right, you do see a spike of almost pure white, representing the sky.

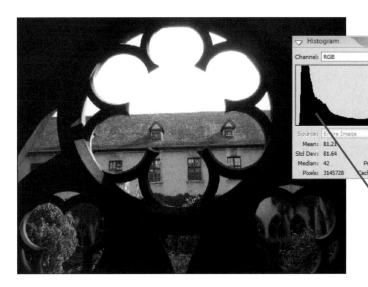

Overall, however, the histogram is skewed to the left, clipping off the black.

As the histogram shows, the photo of the two storks has a full range of tones from pure black to pure white.

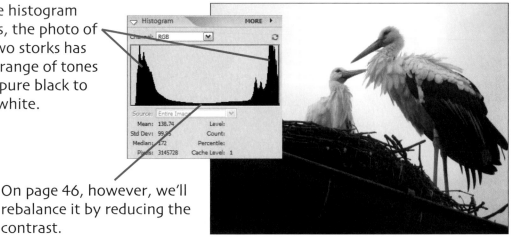

On page 46, however, we'll rebalance it by reducing the contrast.

correct exposures

The flower histogram shows
an almost ideal exposure:
an evenly spread, full range
of tones.

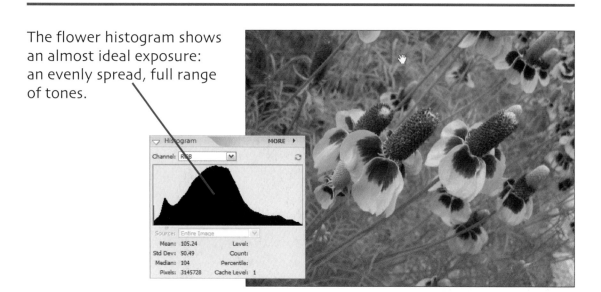

Now that you can read the histogram,
let's use it to fix the stork photo.

reduce contrast

The stork photo on page 44 suffers from too much contrast, with all blacks or whites and few midtones. By watching the histogram as we use the Shadows/Highlights dialog box, we can accurately reduce the contrast.

1 Open the photo you want to fix in Standard Edit mode and make sure the histogram is visible (Window > Histogram). Choose Enhance > Adjust Lighting > Shadows/Highlights.

2 When the Shadows/Highlights dialog box opens, it automatically lightens the shadows by 50 percent.

3 The histogram's gray areas show how the photo's darkest areas were bunched up on the left before the Lighten Shadows adjustment.

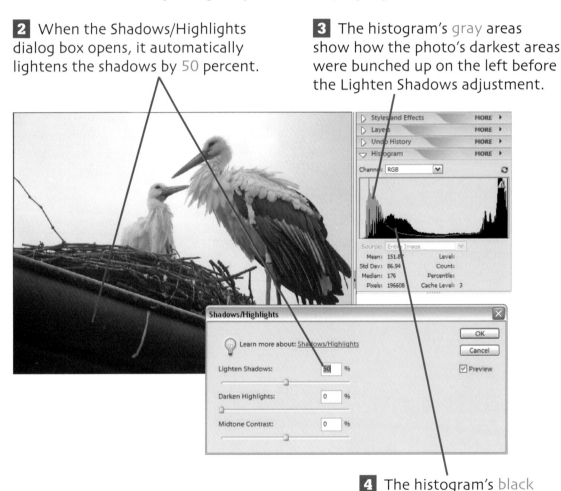

4 The histogram's black areas show the new settings.

5 Because the shadows were lightened a little too much, we'll reduce the setting from 50 to 35 percent, based on some trial and error. We'll also darken the highlights by 9 percent. Most importantly, we'll reduce the Midtone Contrast by 13 percent (−13).

6 The histogram shows that the lightest areas have shifted toward the middle, and the midtones have also increased, compared to the light line marking their original levels.

7 The entire photo is less contrasty, especially in the sky and feathers.

8 While you could make these adjustments by eyeball, the histogram provides feedback that you're on the right track. Save your changes before closing the photo.

use levels

Sometimes, you may need a bit more control than the Shadows/Highlights commands can offer. That's the time to use Elements' Levels command. Take a look at the Levels dialog box for any photo by pressing [Ctrl][L]. The changes in the example photos below are far greater than normal, just to clearly show their effects. (See extra bits on page 59.)

The Levels dialog box has its own histogram, plus sliders and text fields for adjusting a photo's brightness levels.

Before any adjustments are made, the Input Levels are set to 0, 1.00, and 255, which represent respectively the brightness/contrast levels for the shadows, midtones, and highlights.

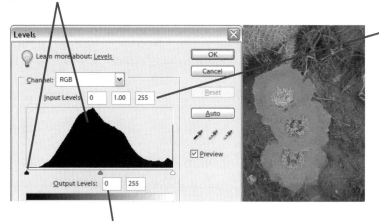

In general, the Output Levels are seldom used to control exposure.

correct exposures

The sliders for the Input Levels control the range of tones (or contrast) in the photo by setting the values for the darkest shadows (the black point) and lightest highlights (the white point). The respective text fields can do the same with more precision.

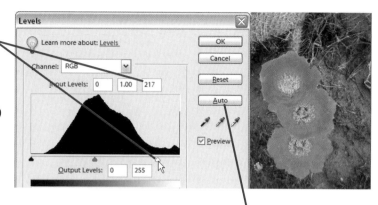

As in Quick Fix mode, the Auto button offers a one-click-to-fix option.

The Input Levels' middle slider (and text field) control the brightness of the photo's midtones—without affecting the shadows or highlights.

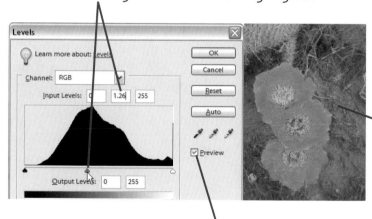

The Preview button lets you compare before and after views of the changes.

Think of the middle slider (the gray one) as the base of a see-saw: Ideally, you position it so that half the histogram's volume sits to the left (the shadows) and half to the right (the highlights). Compare this photo to the one on page 48, and you'll see that the shadow area remains the same while the midtones are brighter.

correct exposures

fix levels with layers

While you can adjust the levels directly, it's much better to do it with an adjustment layer. That's because it lets you change the levels at any time without permanently tossing away any exposure information. If you change the levels directly, the changes are locked in and cannot be tweaked later. Let's see how adjusting the levels can improve the canyon photo on page 43. We'll start by boosting the contrast since the histogram shows few true blacks.

1 In Standard Edit mode, open the photo you want to fix and make sure the Histogram and Layers palettes appear in the Palette Bin (Window > Layers). Click the Adjustment Layer button and choose Levels in the drop-down menu.

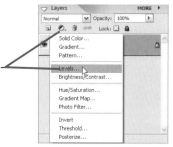

2 Click OK in the dialog box that appears and the new adjustment layer will be automatically selected in the Layers palette and the Levels dialog box will open.

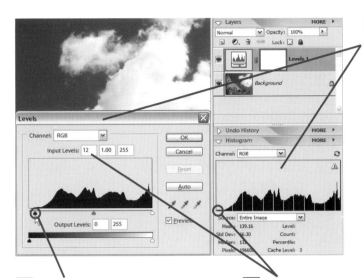

3 Reposition the Levels dialog box so that you can also see the Histogram palette, which will update as you adjust the levels.

4 Drag the black point slider right to where the Levels histogram meets the baseline.

5 Now look at the live Histogram palette and you'll see that the graph has spread to the left edge. This will adjust the previous Input Level of 12 (dark gray) to black (0) and boost the photo's tonal range and contrast.

6 Remember the notion of balancing the histogram on the middle gray slider, like a see-saw? Since we've shifted the photo's overall tonal range slightly to the right, we've also bumped the gray slider slightly right as well (from 1.0 to 1.1), which slightly brightens the midtones.

Be sure to save your work when you're done.

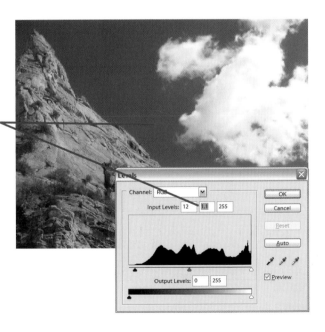

fix flashed-out areas

This photo shows one of the most common flash problems. The powdered sugar of the New Orleans beignet has been blasted by the flash, leaving little detail in the highlights. You can use an adjustment layer to fix it. (See extra bits on page 59.)

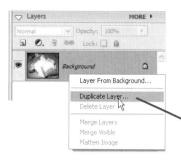

1 Open your flashed-out shot in Standard Edit mode and make sure the Layers palette appears in the Palette Bin (Window > Layers). Right-click the Background layer and choose Duplicate Layer from the drop-down menu.

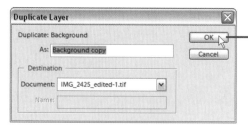

2 Elements names the duplicate Background copy; click OK to close the dialog box and the new layer will be automatically selected in the Layers palette.

3 In the Layers palette, click the Normal drop-down menu and choose Multiply.

correct exposures

4 Any black in the layer is multiplied, darkening the photo overall—along with the flashed-out area. If the flashed-out area was still too bright, you could add another duplicate layer and repeat the multiply effect. Here, however, even a single duplicate layer darkens the photo too much.

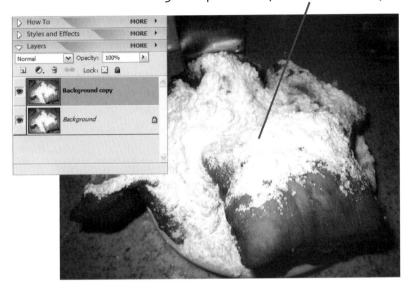

5 To adjust the amount, click the Opacity drop-down menu and drag the slider to the left.

6 In this case, after a bit of trial and error, an opacity of 77 percent looks best.

7 Save the changes when you are done.

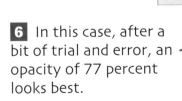

correct exposures

add fill flash

NEW The yucca bloom photo shows what happens when you should use fill flash but forget: the foreground is too dark because the sky threw off the exposure. This too can be fixed using an adjustment layer, along with two tools: the new Magic Selection Brush and the related Selection Brush. (See extra bits on page 59.)

1 Open your photo in Standard Edit mode and make sure the Layers palette appears in the Palette Bin (Window > Layers). Right-click the Background layer and choose Duplicate Layer from the drop-down menu.

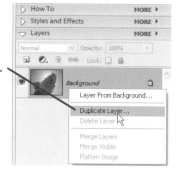

2 Elements names the duplicate Background copy; click OK to close the dialog box and the new layer will be automatically selected in the Layers palette.

3 With the Background copy layer still selected, select the Magic Selection Brush Tool.

4 Use the Options bar to set the brush size relatively large (42).

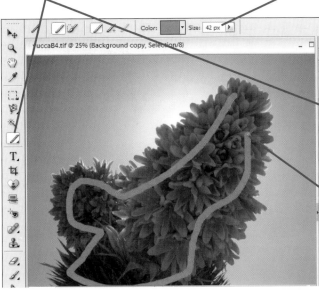

5 Drag the brush over the photo to select the general area where the exposure needs adjusting.

6 Release the cursor to trigger the selection, marked here by a dashed outline.

7 If you need to exclude any areas accidently selected—in this case a bit of sky—first magnify the unwanted area using the Zoom Tool.

add fill flash (cont.)

8 Keep the Background copy layer selected. We need more brush control to exclude that bit of sky, so in the Options bar click the Selection Brush Tool and the subtract-from-selection button.

9 Once you do, photo areas that are not part of the selection will be overlaid with a pink mask, which makes it easier to see what needs to be subtracted from the selection, such as that bit of sky.

10 Use the drop-down menu in the Options bar to choose a small brush (21-pixel diameter) with a soft, rounded-tip, which will avoid drawing a hard line between areas included and excluded (the pink) in the selection. Make several brush strokes to exclude the patch of blue sky.

correct exposures

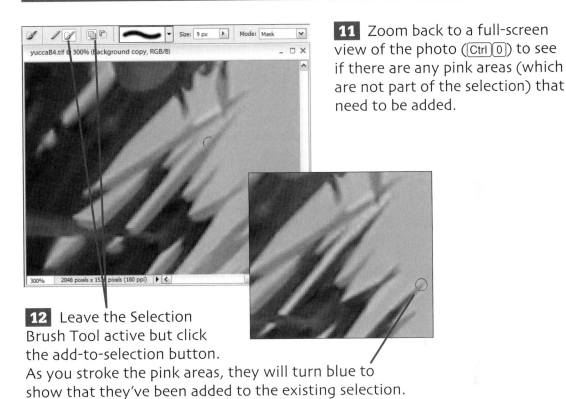

11 Zoom back to a full-screen view of the photo ($\boxed{Ctrl}\boxed{0}$) to see if there are any pink areas (which are not part of the selection) that need to be added.

12 Leave the Selection Brush Tool active but click the add-to-selection button. As you stroke the pink areas, they will turn blue to show that they've been added to the existing selection.

13 Zoom out for another full-screen view ($\boxed{Ctrl}\boxed{0}$) to check if you're happy with the selection. With the Background copy layer still selected, right-click the adjustment layer button and select Levels.

add fill flash (cont.)

14 The new adjustment layer automatically will be named Levels 1. Select the Group With Previous Layer checkbox and click OK to add the layer.

15 The Levels 1 adjustment layer becomes the top layer in the Layers palette with the white area in the mask representing the selection.

16 The Levels dialog box also opens so that you can use the sliders, especially the middle gray slider, to adjust the exposure of your selection. When you're happy with the changes, click OK to close the Levels dialog box. Having added fill flash to the photo, save your work (Ctrl S).

correct exposures

extra bits

lighten shadows p. 39

- Stay away from using the Enhance > Adjust Lighting > Brightness/Contrast control, because its changes do not distinguish between shadows, highlights, and midtones.

- It's hard to adjust the sliders precisely. Instead, click in the number text window and use the ⬆ or ⬇ keys to change the number a digit at a time. Use Shift⬆ or Shift⬇ to move in 10-digit steps. The Lighten Shadows and Darken Highlights sliders also appear in the Quick Fix Lighting pane—but without the text windows.

read the histogram p. 43

- To save memory, Elements does not continuously update the histogram. If a yellow triangle appears, click it to update the histogram's display.

use levels p. 48

- Because the histogram's top-to-bottom axis reflects the amount of each value, the balance point will not always fall halfway between the right and left end points.

fix flashed-out areas p. 52

- Finding the right levels often takes some trial and error. That's the great thing about adjustment layers: You can change your mind. Just double-click the adjustment layer to re-open its Levels dialog box.

add fill flash p. 54

- If you never make mistakes, you could do this without creating a copy of the Background layer. But for the rest of us, working on a copy of the layer helps avoid wiping out the original.

- Even a rough squiggle of the Magic Selection Brush Tool will usually allow it to grab what you need selected. The first time you use the brush, an explanatory dialog box will appear. Select the Don't show again checkbox and click OK to keep it from popping up constantly.

- This layer-and-brush trick works for fixing a portion of a photo. If you need to lighten the entire photo, click the Normal dropdown menu in the Layers palette and choose Screen. The steps from there are the same as fix flashed-out areas—except that it lightens instead of darkens.

4. adjust colors

Most of the time, the colors in your photos are spot on. Still, sometimes even the smartest camera gets fooled. Maybe the white balance is set for outdoors and you're inside, perhaps a flash has turned a scene cold, or nearby objects have reflected odd colors onto faces. Scanned photos or faded family shots may need some correction or rejuvenation. Before using the Standard Edit mode's color tools covered here, first try the Auto button in the Quick Fix Color palette, as explained on page 31. If you haven't already checked your monitor's settings and calibration, see page 9 before digging into this chapter.

set color management

Few things are as subjective as color perception. What's deep blue to you may look purple to me. To cope with this issue, manufacturers have created numerical color profiles for every image source (your computer, scanner, camera) and color output device (monitor or printer). Using this color management feature (sometimes called an ICC profile), Photoshop Elements embeds a color profile in each of your images. It's not perfect, but the idea is to keep colors from fluctuating as your photo moves from camera to monitor to Web page or snapshot.

In Standard Edit mode, press ⇧Shift Ctrl K to open the Color Settings dialog box. By default, No Color Management is selected. See the first extra bit on page 80 to decide which option to choose. In most cases, Always Optimize Colors for Computer Screens is best.

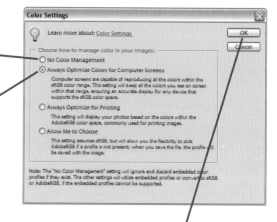

Click OK to close the dialog box and you're set. If you have a photo onscreen, you may notice an immediate, but subtle color shift.

Now, whenever you save a photo, Elements will automatically embed the chosen color profile in the file.

adjust colors

learn color basics

Take a minute to understand how colors are generated and you'll get a head start on how to adjust colors in photos. Three terms are used to describe how we perceive colors: Hue, Saturation, and Brightness, known as the HSB model of color. Hue is what most of us think of as color: red, yellow, blue, green are all different hues. Saturation refers to the vividness or purity of a particular color. Brightness, obviously, depends on how much light or dark a photo contains.

Whether it's on a computer screen or a printed page, a color photo never looks quite as rich as the real thing. That's because our eyes perceive a much greater range of hue, saturation, and brightness than any machine can reproduce. Your computer monitor tries to duplicate that range by mixing red, green, and blue light (using the RGB model) to generate all other colors. Printers take a stab at it by mixing pigments or inks of cyan, magenta, yellow, and black (using the CMYK model). While you might change colors for artistic reasons, the main point of adjusting colors is getting your monitor and/or printer to match the color you saw when you took the photo. To clearly show how hue, saturation, and brightness affect color, the sliders for the photos on this and the next page have been moved beyond the normal adjustment range in the Hue/Saturation dialog box.

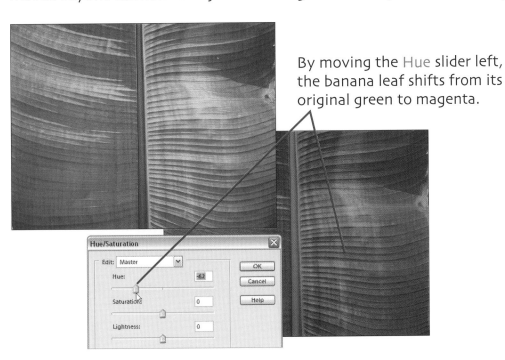

By moving the Hue slider left, the banana leaf shifts from its original green to magenta.

learn color basics (cont.)

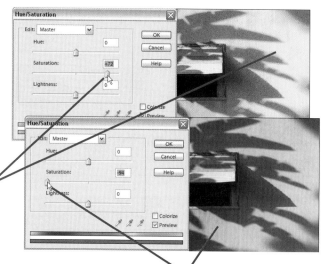

Increasing the Saturation shifts the wall's original light yellow to an orange.

Greatly decreasing the saturation, the wall becomes almost black and white.

The Lightness slider works just as you'd expect: Moving the slider right lightens the photo.

Moving the slider left darkens it.

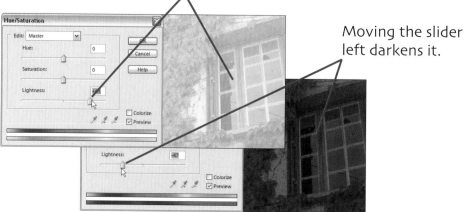

adjust colors

adjust with variations

The Color Variations feature offers a great starting point when you're still getting a feel for how hue, saturation, and brightness affect colors. It lets you compare one choice against another, making it easier to move step-by-step to the right color balance. Use this method for a while and you'll develop a good sense of how to fix a photo's color problems. (See extra bits on page 80.)

1 In Standard Edit mode, open the photo you want to fix, then from the menu bar, choose Enhance > Adjust Color > Color Variations to open the Color Variations dialog box.

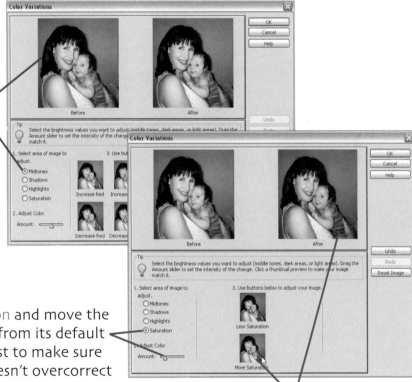

2 Midtones is automatically selected, but our photo looks washed out, so we'll fix that.

3 Select Saturation and move the Amount slider left from its default middle position, just to make sure our adjustment doesn't overcorrect the saturation.

4 Click the More Saturation thumbnail and the After image will reflect the change.

5 Examine the results and, if needed, click the More Saturation thumbnail again. You can click Undo any time to move back a step.

adjust colors

adjust with variations (cont.)

6 Once you've fixed the saturation, reselect Midtones and click the thumbnail that seems to best correct the color (in this case, Decrease Red). You may need to click another thumbnail to fine-tune the adjustment.

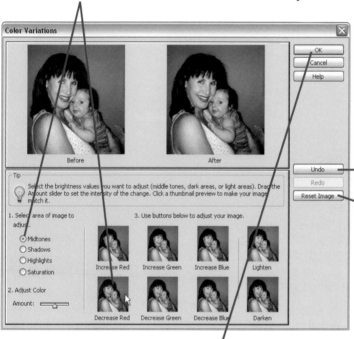

7 Click Undo if you want to go back a step or click Reset Image if you want to start over from the beginning.

8 Once you're happy with the results, click OK to close the dialog box. Be sure to save your changes.

adjust colors

fix hue with layer

Just as we did with levels in the previous chapter, adjustment layers can be used to change the hue, saturation, or brightness while leaving the original photo's pixels untouched. (See extra bits on page 80.)

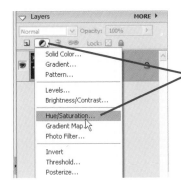

1 In Standard Edit mode, open the photo you want to fix and make sure the Layers palette appears in the Palette Bin (Window > Layers). Click the Adjustment Layer button and choose Hue/Saturation in the drop-down menu.

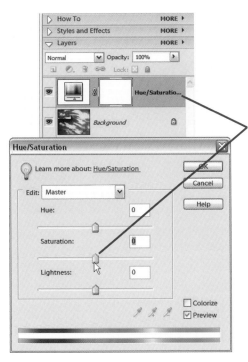

2 Click OK in the dialog box that appears and the new adjustment layer will be selected automatically in the Layers palette and the Hue/Saturation dialog box will open.

fix hue with layer (cont.)

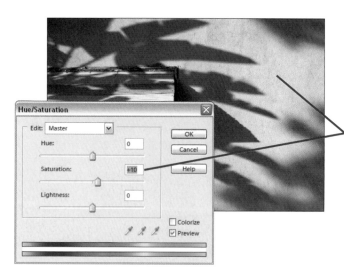

3 Click any of the three sliders or their related text windows to adjust the setting. In this case, the Saturation was boosted to +10 and the photo shows the effect.

4 To see how the change compares to the original photo, uncheck the Preview box and the photo will return to its previous color.

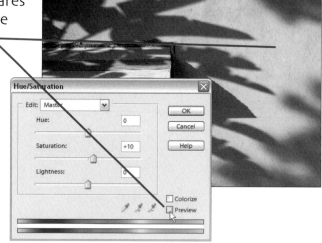

5 Recheck Preview to see the fix. Once you're satisfied with the changes, click OK to close the dialog box. Be sure to save your changes.

adjust colors

fix skin tone with mask

By creating an adjustment layer with a mask (another overlying protective layer), we can apply color fixes to just part of a photo. This is particularly useful when, as in this example, light reflecting off the nearby hydrangeas adds a pink cast to the skin tone. We used this same method to add "fill flash" on page 54. (See extra bits on page 80.)

1 In Standard Edit mode, open your photo and make sure the Layers palette appears in the Palette Bin (Window > Layers). Right-click the Background layer and choose Duplicate Layer from the drop-down menu.

2 Elements will name the duplicate Background copy; click OK to close the dialog box and the new layer will be automatically selected in the Layers palette.

fix skin tone (cont.)

3 With the Background copy layer still selected, choose
Enhance > Adjust Color > Adjust Hue/Saturation (Ctrl U).

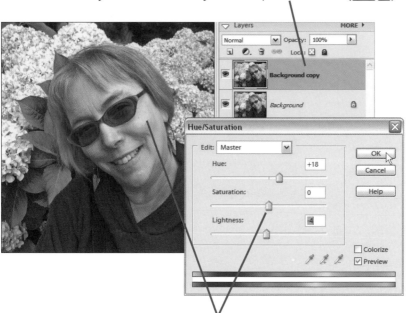

4 When the Hue/Saturation dialog box appears, use all
three sliders, if necessary, to adjust the skin tones to what
looks best in the photo. Don't worry if the non-skin areas
now look wrong. Click OK to close the dialog box.

5 With the Background copy layer still selected in the Layers palette, press Ctrl while clicking the New Layer button.

A new blank Layer 1 will appear between the Background and Background copy layers.

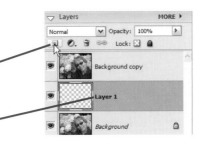

6 Select the Background copy layer again. Press Ctrl G and the Background copy layer will be grouped with Layer 1, as indicated by the downward pointing arrow. For the moment, the photo will return to its original colors. With the two layers grouped, changes to Layer 1 will affect the Background copy layer.

7 Press B to select the Brush Tool in the Toolbox, and set the foreground color to black by clicking the reset icon.

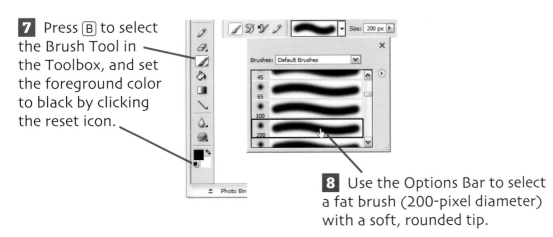

8 Use the Options Bar to select a fat brush (200-pixel diameter) with a soft, rounded tip.

fix skin tone (cont.)

9 In the Layers palette, make sure that the blank Layer 1 is selected.

10 Begin painting in the middle of the skin area.

11 When you're done, the middle layer will show a black area shaped like the area you painted out.

12 The layer mask blocks the face in the Background layer from appearing so that you only see the corrected skin tones in the Background copy.

Be sure to save your changes before closing the photo.

adjust colors

remove color cast

Sometimes a photo has a color cast in which even pure blacks and whites show a bit of color. When importing with a scanner, it's common for the photos to take on a slight blue cast.

When you compare the before and after versions, you realize how much color cast the original contains. In this case, the original has a slight blue-purple cast in the shadows. If you're not sure if a photo has a cast, give it a try since the technique is reversible.

1 In Standard Edit mode, open the photo that you suspect has a color cast. Choose Enhance > Adjust Color > Remove Color Cast to open the Remove Color Cast dialog box. The cursor becomes an eye dropper that you click in a part of the photo that's supposed to be pure white or black.

2 When you click the dropper, any color cast will disappear. If nothing happens, the photo may have no cast. If the photo gains color, you didn't click on a pure black or white spot. Click Reset if you need to start over. Once you've removed the cast—or realized the photo has none—click OK. Save your changes.

adjust colors   **73**

remove color noise

Sometimes photos will show a lot of splotchiness in the sky or other broad patches of color, particularly if you zoom in. Called noise, this splotchiness is the digital equivalent of film grain. As with film, noise is only a problem in low light when your camera's ISO setting exceeds 150. ISO measures light sensitivity, akin to film's old ASA. To gather more light, your camera may automatically boost the ISO—or you do it manually. Either way, you can shoot in less light but at the cost of more noise. Thankfully, the noise is easy to remove. (See extra bits on page 80.)

1 In Standard Edit mode, open the problem photo and, from the menu bar, choose Filter > Noise > Reduce Noise to open the Reduce Noise dialog box. The dialog box's initial settings are applied immediately but we'll adjust them in a second.

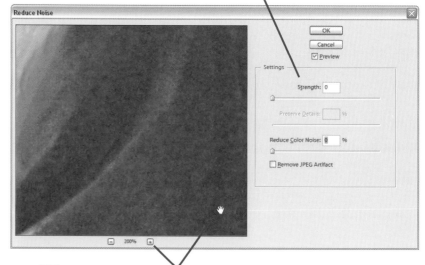

2 First use the Hand Tool and the ⊕ or ⊖ buttons to zero in on the problem area.

adjust colors

3 The trick is to reduce the noise while preserving as much detail as possible. Use the Strength, Preserve Details, and Reduce Color Noise sliders to find the best compromise.

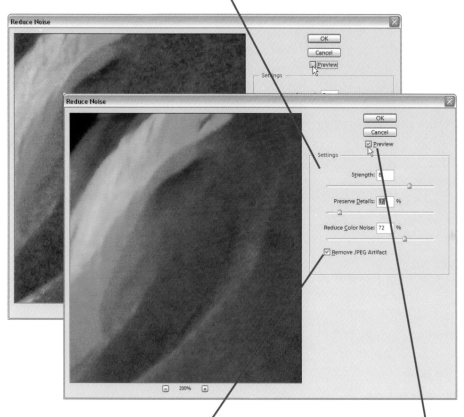

4 If your photo is formatted as a JPG/JPEG image, also try selecting the Remove JPEG Artifact checkbox.

5 Compare the before and after results by checking and unchecking the Preview box.

6 Once you're satisfied, click OK to close the dialog box. Be sure to save your changes.

adjust colors

warm or cool colors

Back in the days of film, photographers had to pay attention to whether they were shooting outdoors or indoors, and whether the lighting was incandescent

or fluorescent. Most digital cameras now have auto white balance, which handles this for you—unless you turn it off. That's one instance when you might need to warm or cool a photo's color. The example photo shows another: on a cloudy day you may need a little warmth to take the shivers off. (See extra bits on page 80.)

1 Open the problem photo in Standard Edit mode and, from the menu bar, choose Layer > New Adjustment Layer > Photo Filter. In the dialog box that appears, check Group With Previous Layer and click OK to create a new adjustment layer named Photo Filter 1. When the Photo Filter dialog box appears, Elements by default immediately applies the Warming Filter (85) at a Density of 25 percent.

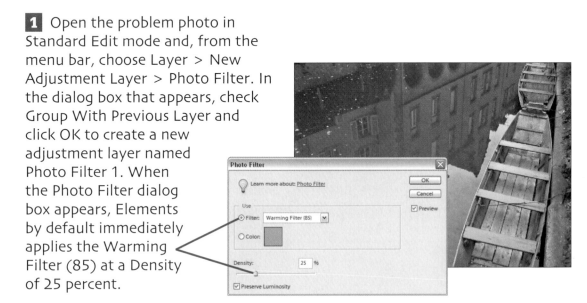

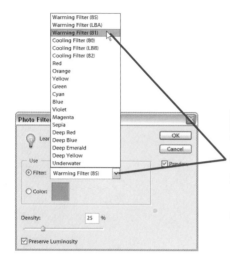

2 For this example, that seems a bit too warm, so click the Filter pop-up menu and choose Warming Filter (81), which is more subdued than Warming Filter (85). If you need to cool a photo, choose one of the two cooling filters. Cooling Filter (80) is more intense (bluer) than Cooling Filter (82).

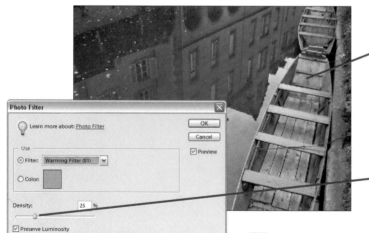

3 Once you choose the new filter, the effect appears immediately in the photo.

4 Adjust the density slider if needed.

5 Once you're satisfied, click OK to apply the change and close the dialog box. Save your changes.

adjust colors

convert colors

In a world awash with color photos, sometimes you can make an image stand out by converting it to a black-and-white shot or an old-fashioned sepia-toned photo.

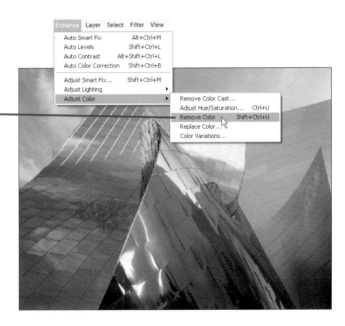

1 Open the photo in Standard Edit mode and, from the menu bar, choose Enhance > Adjust Color > Remove Color. The photo will convert to a gray-scale image.

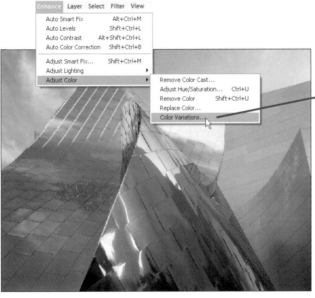

2 From the menu bar, choose Enhance > Adjust Color > Color Variations.

adjust colors

3 In the Color Variations dialog box, Midtones will already be selected.

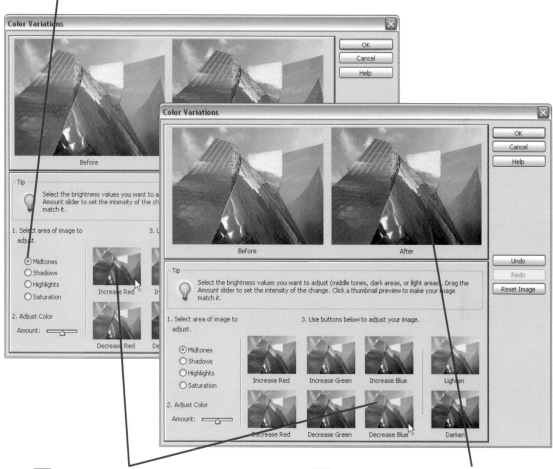

4 Click the Increase Red thumbnail, then the Decrease Blue thumbnail.

5 The now sepia-toned version will appear in the After thumbnail. Tweak the other values if you like.

6 Once you're happy with your adjustments, click OK to close the dialog box. Save your changes.

adjust colors

extra bits

set color management p. 62

- The Always Optimize Colors for Computer Screens choice makes the most sense when you're creating onscreen slide shows, photos for emailing, posting on the Web, and even ordering prints online. If, however, you always create photos for your own local (desktop) printer then choose Always Optimize for Printing.

adjust with variations p. 65

- It's common to bounce between the Midtones and Saturation choices in the Color Variations dialog box.
- If you have a faded print or slide try boosting the saturation in the Variations dialog box.

fix hue with layer p. 67

- You can readjust the hue/saturation any time by double-clicking the adjustment layer.
- If you want more control, click in the number text window and use the ⊕ or ⊖ keys to change the number one digit at a time. Use (Shift)⊕ or (Shift)⊖ to move in 10-digit steps.

fix skin tone p. 69

- Feel free to try the new Enhance > Adjust Color > Adjust Color for Skin Tone feature on page 32. In this example, that feature fixed the skin tones—but skewed the color of the flowers.
- With a mask, you can adjust the color and exposure. Depending on which layer you select, you can apply color/lighting changes to the Background or Background copy.
- Depending on the photo, it may be quicker to create the layer mask using the Magic Selection Brush Tool (see page 54–55).

remove color noise p. 74

- The remove color noise feature also can be a lifesaver if you're using a low-resolution camera phone. Faces in particular can wind up looking splotchy.

warm or cool colors p. 76

- While you could apply a warming or cooling filter to the photo's Background layer, the adjustment layer preserves your original pixels.
- Whether you're warming or cooling a photo, feel free to readjust the Density slider from the standard 25 percent. For a realistic effect, keep it below 40 percent.

adjust colors

5. repair & transform photos

Repairing photos lets you restore something similar to what used to be there. Many of the same repair tools and methods also enable you to transform photos into something not seen when you snapped the picture. Some of the repair techniques require a lot of steps, but they're worth the effort because they'll give you dramatic control over all your photos.

remove dust & scratches

Dust and scratches are a constant problem any time you scan slides or prints. While this example shows dust being removed, the same method can be used for small scratches.

Unmagnified, this slide looks fairly clean.

But when you zoom in, the light sky area is full of junk.

repair & transform photos

While Elements includes a special filter for this (Filter > Noise > Dust & Scratches), it's applied to the entire photo. You could select only the dust areas and then apply the filter, but that's too much trouble.

1 Instead, zoom in on a problem spot in Standard Edit mode.

2 Select the Spot Healing Brush Tool.

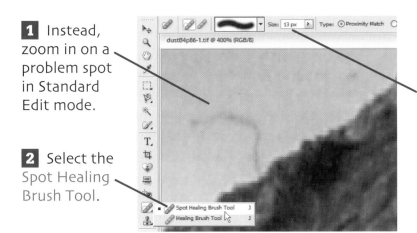

3 Use the Options Bar to pick a soft-edged brush (13 pixels is a good size) and make sure the Type is set to Proximity Match.

4 Position the brush over the dust spot (or in our example, a strand of fuzz).

5 If it's a single spot, click once. If it's a strand, as here, click and drag.

6 Release the cursor and the spot disappears into the surrounding color.

Use the Hand Tool to move to the next bit of dust and repeat the steps above until you've cleaned up all the problem areas. Save your changes.

repair & transform photos

fix blemishes

Fixing blemishes is not much different from eliminating dust spots: The Spot Healing Brush Tool is the best tool for both since you're blending a spot to match its surroundings.

1 Use the Zoom and Hand tools to get close enough to the blemish area that you can see what you're doing.

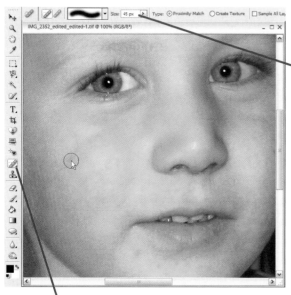

3 Use the Options Bar, pick a soft-edged brush just slightly larger than the blemish (in our example 45 pixels is a good size), and make sure the Type is set to Proximity Match.

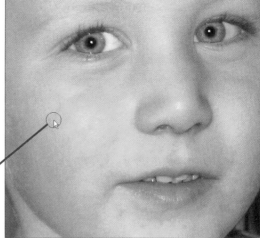

2 Select the Spot Healing Brush Tool.

4 Position the brush over the blemish and click once. The blemish disappears as the area takes on the color of the surrounding area.

Use the Hand Tool to move to the next blemish and repeat the steps above until you've removed the most obvious spots. Save your changes.

repair areas

The Spot Healing Brush Tool performs miracles, but it has limits. Old prints, for example, often have subtle cracks in their finish, which a scanner winds up making even more apparent. The Spot Healing Brush, set to Proximity Match, would duplicate any nearby cracks, making the problem worse. If set to Create Texture, it would erase the cracks—along with all the underlying pixel variation. To repair such damage while preserving the underlying texture, your best bet is the Healing Brush Tool. (See extra bits on page 115.)

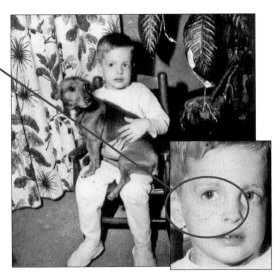

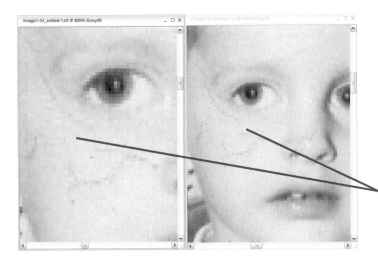

1 From the menu bar, choose View > New Window for Image, which opens a second view of the image. Use the Zoom and Hand tools to position the two windows side by side; one with a pixel-level view of the damage, the other zoomed out enough to give you an overall view of how the fix will look in the final photo.

repair areas (cont.)

2 Select the Healing Brush Tool, which shares a Toolbox berth with the Spot Healing Brush.

3 Use the Options Bar to set the brush's Diameter (fairly small, 5 pixels in our example), Hardness (23 percent is a good place to start), and leave the Mode set at Normal.

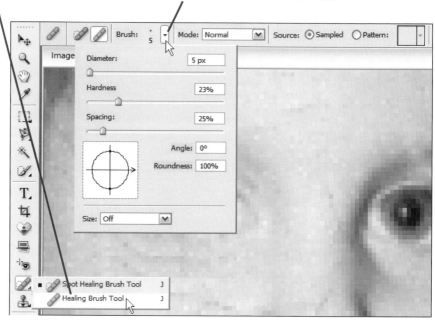

4 While pressing [Alt], click the cursor in an area with the mix of light/dark pixels you want applied to the damage. (Don't worry about matching the color; the tool will perform that magic.) The cursor turns into a cross-hair tool to help you pinpoint exactly what you're sampling. Release the cursor and [Alt] key once you've taken the sample.

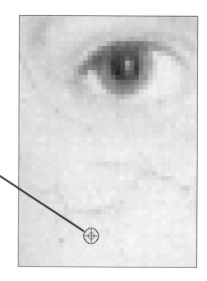

5 Position your cursor over a damaged area and click to repair it. A circle marks where the repair is being applied; a cross marks which pixels are being sampled for the fix.

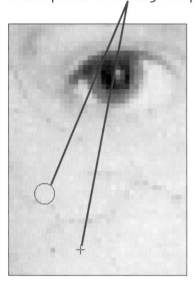

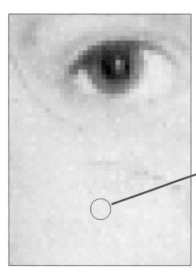

6 Continue applying the repair one click at a time, or click and drag the cursor to fix a whole line at once. When you release the cursor, it may take a second for the fix to be applied.

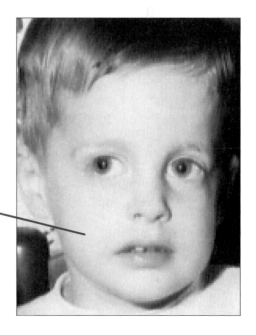

7 When you think you've repaired all the damaged areas, check your second zoomed-out view of the photo to be sure.

Save your changes.

repair & transform photos

restore missing areas

If half a photo is missing, you can't recreate something from nothing. But it's surprising how often you can restore smaller missing areas using the Clone Stamp Tool to duplicate nearby areas bit by bit. In the example, we start by fixing an area of uniform color, then take on a harder-to-fix striped area. (See extra bits on page 114.)

2 Use the Options Bar to pick a small soft-tip brush. In our example, a size 9 pixel brush will work well.

1 Zoom in a bit on the easier-to-fix area and select the Clone Stamp Tool in the Toolbox.

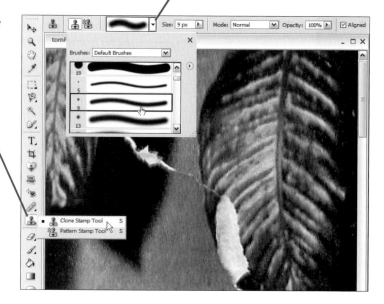

3 While pressing Alt, click the cursor near the damage to grab a similarly colored sample.

4 Release the cursor.

5 Click on the damaged area. A circle marks where the repair is being applied; a cross marks the sample source.

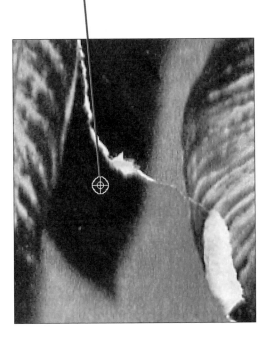

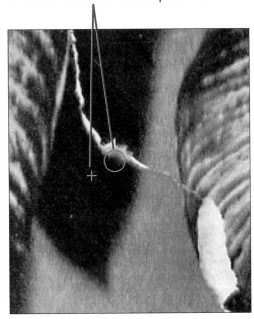

6 Continue applying the sample to the damaged area, either one click at a time or in tiny brush strokes. Resample and repeat the process for other uniformly colored areas.

restore missing areas (cont.)

7 We need to get closer to restore the striped leaf, so choose View > New Window for Image to open a second view of the image. Use the Zoom and Hand tools to position a zoomed-in view next to an overall view.

8 Use the Options Bar to pick a brush with a fuzzy tip in a larger size (21 pixels in our example).

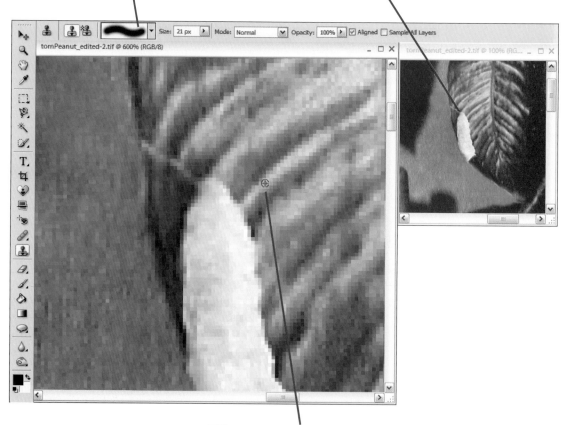

9 While pressing [Alt], click the cursor in the middle of a striped leaf.

10 Release the cursor.

repair & transform photos

11 Align your brush tip with the middle of the stripe but extending into the blank area. Its reach will be indicated by a 21-pixel-wide circle—the diameter of the Clone Stamp Tool's brush. Click once and the stripe will be applied to the blank area.

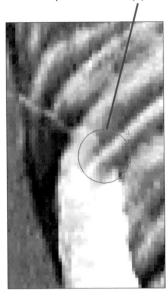

12 Use the cross marking the sample source to keep the brush aligned with the middle of the stripe. Continue painting into the blank area one click at a time. Stop short of the opposite edge of the blank area.

13 While pressing Alt, grab a sample of the next stripe.

14 Repeat the process of extending the stripe out into the blank area.

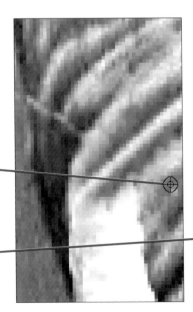

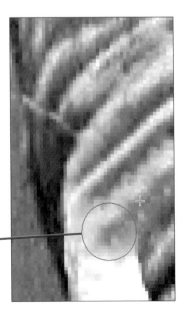

restore missing areas (cont.)

15 Once you've filled in the main area, select a smaller brush and continue using the Clone Stamp Tool to patch details along the edge.

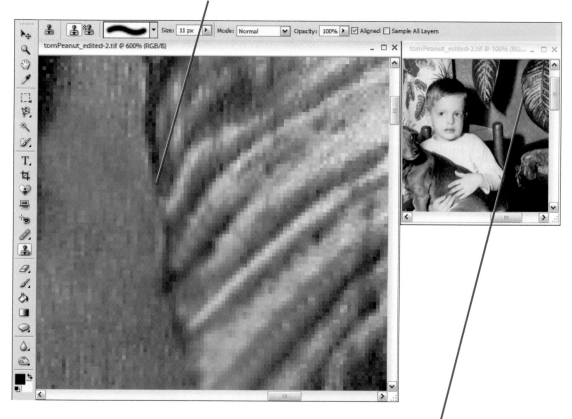

16 When you think you've repaired all the damaged areas, check the zoomed-out view to be sure. If not, zoom back in and finish up any repairs with the Clone Stamp Tool.

17 Save your changes.

repair & transform photos

select part of photo

NEW Elements offers five tools for selecting parts of a photo—the Marquee, Lasso, Magic Wand, Selection Brush, and the new Magic Selection Brush. Once a selection's made, it can be deleted, copied, or changed without affecting the rest of the photo. (For details on using the Magic Selection Brush, see pages 55–57.)

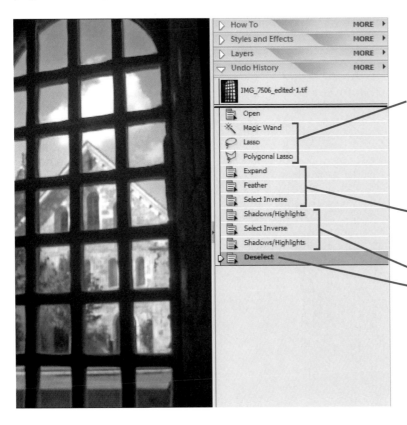

As the Undo History palette for this photo shows, it's common to use a combination of selection tools. Once you've selected an area, you then apply various commands to expand, shrink, or reverse the selection. In the typical retouching session, you then apply several fixes before finally deselecting the area. Trial and error soon shows you which tools and methods suit your style.

select part of photo (cont.)

With the circle-version of the Marquee Tool set to Fixed Aspect Ratio, it's easy to select the round logo on this German telephone booth.

You can then apply such transformations as Image > Transform > Free Transform to pivot the circle open like a window.

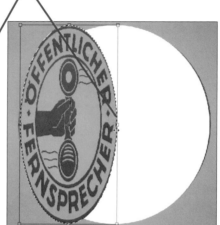

With the Magic Wand Tool set for a wide range of color (Tolerance 64) in a single area (Contiguous), you can quickly select the block of blue-purple hyacinths.

Then you can use the Shadows/Highlights dialog box to lighten only that color.

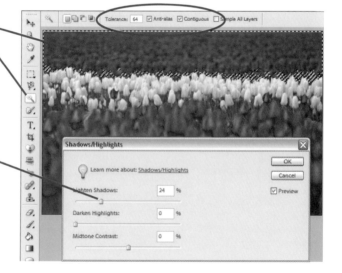

With the Selection Brush Tool set for a large brush with a very defined tip (Size 19 pixels), you can just brush over an area to select it. In this example of extreme red eye, however, Elements may have met its match.

All three variations of the Lasso Tool work by drawing a loop around an area to select it. While it can be as tricky to use as double-sided tape, the Magnetic Lasso works well for laying a line down along the irregular edge in the example.

repair & transform photos

modify selection

After selecting part of a photo, it's easy to modify that selection. You add to the selection or remove some of it. The Select menu lets you change the boundary between the selection and the rest of the photo.

All the selection tools let you add to your selection by using the tool while pressing Shift.

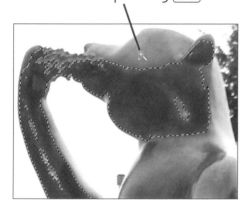

You can remove from the selection while using the tool by pressing Alt.

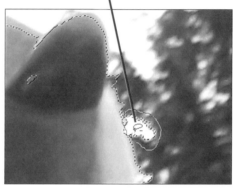

To change the boundary of a selection, choose Select > Modify and pick from the drop-down menu.

Our cookie selection with the Magnetic Lasso was a little ragged, so we choose Select > Modify > Smooth. A dialog box controls the amount of smoothing.

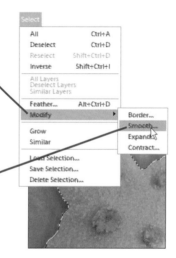

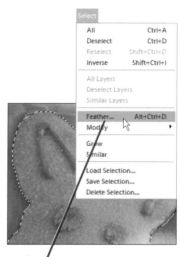

Having smoothed the selection, we want to soften its edge by choosing Select > Feather.

repair & transform photos

When you choose Select > Feather, a dialog box controls the width of the feathering in pixels.

Set to 0 pixels leaves a distinct boundary,...

...10 pixels blurs it a bit,...

...and 50 pixels creates a very soft edge.

Sometimes it's much easier to select what you don't want and then reverse the selection. To adjust the exposure outside the window, for example, would require selecting each pane of glass.

Instead, use the Magic Wand to select the surrounding black, then choose Select > Inverse.

That reverses the selection to the view outside.

remove objects

The Healing Brush and Clone Stamp examples earlier in the chapter gave you a sense of how easy it might be to remove objects in a photo. With your new selection skills, we'll start small by removing some distracting wires. (See extra bits on page 114.)

1 To ensure we don't remove any of the sign, select the sky above and below it.

2 Choose Select > Save Selection so that all your work making the selection doesn't disappear with the click of a wrong key.

3 Name the selection and click OK to close the dialog box.

repair & transform photos

4 Choose the Clone Stamp Tool.

5 Set the brush tip small enough to work amid the wires (13 pixels is a good size), then Alt-click to grab a sample of the sky. Release the cursor.

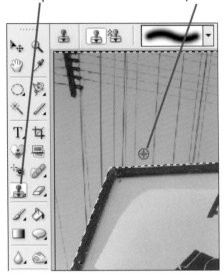

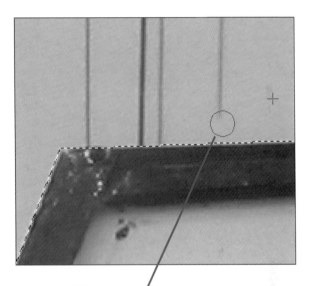

6 Start erasing the wires one click at a time. A circle marks where the stamp is applied; a cross marks the sample source. Because only the sky's selected, we can click right up to the sign without turning it blue.

remove objects (cont.)

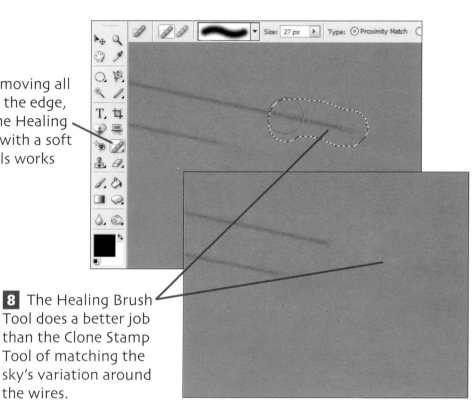

7 After removing all wires along the edge, switch to the Healing Brush Tool with a soft tip (27 pixels works well here).

8 The Healing Brush Tool does a better job than the Clone Stamp Tool of matching the sky's variation around the wires.

Though it takes time, the final photo shows no sign of the previous tangle of wires.

extract & defringe objects

NEW In the previous section, we carefully removed just the wires while preserving the blue sky. But suppose, we wanted to remove all the sky and work only with the remaining sign and building? The new Magic Extractor is perfect for that sort of task, especially since it includes a Defringe option to automatically remove the boundary fringe of pixels often mistakenly selected with an object. (See extra bits on page 114.)

1 Open a photo from which you want to extract a particular area. In our example, we'll start by opening the same wire-free photo we created on pages 98–100. Choose Image > Magic Extractor and the image appears within the Magic Extractor dialog box.

2 The Foreground Brush Tool will be selected by default with a Brush Size of 20 pixels.

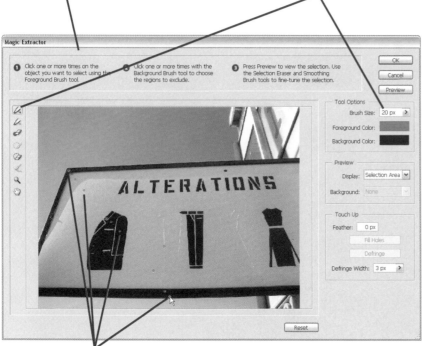

3 Click within the photo on all the areas you want to add to your selection. Each of the areas will be marked by a red dot.

extract & defringe (cont.)

4 Now select the Background Brush Tool, leave the Brush Size as is, and click on the areas you want to place outside (subtract from) the selection. These areas will be marked by blue dots. Click Preview to start the extraction.

5 A progress bar will appear as Elements extracts the area you want from the rest of the photo.

6 When the extraction's finished, check to see if any areas were mistakenly left out or included in your selection.

7 Use the Zoom Tool (🔍) to zero in on areas missed in your initial selection. (If the only problem involves a small fringe of pixels around the object, skip to step 11.)

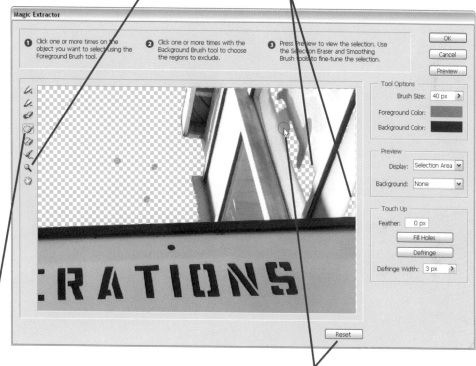

8 Select the Add to Selection Tool (✏️) and choose a Brush Size that's big enough to quickly cover the missing areas and small enough to not spill into adjacent areas. In our example, 40 pixels seems about right.

9 Use the tool to paint in any areas you want to add to the selection. If you ever want to start from scratch in creating the selection, click Reset.

10 If the Magic Extractor picks up any areas you do not want included in the selection, select the Remove from Selection Tool (✏️), choose a Brush Size, and paint in any areas you want to subtract from the selection.

repair & transform photos

extract & defringe (cont.)

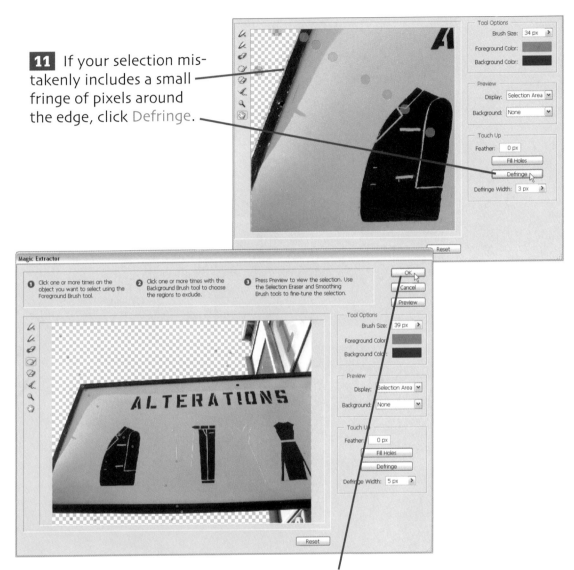

11 If your selection mistakenly includes a small fringe of pixels around the edge, click Defringe.

12 Once you're happy with the results, click OK to close the Magic Extractor dialog box and return to the Standard Edit main window. Be sure to save your work (Ctrl S). We'll use this same photo in the next section and fill the transparent areas with pixels from another photo.

repair & transform photos

combine photos

Using layers, we're going to move items from one photo to another. It takes a lot of steps. But, once you master this method, you can combine bits and pieces from multiple images in a single photo. (See extra bits on page 114.)

1 Open the photo to which you want to add items from another photo. Our example is the same alterations sign we used in the previous section.

combine photos (cont.)

2 Switch to your second photo and select what you want to move to the first photo, in this case a more dramatic sky.

3 Choose Layer > New > Layer via Copy.

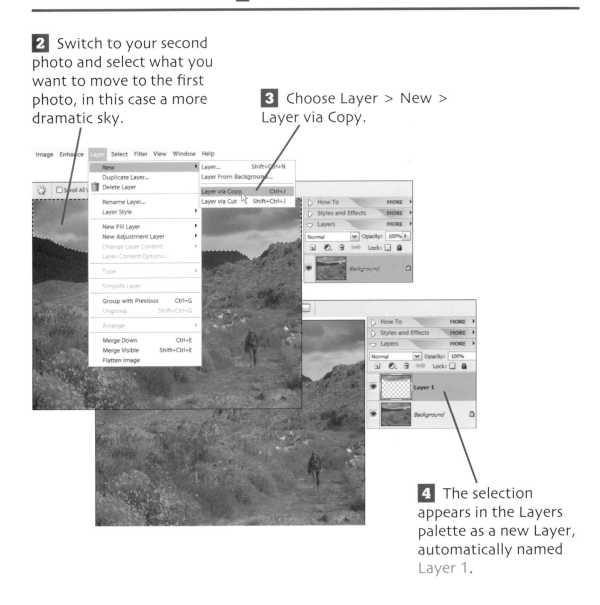

4 The selection appears in the Layers palette as a new Layer, automatically named Layer 1.

repair & transform photos

5 Use the Photo Bin to bring up the still-open first photo. Position the windows so that the first photo is visible right below the second photo.

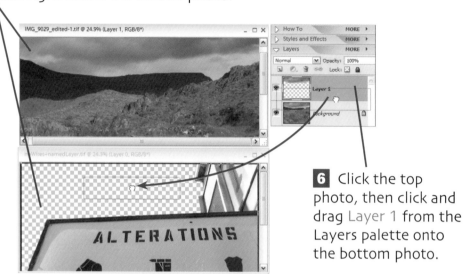

6 Click the top photo, then click and drag Layer 1 from the Layers palette onto the bottom photo.

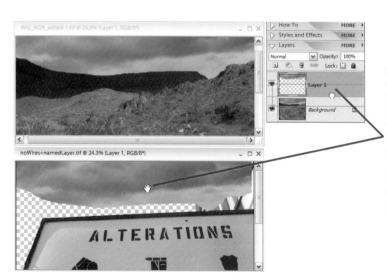

7 Release the cursor and Layer 1 will be pasted into the bottom photo. It also will appear in the Layers palette. Minimize or close the other photo to give you more room to work.

repair & transform photos

combine photos (cont.)

8 Click the Move Tool in the Toolbox (or press V).

9 A dashed line borders the new layer, with square "handles" at its corners and sides.

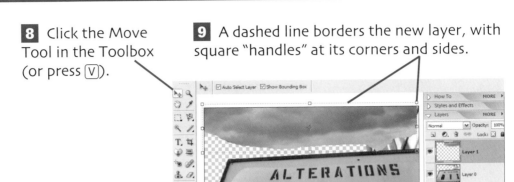

10 Click and drag the various side and corner handles to fit Layer 1 over the transparent area.

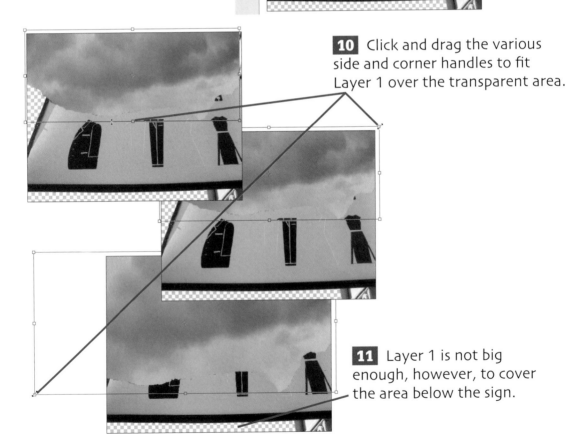

11 Layer 1 is not big enough, however, to cover the area below the sign.

repair & transform photos

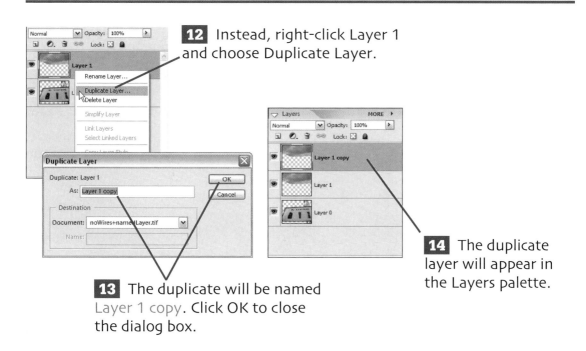

12 Instead, right-click Layer 1 and choose Duplicate Layer.

13 The duplicate will be named Layer 1 copy. Click OK to close the dialog box.

14 The duplicate layer will appear in the Layers palette.

15 To see the original image, click and drag Layer 0 to the top of the Layers palette.

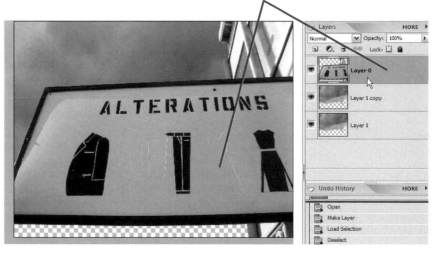

combine photos (cont.)

16 Select Layer 1 copy in the Layers palette, then click the Move Tool in the Toolbox (or press [V]).

17 Use the [↓] key to shift Layer 1 copy down enough to cover the area below the sign. (Don't click on the image or you'll wind up reselecting the visible Layer 0.) A dashed line marks the edge of the layer as it moves down the image.

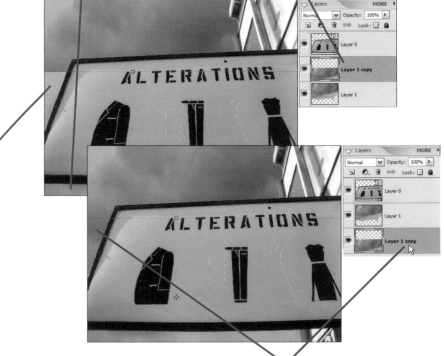

18 A bit of brighter sky mars the effect, but that's easy to fix.

19 Click and drag Layer 1 copy to the bottom of the Layers palette. This puts it beneath Layer 1, blocking out the lighter area to create a seamless new sky.

20 Merge the layers by choosing Layer > Flatten Image. Save your changes ([Ctrl][S]).

repair & transform photos

create a panorama

Nothing puts the viewer into a scene more dramatically than a panorama photo. Many digital cameras include features to help you create a panoramic picture by overlapping a series of photos. Photoshop Elements' Photomerge feature then takes those multiple photos and stitches them into a single photo.

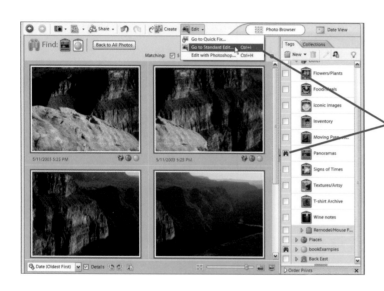

1 In Standard Edit mode, open the photos with which you'll build the panorama (Ctrl O). Or use the Elements Organizer and its tags to find what you need, then choose Go to Standard Edit from the Edit drop-down menu.

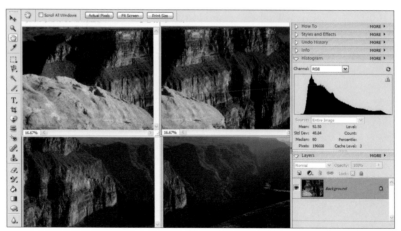

2 After the photos open in Standard Edit mode, position them so you can compare their exposure and color. Fix any differences now—before you start creating the panorama.

create a panorama (cont.)

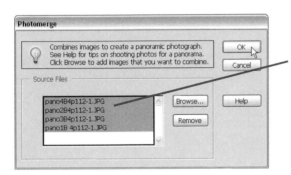

3 Choose File > New > Photomerge Panorama to open the Photomerge dialog box. The open photos will be listed in the dialog box, but you must select each one before clicking OK.

4 If Elements cannot merge all the photos, it puts the leftover images at the top.

5 Click and drag the first leftover photo to the correct spot in the panorama.

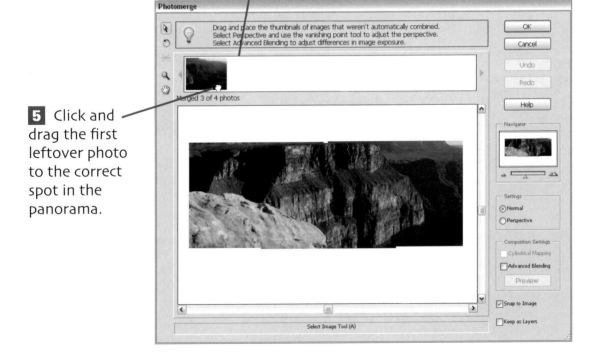

6 You don't need to be that precise when you drag the image into place. It will jump into position because Snap to Image is checked by default.

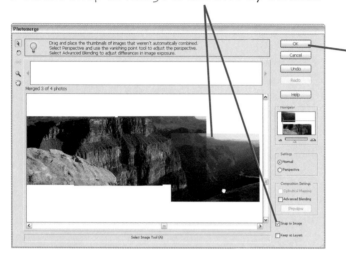

7 Drag any remaining photos into place and click OK.

8 If the original pictures were not perfectly aligned, there may be some ragged borders in the panorama image. Clean them up with the Crop Tool.

The panorama is a new file, so be sure to save your work.

extra bits

repair areas p. 85

- In picking a Healing Brush size, remember: the larger the flaw, the bigger the brush.
- As you move around the photo and repair areas, use [Alt]-click to grab new pixel samples nearer the area being fixed.

restore missing areas p. 88

- Though the example is black and white, the same steps apply working with full-color photos.
- When you change the brush size, stay with a fuzzy tip so each click/stroke blends well.

remove objects p. 98

- To paint out an object wider than the Healing Brush Tool's tip, switch to the Clone Stamp Tool. The Healing Brush tries to blend the object with the surrounding color, making a mess.
- The same methods can add objects to a photo. It's just a matter of what you sample.

extract & defringe p. 101

- Avoid starting over by using the Point Eraser Tool to remove dots placed by the Foreground Brush Tool or Background Brush Tool.
- The Touch Up pane's Feather and Defringe options work in opposite ways: Feather expands the boundary of your selection while Defringe shrinks it.
- Start with a Defringe Width of 3 pixels. If that doesn't fix the problem, increase the width and click Defringe again.

combine photos p. 105

- If the Background layer shows a lock in the Layers palette, you must unlock it to add transparent areas: Double-click the layer and click OK in the New Layer dialog box to unlock the layer.
- You also must unlock the Background layer to change its order in the Layers palette. The layer order works like a stack of windows. Transparent portions of the upper layers let you see any layers beneath them; solid portions on top block the appearance of those below.
- To reposition the bounding box, click and drag the red crosshair.

repair & transform photos

6. share photos

The payoff for all that work fixing your photos comes when you can share them with friends and relatives. Some of them will want prints, others will prefer to see them on a computer screen. Either way, Elements makes it easy.

print photos

Printing photos with Elements couldn't be easier: Open the photo or photos you want to print, choose File > Print, pick a size, and click Print.

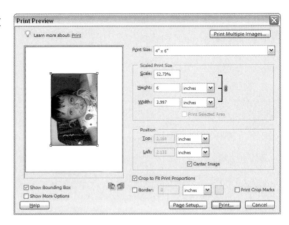

But Elements also has a less-obvious, paper-saving option called the Picture Package, which lets you print different-sized photos on a single sheet. You can use the same photo or several photos. Either way, you wind up with a photo package akin to those offered by school and wedding photographers. (See extra bits on page 129.)

Open the photo or photos you want to print in Quick Fix or Standard Edit mode and choose File > Print Multiple Photos. In the Print Photos dialog box, your open photos run down the left.

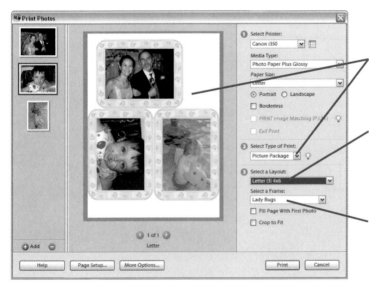

Choose Picture Package and the center layout will reflect the choice.

Choose a photo-layout combination. (In our example, a 4 x 6 print of three different photos will appear on a single letter-sized sheet.)

If you like, you can select a fanciful frame for the photos.

If you want multiple, but different-sized, copies of the same photo on the same page of paper, check Fill Page With First Photo. Use the first drop-down menu in the Select a Layout section to choose a mix of photo sizes. In our example, that change means we'll have two 4 x 5 prints, two 2.5 x 3.5 prints, and four 2 x 2.5 prints of the same image on a single page. The same mix of sizes will be used for the other two images, using a total of three sheets of paper.

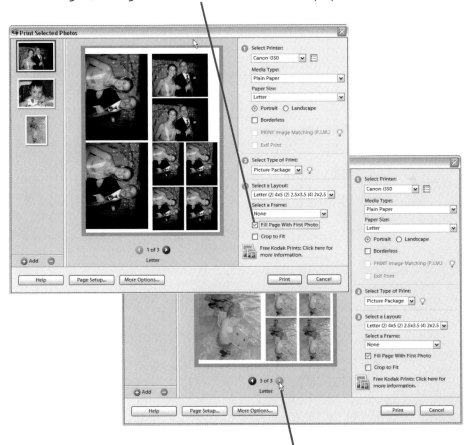

If you're printing multiple sheets, click the arrows to see the other sheets. Here, the third sheet shows the same mix of sizes for the third photo. Once you've set your combination, click Print.

set email preference

When preparing to email photos, the Preferences dialog box in Elements offers you four choices. Each is explained below. Try several to discover which works best for you.

1 Start by setting the email preferences for Elements. If you are working in the Editor (in Quick Fix or Standard Edit mode), choose Edit > Preferences > Organize & Share. If you're working in the Organizer, choose Edit > Preferences > Sharing.

2 In the Preferences dialog box, select Sharing. (If you were in the Organizer, it already will be selected.) Choose an E-mail client from the drop-down menu.

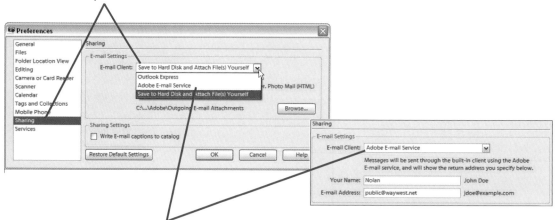

3 If you choose Outlook Express, Elements automatically attaches photos to a blank outgoing Outlook message.

Choosing Adobe E-mail Service creates a message that's sent by Elements itself. If you decide to use the Adobe service, make sure you're connected to the Internet, fill in your name and email address, and see the next step.

The Save to Hard Disk choice stores the converted photo on your computer for sending manually with any email program.

Once you make a choice from the drop-down menu, click OK to close the dialog box.

4 If you choose the Adobe E-Mail Service, Elements automatically asks you to re-confirm your email address by entering a special code that's sent to you by email.

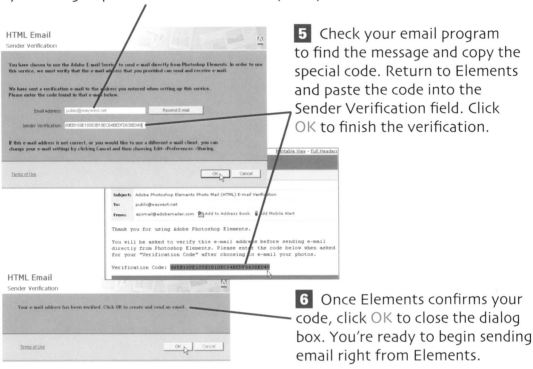

5 Check your email program to find the message and copy the special code. Return to Elements and paste the code into the Sender Verification field. Click OK to finish the verification.

6 Once Elements confirms your code, click OK to close the dialog box. You're ready to begin sending email right from Elements.

7 After setting the preferences, open the photo(s) you want to send. If you are working in the Editor (Quick Fix or Standard Edit), click the email icon in the shortcuts bar. Elements then switches to the Organizer. If you're already working in the Organizer, click the Share icon in the shortcuts bar and choose E-mail.

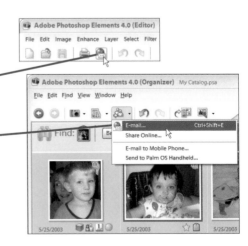

8 The appearance of the Attach to E-mail dialog box varies, depending on your choice in step 3.

send as attachments

If you chose Save to Hard Disk on page 118, the Attach to E-mail dialog box lets you adjust the size and quality of the photos that will be attached.

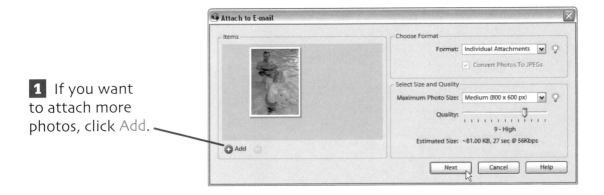

1 If you want to attach more photos, click Add.

2 The Add Photos dialog box lets you quickly look through and choose photos from your entire catalog or using particular tags and collections. Once you narrow your search on the left, check individual boxes to the left of the photos or use the Select All button. Click Done to close the dialog box and the selected photos appear in the Attach to E-mail dialog box.

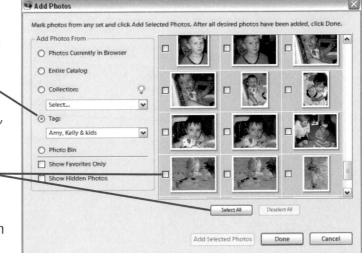

3 In the Attach to E-mail dialog box, click Next and you'll see that the photo(s) are saved in a separate folder. Click OK to close that dialog box and then use the email program of your choice to send the photos.

share photos

use Adobe service

If you chose the Adobe E-mail Service on page 118, Elements offers you two choices. The plainer option (described below) lets you send photos as individual attachments. The fancier option (described on page 122) allows you to insert photos right into the body of your message and apply special text formats.

1 Leave Format set to Individual Attachments.

2 Choose recipients from the list.

3 Add new recipients by clicking Edit Contacts and using the dialog box that appears.

4 To attach more photos, click Add (see step 2 on the previous page).

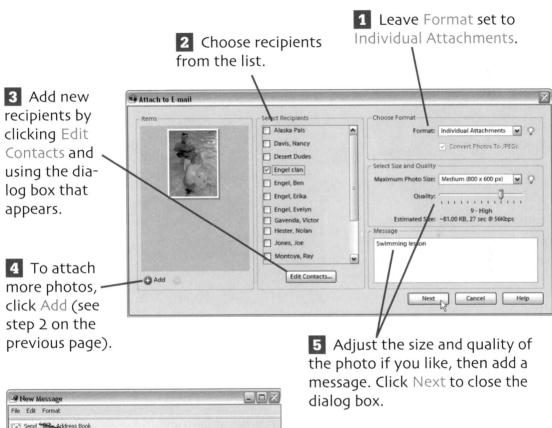

5 Adjust the size and quality of the photo if you like, then add a message. Click Next to close the dialog box.

6 The New Message dialog box appears; this gives you the option of formatting your text. When you're done, click Send and Elements dispatches the message.

use Adobe service (cont.)

◆ NEW If you chose the Adobe E-mail Service on page 118, Elements also lets you use photo mail (or HTML mail as it's sometimes called). It allows you to insert photos directly in the body of your message instead of as separate attachments. You also can add decorative backgrounds or icons and apply fancy text formatting. (See extra bits on page 129.)

1 Make sure you've already set your email preferences. (See steps 1–4 for email photos on page 120.) Open the photo(s) you want to send, and if you are working in the Editor (Quick Fix or Standard Edit), click the email icon in the shortcuts bar. If you're already working in the Organizer, click the Share icon in the shortcuts bar and choose E-mail.

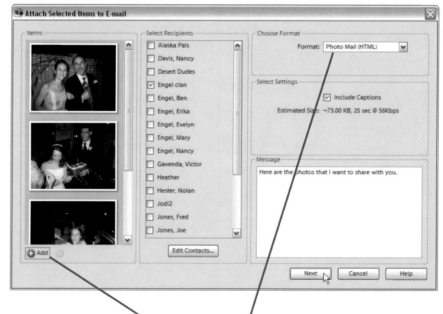

2 When the Attach to E-mail dialog box appears, use the Add button to gather any additional photos you want to include. (See step 10 page 120.) Then click the Format drop-down menu and choose Photo Mail (HTML). Click Next to close the dialog box.

share photos

3 In the Stationery & Layouts Wizard, scroll through the list of stationery styles to find one to your liking. Click Next Step.

4 Customize your layout by selecting the Photo Size and Layout for your photos.

5 Skip the Text section since you can change that later. Finally, check any options you want applied, such as drop shadows. Click Next.

use Adobe service (cont.)

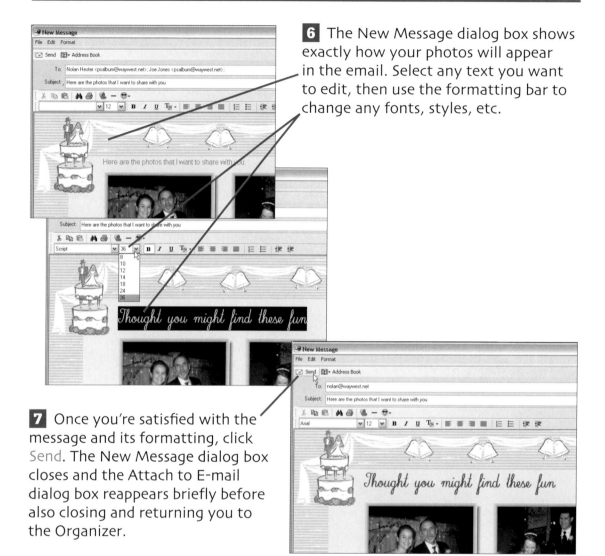

6 The New Message dialog box shows exactly how your photos will appear in the email. Select any text you want to edit, then use the formatting bar to change any fonts, styles, etc.

7 Once you're satisfied with the message and its formatting, click Send. The New Message dialog box closes and the Attach to E-mail dialog box reappears briefly before also closing and returning you to the Organizer.

8 A progress bar appears briefly as Elements prepares the message. Finally another smaller progress bar appears as the message and its photos are actually mailed.

save for the web

Posting photos on a Web page is a great way to share them. When you make prints, you try to preserve every last detail to get the most faithful photo reproduction. But when you prepare an image for the Web, it's almost the opposite: You try to slim the file down so it will download quickly to the viewer's computer. The slimming process is called optimization, and the Save For Web dialog box makes it easy. (See extra bits on page 129.)

1 In Quick Fix or Standard Edit mode, open the photo you want to use on the Web and choose File > Save for Web. The photo appears in the Save For Web dialog box.

2 By default, the photo opens at 100 percent, so use the Hand Tool to maneuver the main part of your photo into view.

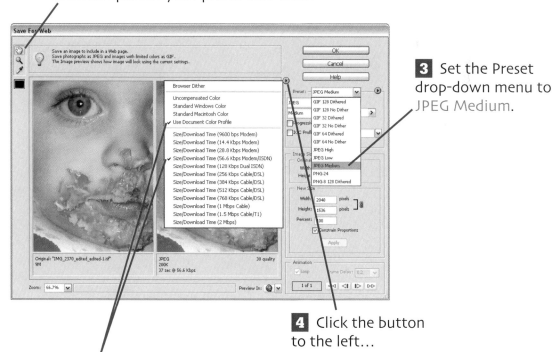

3 Set the Preset drop-down menu to JPEG Medium.

4 Click the button to the left...

5 ...and make two selections in the drop-down menu: Use Document Color Profile and Size/Download Time (56.6 Kbps Modem/ISDN).

save for the web (cont.)

6 Check two more boxes: Progressive and ICC Profile.

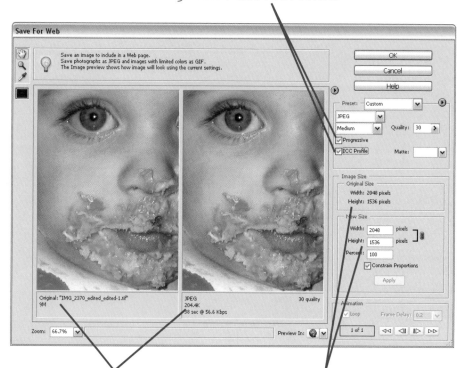

7 Listed at the bottom left is the photo's present size in the TIFF format (in this case 9 megabytes). To the right is its size (204.4 bytes) as a JPEG file and how long it would take to download (38 seconds at 56.6 Kbps) if we click OK.

8 But wait, even though the format's different, the dimensions of the original and the new version remain the same: 2048 x 1536. Since the new version is going to be on a Web page, it could be a lot smaller. Otherwise, you'll wind up with a giant screen-filling photo, like this cake fan's face.

9 Use the Zoom drop-down menu to find a setting closer to how large you want the photo to appear on the Web page. In our example, a Zoom setting of 12.5 percent looks about right.

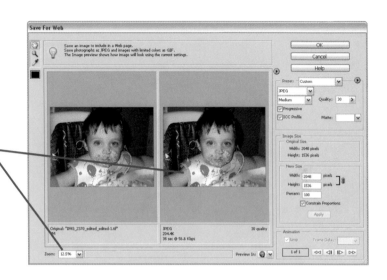

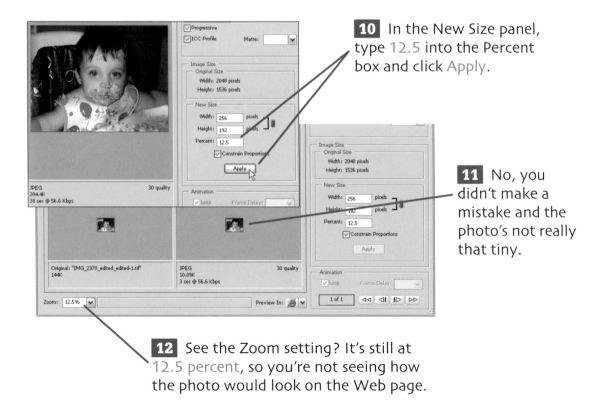

10 In the New Size panel, type 12.5 into the Percent box and click Apply.

11 No, you didn't make a mistake and the photo's not really that tiny.

12 See the Zoom setting? It's still at 12.5 percent, so you're not seeing how the photo would look on the Web page.

save for the web (cont.)

13 Set the Zoom level back to 100 percent and you can see exactly how big the photo will appear on the Web.

14 The New Size panel lists its physical dimensions at 256 x 192 pixels. That's 3.5 x 2.6 inches—just about right for viewing on a computer screen.

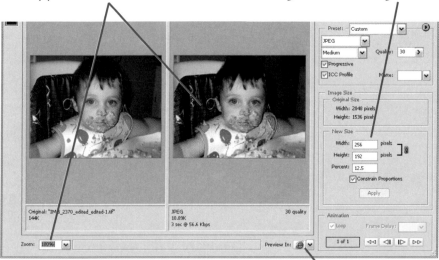

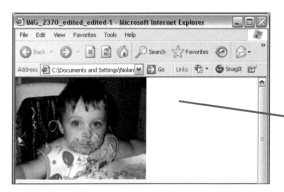

15 If you're still skeptical, click the Preview In button. Your Web browser launches and shows how the photo will look on the Web.

16 Click OK to save the optimized image. Name it, pick where to store it, and click Save. It will not affect your original photo. You'll need a Web program to upload the new image.

extra bits

print photos p. 116

- If a dialog box appears and warns that the image will print at less than 220 dpi (dots per inch), the printer probably is still set to print letter-sized documents. Choose File > Page Setup and in the Page Setup dialog box click the Printer and then Properties buttons to check and change the settings.

use Adobe service p. 121

- To thwart spam, a few people set their Web browsers and email programs to block the display of HTML-based graphics. Any email you send them will appear without fancy text formats and the photos will be included as plain attachments.

save for the web p. 125

- You can trim so much digital fat from a Web-bound photo because of the difference between printers and computer monitors. For a print to look good, printers need to lay down at least 150 dots per inch (dpi). Photos on a monitor, however, look great at just 72–96 dpi. For onscreen Web pages, the rest of those dots can be tossed, during optimization.

- Your Size/Download Time choice doesn't change the photo in any way. It simply helps you gauge how long a viewer will have to wait to see your image.

- Choosing Progressive in the Save For Web dialog box helps Web surfers with slow connection speeds see a sketchy version of the photo as it downloads. That way they can decide if they want to wait for the whole picture or move on to another page.

- Choosing ICC in the Save For Web dialog box embeds color profile data in the photo—making it easier for other profile-enabled computers to display the photo properly.

- If you haven't set a default Web browser, Elements will show you how to set one when you click Preview In.

- If anyone tried to print out the Web image of the baby's face, it would be postage-stamp size. That's the difference between the resolution of a computer screen (72 or 96 dpi) and a photo print (150–300 dpi). To post photos for prints, use your Web-site creation software to create a separate download link to the big original file.

index

index   **131**

index

ull-color projects
rom the folks
ho bring you
isual QuickStart
uides…

Visual QuickProject

Creating a Photo Album
in Photoshop Elements
for Windows

KATHERINE ULRICH

creating a photo album
in photoshop elements
for windows

Visual QuickProject Guide

by Katherine Ulrich

Peachpit
Press

Visual QuickProject Guide
Creating a Photo Album in Photoshop Elements for Windows
Katherine Ulrich

Peachpit Press
1249 Eighth Street
Berkeley, CA 94710
510/524-2178
800/283-9444
510/524-2221 (fax)

Find us on the World Wide Web at: www.peachpit.com
To report errors, please send a note to errata@peachpit.com
Peachpit Press is a division of Pearson Education

Editor: Nancy Davis
Production Editor: Lisa Brazieal
Compositor: Katherine Ulrich
Indexer: Karin Arrigoni
Technical Review: Victor Gavenda
Cover design: The Visual Group with Aren Howell
Interior design: Elizabeth Castro
Interior photos: Katherine Ulrich
Cover photo credit: Photodisc

Notice of Liability
The information in this book is distributed on an "As Is" basis, without warranty. While every precaution has been taken in the preparation of the book, neither the author nor Peachpit Press shall have any liability to any person or entity with respect to any loss or damage caused or alleged to be caused directly or indirectly by the instructions contained in this book or by the computer software and hardware products described in it.

Trademarks
Visual QuickProject Guide is a registered trademark of Peachpit Press, a division of Pearson Education.
All other trademarks are the property of their respective owners.

Throughout this book, trademarks are used. Rather than put a trademark symbol with every occurrence of a trademarked name, we state that we are using the names in an editorial fashion only and to the benefit of the trademark owner with no intention of infringement of the trademark. No such use, or the use of any trade name, is intended to convey endorsement or other affiliation with this book.

ISBN 0-321-27081-9

Printed and bound in the United States of America

To my parents, Reva and John,
who shared with me their love of
nature and the joys of observation,
from the very beginning.

Special Thanks to...

Perry Whittle, whose ongoing support, both moral and technical, smoothed out the bumps in the road to writing this book.

David Van Ness, my InDesign guru, for guiding me through the page-layout process.

Victor Gavenda, for combing through these pages for errors and goofs of a technical nature.

Bob Gager, Group Product Manager, Adobe Photoshop Services, for his generous help with my questions about creating albums in Photoshop Elements.

Nancy Davis, my editor, for her consistently upbeat spirit, words of encouragement, and editorial direction.

Lisa Brazieal, for her production expertise and shepherding these pages through the process.

Marjorie Baer, for her friendship and for thinking this project might be for me.

Karin Arrigoni, for creating the book's index on a tight timeline.

San Francisco Botanical Garden at Strybing Arboretum, where most of the photos in this book were taken. I'm grateful to the gardeners, volunteers, and staff, for creating a beautiful living museum of plants, a haven for small creatures of every sort, an oasis of calm in the midst of the bustling city.

contents

contents

introduction

The Visual QuickProject Guide that you hold in your hands offers a unique way to learn about new technologies. Instead of drowning you in theoretical possibilities and lengthy explanations, this Visual QuickProject Guide uses big, color illustrations coupled with clear, concise step-by-step instructions to show you how to complete one specific project in a matter of hours.

Our project in this book is to assemble your digital photos into an album using Adobe Photoshop Elements for Windows. Using the Album Creation wizard in Elements, we'll arrange photos in layouts for printing on a home printer, on high-quality photo paper. You can assemble these pages into albums using three-ring notebooks, portfolio binders, or any cover materials that appeal to you. We'll also use the Album Creation wizard to arrange photos in layouts that you can order as bound hardcover books. In the process, we'll learn about working with Elements Organizer to create catalogs of photos. And we'll learn some basic photo-enhancing techniques using tools in Elements Editor.

Of course, you could always place individual photo prints into commercial albums or homemade scrapbooks. But the Album Creation wizard makes it easy to arrange multiple photos on a single page, and the wizard's templates let you create albums in a variety of styles.There are styles that place photos in special frames, some sophisticated and elegant, others whimsical or theme-based. There are styles that show off the photos on plain white pages. The Album Creation wizard frees you from the drudgery (and in my case, the illegibility) of handwritten captions, making it easy to add high-quality text. Here's another plus: the major work in creating an album is placing the photos on the page. With traditional albums, you must redo that work for each and every album, even if you're just re-creating the same one for different members of your family. In Elements, once the work of creating the album is done, you just print or order the number of copies you need.

what you'll create

Bring your digital photos
into Elements Organizer.

Create a catalog struc-
ture with categories
and tags, then create
collections to gather
the photos you want
to use in your album.

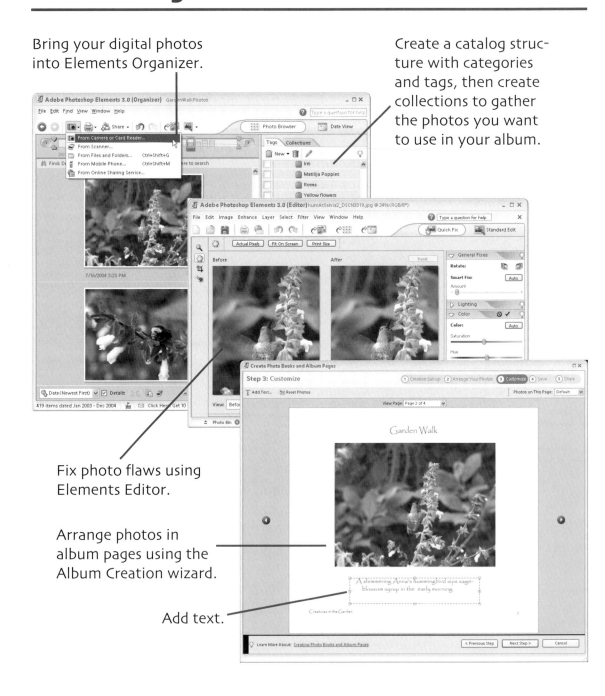

Fix photo flaws using
Elements Editor.

Arrange photos in
album pages using the
Album Creation wizard.

Add text.

Use Adobe Photoshop Services, Provided by Ofoto, to order a hard-cover book printed from your album pages.

Print album pages yourself and create your own binding system.

how this book works

The title explains what is covered in this section.

Orange highlight calls out special terms, names of steps that make up the interface of the Album Creation wizard, and cross references in this book.

Numbers clarify the precise order of steps you need to follow to complete a task.

Dotted arrows show interactive movement, for example, dragging a photo to a new location.

Purple tint connects an area of detail to an enlarged view of that area.

Screenshots illustrate the essential areas of the software interface that you will work with.

put photos in order

You can change the order of your images in Step 2: Arrange Your Photos.

1 Click the photo you want to move, then drag it to a new position. (To move several photos, Ctrl-click each one; if the photos are in a row, click the first one, then Shift-click the last one to select them all. Dragging one photo moves the whole selected group, even if the photos are not contiguous.)

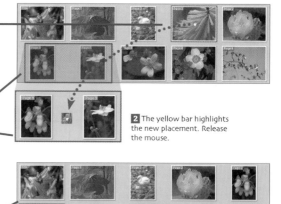

2 The yellow bar highlights the new placement. Release the mouse.

3 The Album Creation wizard reorders the images and reassigns their pages.

creating albums with fixed layouts 61

Captions describe the actions you need to take to complete the task described in the section.

The extra bits section at the end of each chapter contains additional tips and tricks that you might like to know—but that aren't absolutely necessary for creating your photo album.

The page number that follows the heading helps you find the content area in the main text.

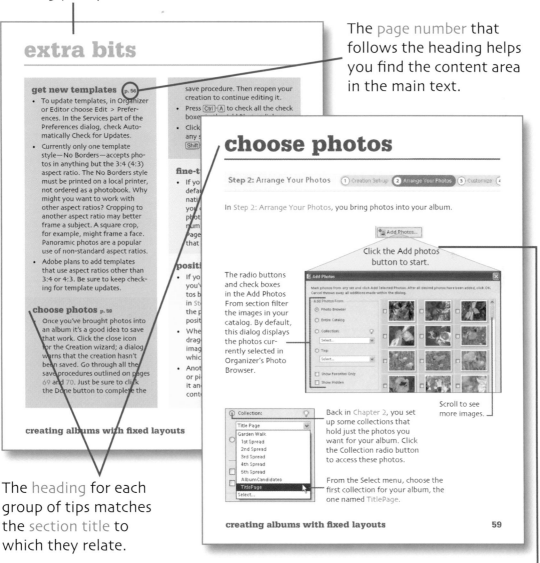

The heading for each group of tips matches the section title to which they relate.

An orange triangle connecting objects indicates cause and effect. Here, clicking the Add Photos button opens the Add Photos dialog.

the next step

This Visual QuickProject Guide gets you started using a variety of tools in Photoshop Elements, but the real focus is on creating photo albums. That means giving short shrift to many of Elements' organizing and editing features. For more in-depth coverage, you might consider adding another book to your library: Photoshop Elements for Windows & Macintosh: Visual QuickStart Guide.

CRAIG HOESCHEN

VISUAL QUICKSTART GUIDE

PHOTOSHOP ELEMENTS
FOR WINDOWS & MACINTOSH

Teach yourself Photoshop ... the quick and easy ... Visual QuickStart ... pictures rather than ... explanations. You'll be ... running in no time!

Changing and Adjusting Colors

Figure 3.32 The Shadows/Highlights dialog box.

Figure 3.33 The top photo is a little under-exposed in the foreground, so detail in the young woman's face is hidden in shadow. In the bottom photo, making adjustments with the Lighten Shadows and the Midtone Contrast sliders selectively brightens and enhances detail in both her face and blouse.

Lighting Your Image

Overexposed background images and under-exposed foreground subjects are a common problem for most amateur photographers. Photoshop Elements provides an elegant tool to help salvage your otherwise perfect compositions. Much like levels, it operates on pixels in specific tonal ranges (either highlights or shadows) while leaving the other tonal ranges alone. A Lighten Shadows slider helps to add detail to areas in shadow, while a Darken Highlights slider can add detail to washed-out areas in the background.

To improve foreground detail:

1. From the Enhance menu, choose Adjust Lighting > Shadows/Highlights. The Shadows/Highlights dialog box appears (**Figure 3.32**).

2. In the Shadows/Highlights dialog box, drag the Lighten Shadows slider to the right to lessen the effect of the shadows, or to the left to introduce shadow back into the image.

3. Drag the Midtone Contrast slider to the right to increase the contrast, or to the left to decrease the contrast.

4. Click OK to close the Shadows/Highlights dialog box and apply the changes (**Figure 3.33**).

✔ **Tips**

- I've found that in many (if not most) images imported from a digital camera, the Shadows/Highlights dialog box defaults work surprisingly well on their own, requiring just minor slider adjustments.

- In any case, use the Midtone Contrast slider sparingly. A little goes a long way, and adjustments of more than plus or minus 10% can quickly wash out or flatten an image's details.

85

LIGHTING YOUR IMAGE

The Visual QuickStart Guide teaches you step-by-step how to use Elements to enhance your photos, improving their quality and heightening their impact. Like all of the books in Peachpit's Visual QuickStart Guide series, it also works as a reference guide when you just need to learn (or remember) the steps for completing a task.

1. getting ready

You've been shooting like mad with your new digital camera, or spending every spare minute scanning old family snapshots. Now you'd like to show off your work and preserve it in a special photo album. You're about to embark on an album-creation project using Adobe Photoshop Elements 3.0 for Windows.

You'll import photos into Elements Organizer; retouch them in Elements Editor; then, using Organizer's Album Creation wizard, arrange them in neat layouts with text. You'll create album pages that can be printed as individual 8.5-by-11-inch pages, using high-quality photo paper, on your own printer. You are free to bind these into an album however you like. For a simple album, punch three holes in each page and put the pages into a three-ring binder from your local Five and Dime. For something a bit fancier, punch just two holes and thread the pages with ribbon or cord. Check local art-supply, crafts, or office-products stores and you'll find many styles of binders, portfolios, and cover materials.

The most luxurious album option is to create layouts for 10.25-by-9-inch pages. Using Adobe Photoshop Services, provided by Ofoto you can order a photobook. Ofoto, a Kodak subsidiary, professionally prints your album pages and binds them into a hardcover book.

general preparations

1 To install Photoshop Elements 3.0 you need

A PC with at least an 800MHz Intel Pentium III or 4 processor (or one that's compatible) and a CD-ROM drive.

Microsoft Windows XP Professional or Home Edition with Service Pack 1; Windows 2000 with Service Pack 4 or later.

At least 256MB of RAM (Adobe recommends 512MB) and 800MB of free space on your hard-drive.

A color monitor and video card capable of handling 16-bit color or greater. (Set your monitor resolution to 1024 by 768 or greater when using Elements.)

2 Calibrate Your Monitor

How do you know that the beautiful colors you see on screen will be the same beautiful colors when you print your photos or album pages or send them out to be printed professionally? Well the truth is, the printed versions will never give you the luminous bright colors you see on your computer monitor. But you can do something to help ensure that your delicate pink rose doesn't come out fire-engine red, and the bright baskets of pollen on a bumblebee's legs are orange not greeny gray. The way to do this is to use color management and to calibrate your monitor. We'll use a simple color-management technique in creating album pages, but monitor calibration is beyond the scope of this book. When you install Elements you also install Adobe Gamma software. The Elements Help feature describes how to use this software to calibrate a CRT monitor. You can also purchase special tools and software specifically for calibrating your monitor. These can get fairly pricey, however, and require devoted attention to achieve the most consistent results.

To run the Adobe Gamma application, use the Windows Start menu to open the Control Panel window. Choose the category named Appearance and Themes. Adobe Gamma is listed with the Control Panel icons. Click the Adobe Gamma icon to start the calibration process.

project materials

1 A digital camera with which to take your photos.

2 A PC computer with Windows.

3 Adobe Photoshop Elements 3.0 for Windows.

4 Adobe Reader for previewing layouts for album pages and hardcover photobooks in Portable Document Format (PDF).

5 A printer. Color ink-jet printers enable you to print your own individual album pages or proof pages in color before ordering a hardcover photobook. Black-and-white printers are good for proofing layouts and text without eating up your stocks of color inks.

6 Low-quality paper for proofing album pages before committing to high-quality paper or ordering a book online.

7 High-quality photo paper for printing finished album pages.

8 An Internet connection for ordering hardcover photobooks through Adobe Photoshop Services, provided by Ofoto.

9 A credit card to complete the online transaction of ordering hardcover photobooks.

project steps

1 Acquire images. For this project, I'll be using photos I shot with a digital camera, but you could just as easily create an album from scans that you've made of older snapshots or documents. You could also use the graphics tools in Elements to create original artwork and use that artwork in your album.

2 Import the photos to Elements Organizer. Organizer is a complete asset-management application within Elements. Organizer keeps track of your photos in a catalog—basically a database of photos.

3 Create structure. You create a hierarchical structure for the database by assigning categories, subcategories, and tags to the photos in the catalog. These structural features work just like keywords in a database, allowing you to identify and ultimately, sort through, your photos. You can filter your catalog to find just the photos you want by asking to see only photos in certain categories or that have certain tags attached.

4 Gather photos for your album. Another quasi-structural feature of Organizer is the collection. A collection is a container (think electronic shoebox) where you can hold a set of photos and arrange them in any order you like.

5 Fix up your photos. No matter how careful you are when shooting in the field, you're bound to take a few shots that could use a little help. Use Elements' editing tools to do such things as crop, fix exposure problems, remove color casts and red-eye syndrome, and retouch minor flaws. Because of a little glitch in the album-creation feature, it's important to edit the photos you want to include in an album before you start creating it. In some cases, editing photos after putting them into an album causes the album to lose all its data.

6 Create album pages. Elements comes with a Creation wizard: a tool that helps you make a variety of printed materials from postcards, to calendars, to our projects—photo album pages and photobooks. Using templates, the Album Creation wizard guides you through the process of creating album pages. These can be printed on your own printer, or sent to a local print shop, or they can be printed professionally and bound into hardcover photobooks.

7 Order a photobook and/or print album pages on high-quality paper designed for your printer, for example, matte or glossy ink-jet photo paper.

getting ready

Elements basics

 To open Elements, double-click its icon on the desktop or choose it from the Windows Start menu.

Elements contains two application areas: Organizer and Editor. Each opens in its own separate work area. Organizer has two viewing modes: Photo Browser and Date View. Editor has two editing modes: Quick Fix and Standard Edit.

Initially, Elements 3.0 opens to the Welcome Screen. This screen is the gateway to all the functional pieces of Elements. Click a button to begin using Elements. The four functions called out below are the ones you'll use in our projects.

Click to open Organizer.

Click to open Editor in Quick Fix mode.

Click to open Editor in Standard mode.

Click to open the Creation wizard.

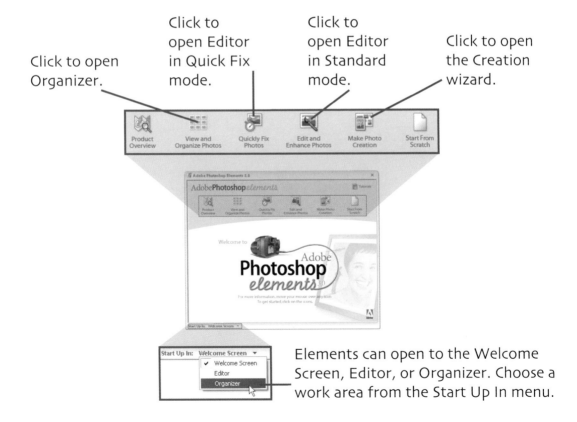

Elements can open to the Welcome Screen, Editor, or Organizer. Choose a work area from the Start Up In menu.

Elements basics (cont.)

1 ORGANIZER

Use Organizer to store and, well, organize your photos. The shortcuts bar offers quick entry to various tasks. Click the appropriate icon to begin.

Open Editor (Chapter 3).

Import photos to catalog (Chapter 1).

Open Creation wizard (Chapters 4 and 5).

View photos by date added to catalog.

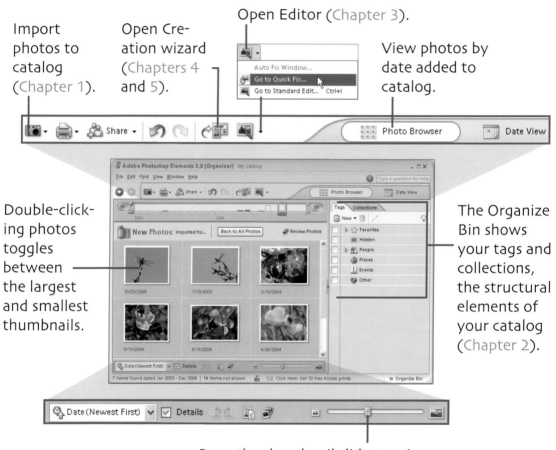

Double-clicking photos toggles between the largest and smallest thumbnails.

The Organize Bin shows your tags and collections, the structural elements of your catalog (Chapter 2).

Drag the thumbnail slider to view thumbnails at intermediate sizes.

2 EDITOR

Use Editor in Quick Fix mode to make simple corrections to your photos. Use Editor in Standard Edit mode to make more complex corrections to your photos and create original artwork.

Open Creation wizard (Chapters 4 and 5).

Open Organizer in Photo Browser mode (Chapter 2).

Enter Quick Fix mode (Chapter 3).

Enter Standard Edit mode (Chapter 3).

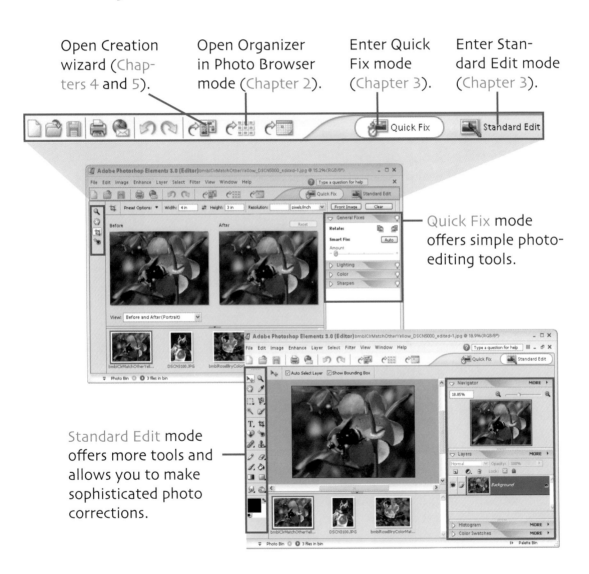

Quick Fix mode offers simple photo-editing tools.

Standard Edit mode offers more tools and allows you to make sophisticated photo corrections.

import photos

There are many ways to get photos into Organizer. You can download photos from a camera or card reader. You can set Elements to download photos automatically when you plug in the camera or insert a memory card into a card reader connected to your PC. You can also grab images that you've downloaded to your hard drive or burned onto CD-ROM. You can set up Watch folders so that any time you add files to a specified folder, Elements grabs them and puts them into Organizer. For this project, I used a card reader.

To start the import process, open Organizer.

Most people use just one catalog, the default My Catalog. If several people, say your whole family, use one computer, you might set up separate catalogs for each user. If you have multiple catalogs, open the one to which you want to add photos. Choose File > Catalog. The Catalog dialog appears.

Click the Open button in the Catalog dialog.

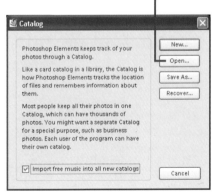

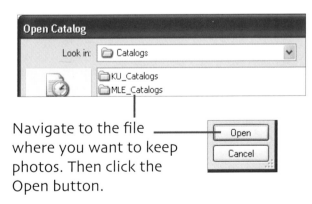

Navigate to the file where you want to keep photos. Then click the Open button.

getting ready

In Organizer, with your catalog open, click the Get Photos button.

Choose a device or location from the menu.

In the Get Photos from Camera or Card Reader dialog, choose the card reader device.

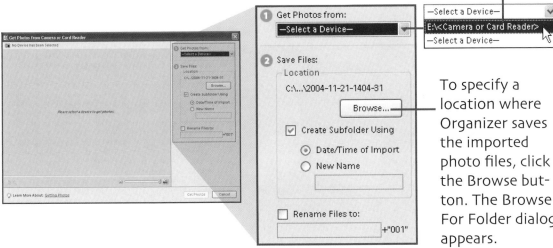

To specify a location where Organizer saves the imported photo files, click the Browse button. The Browse For Folder dialog appears.

In the Browse For Folder dialog, navigate to the folder where you want Organizer to save your photo files.

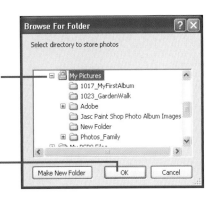

Click OK to close the dialog.

import photos (cont.)

Elements previews the memory card's photos in the Get Photos from Camera or Card Reader dialog.

By default, all images are selected. Click a check box to deselect any photo(s) you don't want to import.

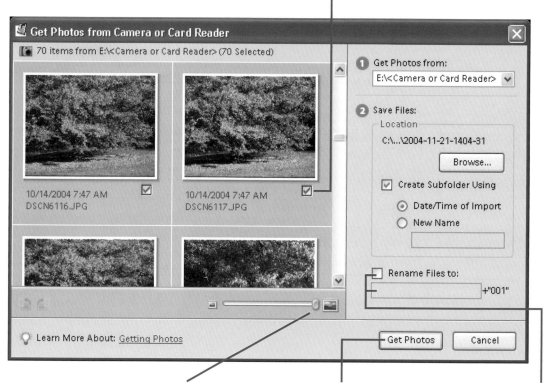

Drag the thumbnail slider to change the size of the preview thumbnail.

Click the Get Photos button to import the selected items to your catalog.

Check the Rename Files To check box and enter a meaningful name for your files. Elements adds sequential numbers at the end of the file name.

Elements imports your photos.

Elements warns you that the catalog shows just the imported images. To avoid seeing this note, click the Don't Show Again check box.

Click OK to close the dialog.

When import is done, you have the option to delete images from your memory card. Click No. It's better to let your camera do the deleting. Plus you can verify that you got all the photos you wanted before deleting them for good.

To display your full catalog, click the Back to All Photos button.

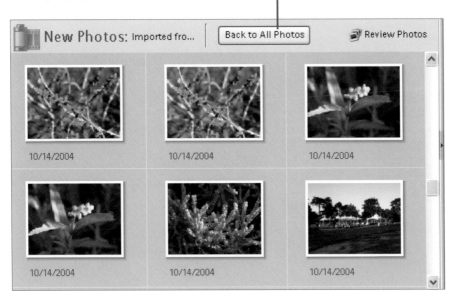

extra bits

general preparations p. 2

- Installing Elements automatically installs Adobe Reader 6.0.1 and Microsoft DirectX 9.0 if you don't already have them installed (these applications are included on the Elements CD).

import photos p. 8

- When Organizer previews the images from your card reader, in the Get Photos from Camera or Card Reader dialog, you can press `Ctrl`-`A` to select all the images.
- Press `Shift`-`Ctrl`-`A` to deselect all the images.
- To select noncontiguous photos, `Ctrl`-click each one.
- To select a range of photos, click the first one, then `Shift`-click the last one.

2. creating structure within your catalog

Once you start having fun with your digital camera, the number of photos you need to keep track of balloons quickly. Organizer's catalogs are really databases in disguise. Use your catalog to bring order to the chaos of your photo files.

Digital cameras record lots of information for each file, for example, the date and time you took the photo, the format, a file name. Organizer automatically enters that information into your catalog. You can add other details in captions and notes. To make it possible to sort your photos, you add categories, sub-categories, and tags. Finally, you can gather a set of photos for a specific purpose by creating collections and collection groups.

Categories and tags are Organizer's version of searchable keywords, while collections and collection groups act more like electronic shoe boxes storing groups of photos for use in a project. We'll make one collection group and several collections to gather photos for our album. Once you place photos in a collection, you can put them in any order you like. The collection contains links to your photo files. Photos in a collection still appear in their original catalog. Catalog searches still find these photos, and you can add them to other collections for other projects. Using tags, we'll narrow the range of candidates for our album, then gather the finalists into collections for each set of facing pages.

add captions and notes

Click the tiny triangle to close and open the Organize Bin.

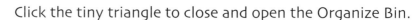

1 In the Photo Browser view in Organizer, click a photo to select it.

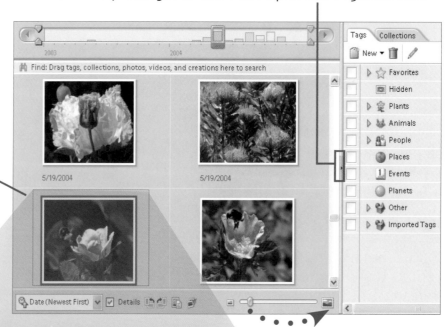

2 Drag thumbnail slider all the way to the right (or double-click the selected image) to view photos individually, at the largest size.

In single-image view, the photo's caption area becomes visible.

5/19/2004 9:55 AM

Click here to add caption

3 Click the caption area to activate the text field.

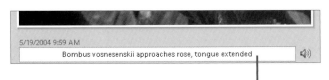

5/19/2004 9:59 AM

Bombus vosnesenskii approaches rose, tongue extended

4 Start typing your caption text. Press enter to confirm the caption.

Organizer automatically enters data from your camera, such as a file name and date, into the Properties window.

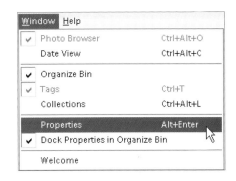

To view the properties of a selected image, choose Window > Properties, or press [Alt]-[Enter]. The Properties window opens in the Organize Bin.

The Caption, Name, and Notes — fields are all editable.

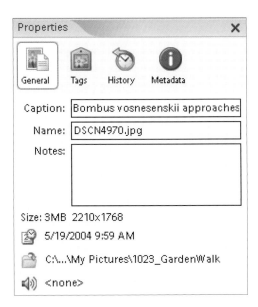

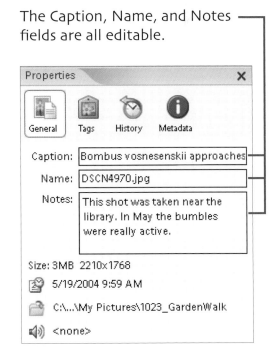

create categories

In the Organize Bin, click the Tags tab.

Click the New button

Select New Category (or New Sub-Category).

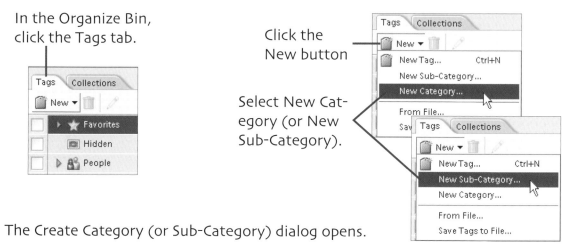

The Create Category (or Sub-Category) dialog opens.

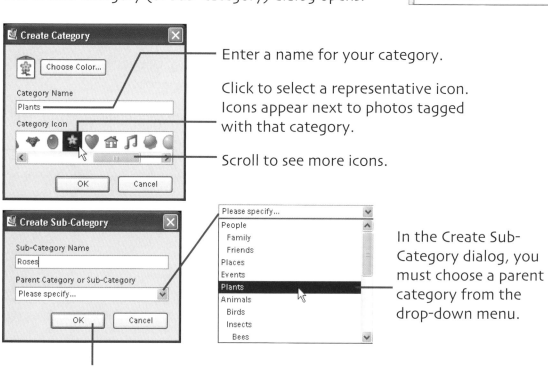

Enter a name for your category.

Click to select a representative icon. Icons appear next to photos tagged with that category.

Scroll to see more icons.

In the Create Sub-Category dialog, you must choose a parent category from the drop-down menu.

Click OK to close the dialog.

The new categories and sub-categories appear in the Organize Bin.

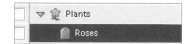

creating structure within your catalog

create tags

Creating tags is similar to creating categories and sub-catgories. Make tags the most specific level of your hierarchy.

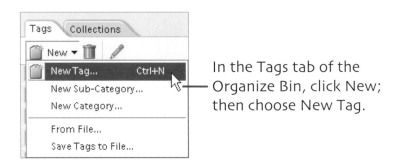

In the Tags tab of the Organize Bin, click New; then choose New Tag.

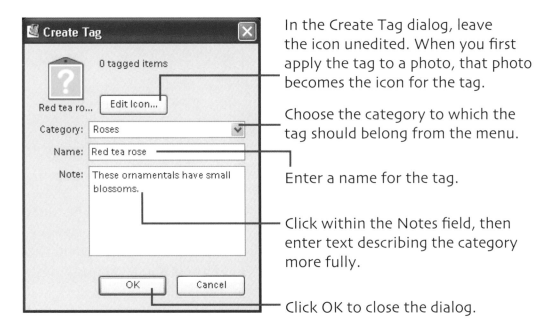

In the Create Tag dialog, leave the icon unedited. When you first apply the tag to a photo, that photo becomes the icon for the tag.

Choose the category to which the tag should belong from the menu.

Enter a name for the tag.

Click within the Notes field, then enter text describing the category more fully.

Click OK to close the dialog.

Tags appear below their parent category in the Organize Bin. Click a triangle to show/hide lower levels.

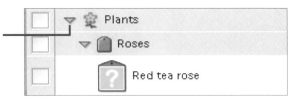

assign tags

Click a photo in the
Photo Browser to
select the photo.

Drag the tag from the Organize Bin onto the selected image.

The icon for the
top-level category
appears beneath
the photo in the
Photo Browser.

A thumbnail of the first image
to which you apply the tag
becomes the tag icon in the
Organize Bin.

Drag a tag to one photo in a
group of selected photos to
apply the tag to all of them.
Use [Shift]-click to select a
range of contiguous photos;
[Ctrl]-click to select noncontiguous photos.

creating structure within your catalog

add collections/groups

Elements' collection feature helps you gather and work with the photos you want to use in an album. When you sort photos by tags and categories, photos appear strictly in date order; in collections you can put images in any order.

1 In the Organize Bin, click the Collections tab.

2 Click New; then choose New Collection Group.

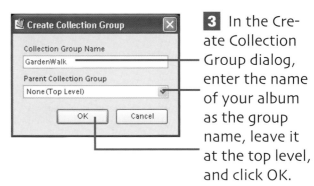

3 In the Create Collection Group dialog, enter the name of your album as the group name, leave it at the top level, and click OK.

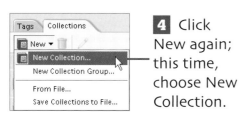

4 Click New again; this time, choose New Collection.

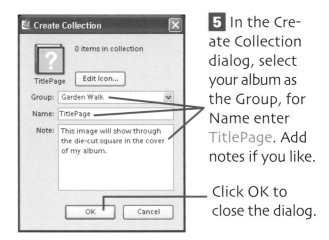

5 In the Create Collection dialog, select your album as the Group, for Name enter TitlePage. Add notes if you like.

Click OK to close the dialog.

Repeat Steps 4 and 5 above to create collections for each spread (a set of facing pages). Our album needs a right-hand title page, nine spreads, and a left-hand last page.

It's useful to have a collection containing all the images you might use in your album. Name it AlbumCandidates. Collections appear in the Organize Bin.

search with tags

Once you have set up tags, use them to search for specific types of photos you'd like in your album. I think I'd like to use some bee photos in mine.

Click the Tags tab to begin your photo search.

Click the check box next to the category, sub-category, or tag you want to find. Ctrl-click to select more than one.

Check the Matching checkbox to display images that match your search criteria.

Binocular icons indicate which categories, sub-categories, and tags are now showing in the Photo Browser. Selecting a category finds all the sub-categories and tags within it.

creating structure within your catalog

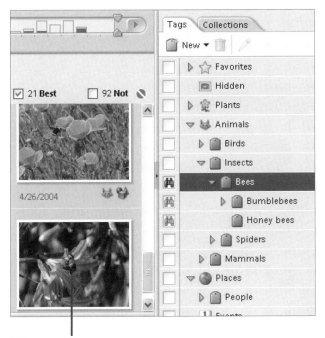

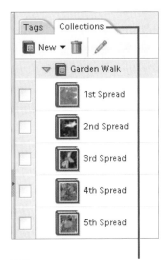

2 Click the Collections tab to view the collections you've prepared.

1 When you find an image that looks like a keeper for your album, click the photo to select it.

3 Drag the AlbumCandidates collection on top of the selected photo to add it to your collection of possible album photos.

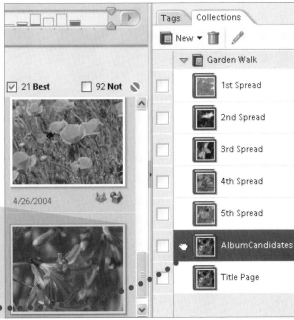

search with tags (cont.)

1 To assign multiple photos to a collection, click the first in a series of consecutive photos, then ⌈Shift⌉-click the end of the range to select them all. Blue highlight shows that they're selected. To add more photos ⌈Ctrl⌉-click them.

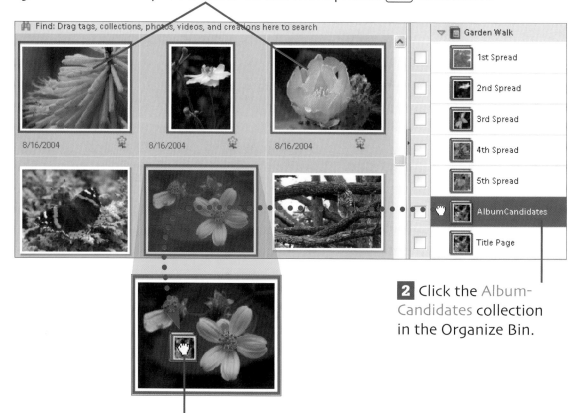

2 Click the Album-Candidates collection in the Organize Bin.

3 Drag the AlbumCandidates Collection onto one of the selected photos.

4 Organizer assigns the selected photos to that collection. The collection icon indicates that a photo belongs to one or more collections.

creating structure within your catalog

put photos in order

It's time to consider the sequence of photos in your album. First view your candidate photos by calling up the AlbumCandidates collection. Play with the order.

To review the photos you've gathered, in the Collections tab in the Organize Bin, click the check box for the AlbumCandidates collection.

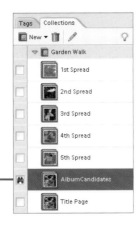

The Photo Browser numbers the collection's contents, but the order is flexible. You can change it.

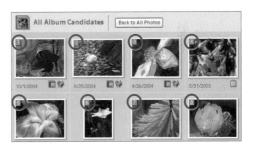

Click and drag a photo; the yellow bar previews the new location.

Release the mouse; the photo order and numbers update.

You can also drag multiple selected photos to a new location.

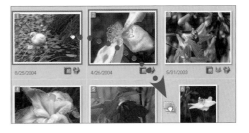

think in spreads

You've got the photos generally in order, now you need to break the order down into specific pages and spreads. Our album consists of a title page (a right-hand page), nine spreads (left- and right-hand pages), and a left-hand page at the end—20 pages in all. Assigning photos that belong together (on a page or on a spread) to a separate collection makes it easier to edit those photos to look good together (see Chapter 3).

Assign your title-page photo to the TitlePage collection you already created (see page 19); drag the TitlePage collection from the Organize Bin to the photo.

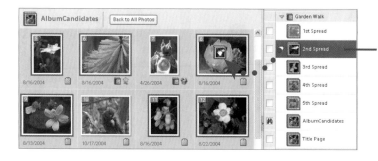

Select the photos that will go together on one spread. (Each page holds up to four photos, a possible total of eight photos per spread). Drag the appropriate Spread collection to one of the selected photos. Assign photos to each collection you created for the album.

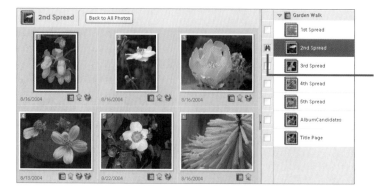

To view just the photos for one spread, click the check box for that collection.

creating structure within your catalog

extra bits

add captions & notes p. 14

- Click an icon at the top of the Properties window to view more data. The Tags view shows categories, tags, and collections to which the photo belongs. The History view shows the photo's place in a version set (see Chapter 3). The Metadata view shows data recorded by your digital camera, such as camera make and F-stop.

create categories p. 16

- In the Create Category dialog, clicking the Choose Color button opens a color picker. Choose the category tag's color; click OK.

- You can change the order of tags, categories, sub-categories, collections, and collection groups in the Organize Bin. In Organizer, choose Edit > Preferences > Tags and Collections. In the Enable Manual Sorting Option section, check the Manual radio button for Collections, for example. You can now drag collections listed in the bin to change their order.

create tags p. 17

- If you want to assign the image that appears in the tag icon right away, you must import it. Click the Edit Icon button in the Cre-ate Tag dialog. The Edit Tag Icon dialog appears. Click the Import button; the Import Image for Tag Icon dialog appears. It's a file-import dialog that displays thumbnails of photo files. Navigate to the photo file you want to use as the icon image. Click the photo's thumbnail in the dialog, then click the Open button. The file-import dialog closes and the photo appears in the Edit Tag Icon dialog; click the OK button to close that dialog. Your selected photo now appears as the icon in the Create Tag dialog. Finish entering your tag name and notes; then click the OK button to close that dialog.

- You can edit a tag's name, notes, and/or icon at any time. Click the tag's name in the Organize Bin to select the tag. Then click the Edit Tag button at the top of the Organize Bin (the small pencil icon) to open the Edit Tag dialog.

- To change the size of icons in the Organize Bin, choose Edit > Preferences > Tags and Collections. Click the radio button for the size you like under Tag Display.

extra bits

add collections/
groups p. 19

- A tag or collection dropped onto an unselected photo applies to that photo only, even if other photos are selected. If you have multiple images selected and drop a tag on one of them, that tag applies to all the selected images.

- Creating collections and groups for each page or spread sounds like a lot of work. It's not absolutely necessary, but because you cannot safely edit images that are included in an album without jeopardizing the album, it's a good idea. These collections facilitate the process of editing images that appear together. If you're not used to working with photos on spreads, consider your first few albums warm ups for getting the hang of how photos can work together.

search with tags p. 20

- To exclude categories or tags from a search, right-click the check box and choose Exclude Photos with . . . from the menu.

3. fixing image flaws

You've made collections for all the pages in your album; but the photos that go on those pages may need some retouching. Elements Editor is your darkroom, providing the tools you need to make your photos look their best. Editor's two modes, Quick Fix and Standard Edit, offer different levels of edit functions, ranging from completely automated to fully user driven. In this project, we want to concentrate on learning to create album pages, not tweaking images to perfection. To fix image flaws quickly, we'll use a mix of automated tools and tools that give the user some control. You'll find most of these tools in Quick Fix mode. A few tools, such as the healing brush, are available only in Standard Edit mode, the mode that gives you the most control over photo retouching. For the sake of space, we'll mostly look at correcting one photo, with one problem, at a time. For your own album, be sure to look at all the photos for a spread together to evaluate what kinds of changes need to be made. If you keep all the images for the spread open simultaneously, you can harmonize them more easily.

enter Quick Fix mode

In Organizer, you're going to call up each collection you made in Chapter 2.

With the Collections tab foremost in the Organize Bin, click the check box for a collection.

The photos in that collection appear in the Photo Browser.

To select a photo for editing, click it.

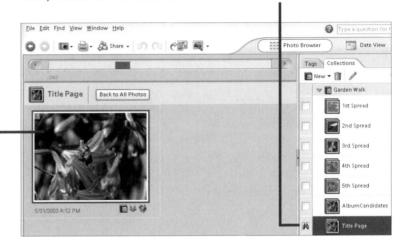

Click the edit button and choose Go to Quick Fix from the drop-down menu.

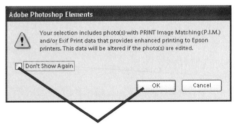

Editor opens its own work area and displays the photo in Quick Fix mode.

Photos from some digital cameras include special printing data. If yours does, this warning appears. Check the Don't Show Again check box, and click OK. You can't edit a photo and keep this information. We'll save each edited photo in a new file; the original retains any special print data should you want to use it to print the photo later.

fixing image flaws

set preview parameters

In Quick Fix mode you have several different views for previewing your edits.

Choose the zoom tool to change magnification. Click the plus icon (+), then click the photo with the tool to zoom in; click the minus icon (-), then click the photo to zoom out.

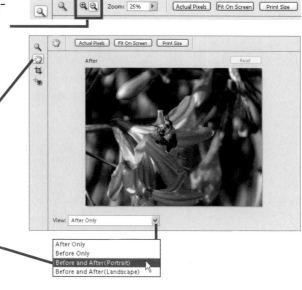

Use the hand tool to position the photo in the viewing area.

From the View menu choose Before and After (Portrait) to compare photos side by side.

With the zoom or hand tool selected, you can choose from three preset view sizes. Click a button to switch sizes.

Actual Pixels view (100%) is good for detail work.

Fit on Screen lets you see full photo context.

Print Size is a good compromise view.

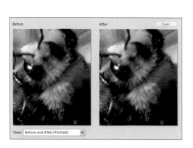

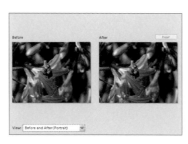

crop your photos

Most photos benefit from cropping (a fancy way to say trimming) to improve the subject's framing. For our project, crop photos to an aspect ratio of 3:4. The crop tool works similarly in both Editor modes. Try it in Quick Fix mode.

Click the crop tool button.

In the Options Bar, for width, enter 4 inches (for landscape orientation) or 3 (for portrait).

For height, enter 3 inches (for landscape orientation) or 4 (for portrait).

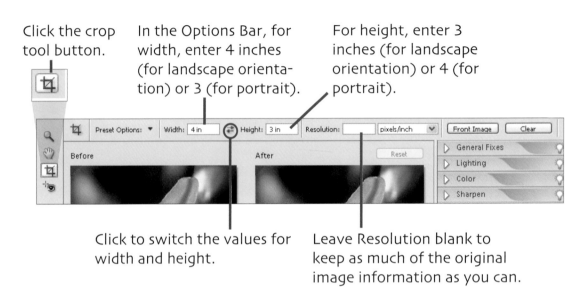

Click to switch the values for width and height.

Leave Resolution blank to keep as much of the original image information as you can.

Position the crop tool over the After photo. (The tool turns into the international No symbol over the Before image.)

Position the crop tool about where you want to begin the new image area.

Drag to create the crop; it need not be exact at first.

The rectangular marquee shows the proposed crop.

Darker, shielded, areas will get trimmed.

To fine-tune the crop, drag any of the four corner handles.

Position the pointer a bit away from a handle to activate the rotate pointer.

Drag to rotate the crop. Use this feature to straighten off-kilter photos.

Drag inside the marquee to move the whole crop rectangle.

Click Reset to start over at any time.

Before and After views help you judge the crop.

To cancel the crop, click the Cancel button.

To complete the crop, click the Commit button.

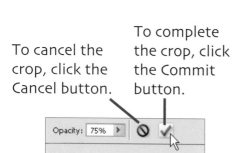

fixing image flaws

save your file

After you finish making edits to a file (in this case, cropping), choose File > Save to save the changes to your file.

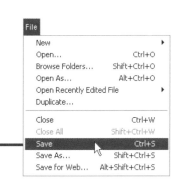

Choose a location for the saved file. By default Elements puts the new version in the same location as the original you just worked from.

Click to view recently used folders or main locations.

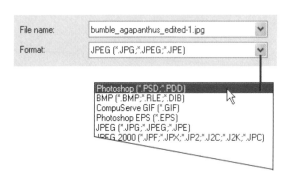

JPEG is a common photo format and will work fine in our album project (see the extra bits, page 52). If you prefer, you can select a new file format from the drop-down menu. We'll work with Photoshop (.psd) format files later in this chapter.

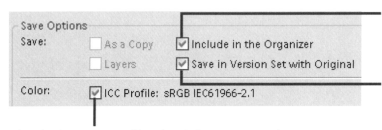

Choose Include in the Organizer and Save In Version Set with Original to preserve your original file. Editor saves changes in a copy, adding the word edited and a version number to the file name.

Check the ICC Profile check box to get the best color management for your album.

fixing image flaws

Click Save to begin saving your file.

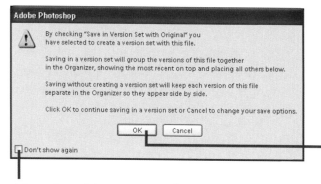

A warning dialog appears describing what saving as a version set entails.

Click OK to close the dialog.

To avoid seeing this message for every photo you edit, check the Don't Show Again check box.

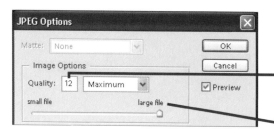

When you save a JPEG file, the JPEG Options dialog appears. Drag the quality slider all the way to the right or enter 12 in the Quality field. Maximum quality and large file size produce the best results in printed albums.

To close the file in Editor, click the Close icon of the item being edited.

While a photo is open in Editor, its thumbnail becomes locked in Organizer's Photo Browser.

After you close the file in Editor, the Photo Browser thumbnail bears a version set icon, meaning this thumbnail represents a group of edited files.

fixing image flaws

fix red eyes

A flash positioned right above the camera lens (as in most point-and-shoot cameras) sends light straight out. If your subject is a face, the light enters the eye, hits the retina, and bounces straight back to the camera, picking up the retina's rich red color. The result: your friends look like angry alien creatures. We'll use the red-eye removal tool in Quick Fix mode; it's available in Standard Edit, too.

Dragging over a value name activates a double-arrow cursor. Drag left and right to change values. Release the mouse to enter the current value.

To open a slider, click the triangle to the right of a value field. Drag to change values. Click outside the slider to enter the current value.

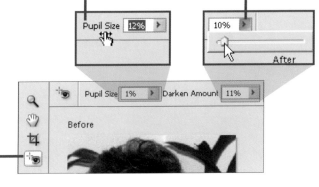

1 Click the cursor-and-eye icon to select the red-eye removal tool.

2 Enter a low value for Pupil Size; 12% is plenty.

Enter a low value for Darken Amount; 10% usually works well.

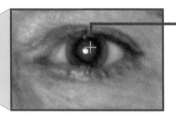

3 Position the pointer over any part of the red pupil in one of the eyes. Then click.

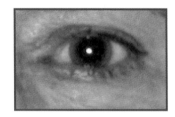

The red in the pupil area changes to black; other red areas retain their red color.

4 Repeat the procedure for the other eye.

The results are quite amazing. Your friends quickly regain their friendly appearance.

fixing image flaws

fix multiple flaws

The correction tools in the bin on the right side of the work area in Quick Fix mode let you correct photo flaws easily (though with less control and sophistication than you can achieve using the Standard Edit tools). The General Fixes section is a good starting place; the Smart Fix tool attempts to correct three problem areas at once: tonal range (exposure), color, and sharpness (focus).

Click the triangle to open General Fixes.

Click the Auto button to let Editor make its best guess at corrections.

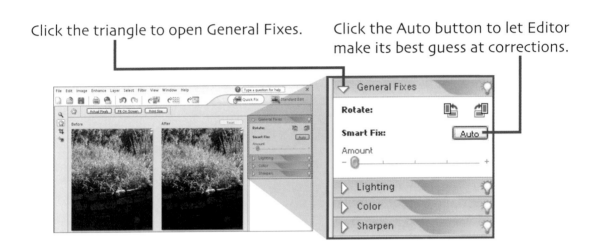

To undo the correction, click the Reset button.

Auto Smart Fix brings out details in the problem area without changing the rest of the photo.

The wall in shadow is underexposed.

fixing image flaws

fine-tune Smart Fix

Here Auto Smart Fix goes in the right direction but too far. The rose's leaves and petals look washed out. Fine-tune the correction with the Amount slider.

After trying an Auto correction, you must click the Reset button to return to your original photo before trying a new correction.

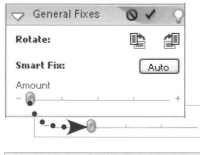

This time, drag the slider to apply Smart Fix. The After photo updates interactively. The farther to the right you drag, the stronger the correction.

Dragging to the first notch looks good.

To undo Amount slider changes, click the Cancel button.

To finalize slider changes, click the Commit button.

fix exposure flaws

Sometimes the Smart Fix correction is just not what you want at all. In this underexposed photo, Smart Fix's Auto correction makes the image too blue.

Click the Reset button to try another fix.

If Smart Fix spoils the color, try the Lighting corrections. Click the triangle to open the Lighting section.

Start with Levels. Click the Auto button.

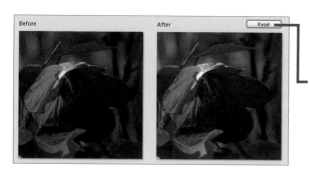

Levels: [Auto]

In this photo, Auto Levels does a little, but not enough. Click the Reset button to try another fix.

Try Contrast. Click the Auto button.

Contrast: [Auto]

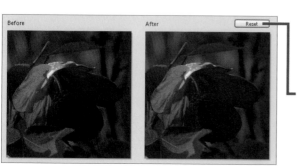

In this photo the Auto Contrast changes are even less helpful. Click the Reset button to try another fix.

It's time to try the interactive correction sliders. You can adjust different parts of your photo separately, judging visually what makes the best correction.

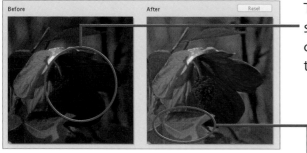

To bring out details where the shadow is too dark inside the flower, drag the Lighten Shadows slider to the right.

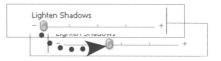

Now detail shows in the shadow, but the bright leaf areas are washed out. Drag the Darken Highlights slider to the right to bring them down.

The leaves look a bit better.

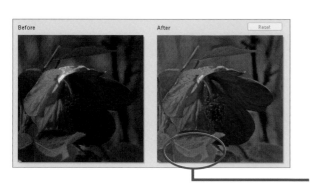

Finally, adjust the Midtone Contrast. Drag the slider to the right to increase contrast, to the left to decrease it. Here adding contrast brings back the leaves more.

With the Lighting sliders set, click the Commit button.

fix exposure flaws (cont.)

You can also use the corrections in the Lighting section to fix overexposed photos. For this photo, none of the automatic corrections (Auto Smart Fix, Auto Levels, or Auto Contrast) went far enough to correct the flat washed-out look.

Drag the Darken Highlights slider to the right to create a darker image with more impact.

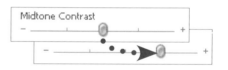

Drag the Midtone Contrast slider to the right to bring out more definition in the feathers and make the hawk stand out more.

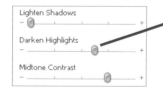

With the Lighting sliders set, click the Commit button.

fix color cast

Photos taken under certain lighting conditions (such as on overcast days or indoors) may take on a color cast. Quick Fix's color-correction tools help you remove a color cast.

Click the triangle to access Quick Fix mode's color-correction tools.

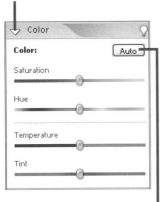

Auto Color did a bad job on this photo. Click the Reset button to start over.

Click the Auto button for Editor's best-guess correction.

Drag the Temperature slider to the right to warm up a photo with a blue color cast.

The result is better, but now it looks too green.

Drag the Tint slider to the right to reduce the green.

fix color cast (cont.)

As a final correction for this photo, dragging the Saturation slider to the left makes the color a bit less intense (a bit closer to black and white), giving the photo more of the mood of the weather the day it was taken, without the odd color cast.

When you've adjusted the photo to your satisfaction with the Color sliders, you must click the Commit button to apply the changes to your file.

If you find the color sliders confusing, try Editor's one-click trick for removing color cast. It's available in both Quick Fix and Standard Edit.

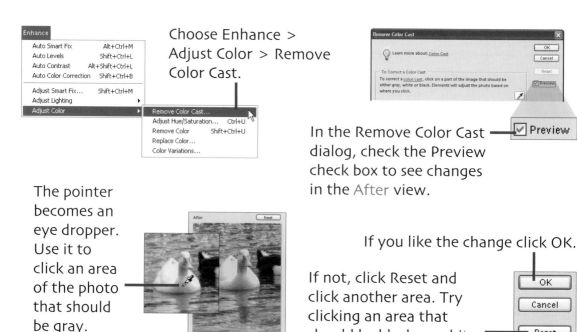

Choose Enhance > Adjust Color > Remove Color Cast.

In the Remove Color Cast dialog, check the Preview check box to see changes in the After view.

The pointer becomes an eye dropper. Use it to click an area of the photo that should be gray.

If you like the change click OK.

If not, click Reset and click another area. Try clicking an area that should be black or white.

harmonize colors

When editing photos that appear together on a page or spread, it's good to open them together. That way you can make sure they look harmonious together.

To view multiple photos simultaneously, you must open them in Standard Edit mode.

1 In Organizer, click the Collections tab to access the collections you made earlier.

2 Choose the check box for a spread whose photos you want to work on.

3 Press Ctrl-A to select all photos.

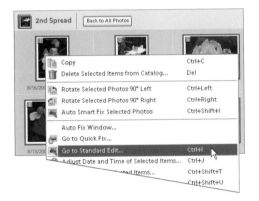

4 To open the photos in separate windows in Standard Edit mode, right-click a photo and choose Go to Standard Edit from the contextual menu.

5 Click the Tile Windows icon to see the photos simultaneously.

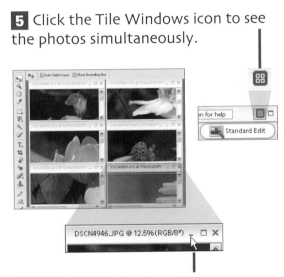

Click the Minimize icon to remove a photo from the work area but keep it available in the Photo Bin.

6 To reopen a photo double-click it in the Photo Bin.

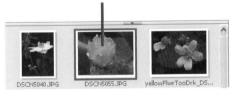

7 Drag any corner or edge of a window to resize the photo.

fixing image flaws

harmonize colors (cont)

Standard Edit mode allows you to work in layers. Using layers is beyond the scope of this book, but one basic layer trick is to make a duplicate layer of your photo before you start editing. If you don't like your edits, just delete the layer.

To copy your photo to a new layer, click the More triangle and choose Duplicate Layer from the Layers palette menu.

The duplicate layer appears in the Layers palette above the original.

Click the Trash icon to delete the active layer.

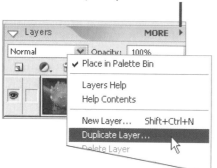

To hide a layer, click its eye icon.

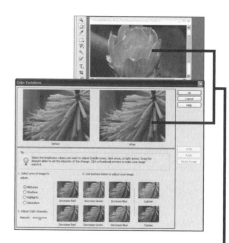

To choose the layer to work on (the active layer), in the Layers palette, click the layer; it highlights.

To start harmonizing colors, choose Enhance > Adjust Color > Color Variations.

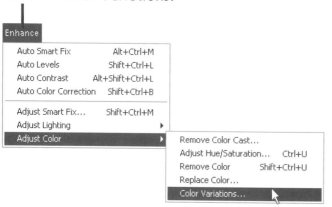

Position the Color Variations dialog so the After preview is near the photo you're trying to match.

The tubular blossoms should be less red to match the cactus flower. Click each radio button in turn to try changing different areas of the photo; view the thumbnails to see if any of them make changes in the direction you want. For this photo, changing the shadows does little; changing the midtones looks like the best bet.

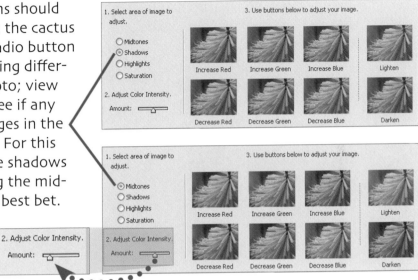

Dragging the Amount slider to the left lets you make the changes in subtle increments.

Click repeatedly to make the change more intense.

After one click.

After two clicks.

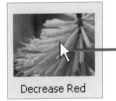

Decrease Red

Click the thumbnail that makes the desired change, here Decrease Red fits best.

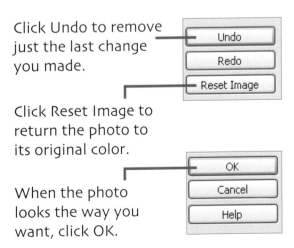

Click Undo to remove just the last change you made.

Click Reset Image to return the photo to its original color.

When the photo looks the way you want, click OK.

fixing image flaws

clean up photos

Even in a lovely spot like the arboretum, trash can spoil a nice shot. Elements' healing brush tool makes it easy to clean up after litter bugs. The healing brush is unavailable in Quick Fix mode. You must open your photo in Standard Edit.

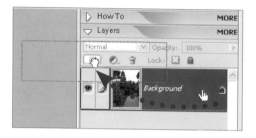

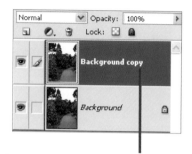

To work on a copy of the image, drag the Background layer to the Create New Layer icon.

Click the Background copy layer to activate it.

Select the zoom tool. You'll want to get a close up view of the area you want to clean up.

Position the zoom tool in the area you want to clean.

Drag a rectangle around the area.

In the tool box, select the healing brush (or spot healing brush) tool.

The spot healing brush works well on small items.

Click the triangle to open the preset brush menu.

Drag to choose brush size.

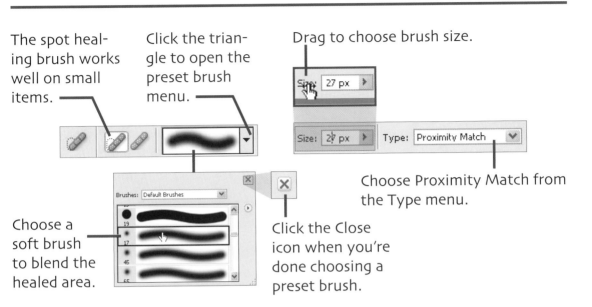

Choose a soft brush to blend the healed area.

Click the Close icon when you're done choosing a preset brush.

Choose Proximity Match from the Type menu.

Unwanted items surrounded by uniform objects, like these dried sticks, heal pretty seamlessly. It may take a few tries to get it just right.

Use the spot healing brush (or healing brush) tool to "paint" over an unwanted item in your photo. Here it's trash lying near the path.

Release the mouse button and the healing takes place.

If some traces of the object remain, paint over them again to make them blend in completely.

fixing image flaws

sharpen in Quick Fix

The final correction to talk about is sharpening—and I do mean final. Sharpen your photo after you've made all other corrections. Sharpening makes the edges of things more distinct and brings out detail. Digital photo prints are often a bit softer than photos printed from film. Sharpening helps bring out that extra touch of focus. But use sharpening sparingly. It's easy to get carried away and sharpen too much, especially using Editor's automated sharpening tools.

Open your photo in Quick Fix mode.

Click the triangle to open the Sharpen section.

Click to select the hand tool. The tool lets you reposition your photo preview to check how various areas look with the sharpening that you add.

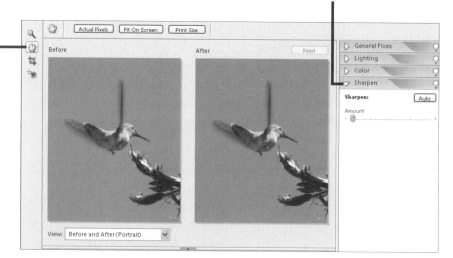

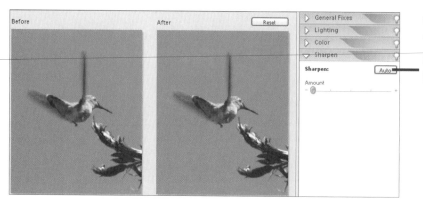

Click the Auto button to apply Editor's best-guess sharpening to your photo.

fixing image flaws

It's important to check the results of sharpening by viewing your photo at 100 percent. This view reveals if oversharpening is happening. Oversharpening creates extra noise and artifacts in your image.

Click the Actual Pixels button to view your photo at 100%.

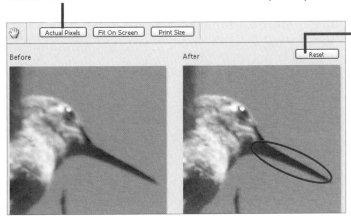

Click the Reset button to try a different correction.

Auto Sharpen frequently takes the correction too far. In this photo, artifacts appear along the top edge of the beak after choosing Auto Sharpen.

Clicking the slider half way to the first notch applies good sharpening for this photo.

Move the slider to the right to apply more sharpening. By the second notch, artifacts already appear. Move the slider any farther right and you start getting a halo effect.

To undo your adjustments, click Cancel.

To accept your adjustments, click Commit.

fixing image flaws

prune your collections

We've been saving each edited photo in a version set with its original. Generally, the Photo Browser stacks a new version on top of its original. When displaying a collection, however, the browser doesn't show version sets. The original photos you assigned to the collection and any edited versions of those photos appear as separate files. Having multiple copies of the photos adds confusion when it's time to place your photos in their album (which we'll do in Chapters 4 and 5). Return to the Photo Browser to prune your collections of outdated photos.

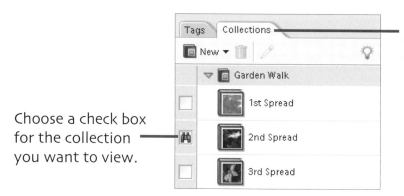

Click the Collections tab at the top of the Organize Bin.

Choose a check box for the collection you want to view.

Originals of any edited photos appear at the beginning of the collection.

Edited photos (and originals of unedited photos) follow the outdated originals and appear in the order that you chose for the collection.

fixing image flaws

To begin the pruning process, right-click a photo that you wan to remove. The contextual menu opens.

Choose Remove from Collection. From the fly-out menu, choose 2nd Spread (or whichever Spread collection the photo belongs to).

When you've done this for each outdated photo in the collection, the Photo Browser displays just the versions of the photos that you will use in your album.

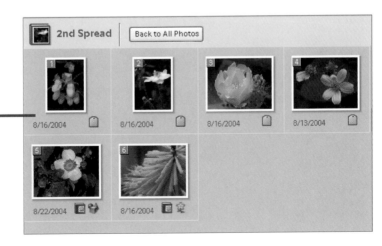

extra bits

crop your photos p. 30

- Most of the Elements albums have built-in borders that frame your photos. The aspect ratio (ratio of width to height) for album borders is 4:3 (landscape) or 3:4 (portrait). This is a common ratio for digital cameras. If a photo has a different ratio, however, Elements' Album Creation wizard simply crops the photo. To keep control over what part of your photo appears in your album, crop photos to 3:4 yourself.

- The No Borders style (for printing album pages on your own printer), accepts photos with any aspect ratio. You might expect that to be the case with No Borders Book and Full Bleed Book styles too, but as this Visual QuickProject went to press, that wasn't true. Photos in those styles get cropped to the 3:4 ratio. Adobe plans to update templates and give you more control over aspect ratio in these styles in the future (see Chapters 4 and 5).

- By default, the cropping shield is black with 75 percent opacity. After you draw a cropping rectangle, you can choose a new color and opacity in the Options bar.

save your file p. 32

- Although JPEG is not usually a suitable format for printed books, Elements translates photo album pages to PDF format for printing (see Chapter 5). Therefore, you don't need to change file formats when you save your edited photos. It's fine to change JPEG (.jpg) files to Photoshop (.psd) files if you prefer. If you edit a photo in Standard Edit mode and add layers, Elements automatically changes the file's format to .psd for you.

- If you have access to an Epson printer that you might want to use for printing your photos, you can restore the P.I.M. warning when you're done with your album project. That way, the warning dialog pops up when you edit a photo that contains embedded Print Image Matching (P.I.M.) data. To restore the warning (and any others you've turned off), from the Organizer work area, choose Edit > Preferences > Editor Preferences. In the Preferences dialog that appears, click the Reset All Warning Dialogs button. If you are already working in the Editor work area, choose Edit > Preferences > General to open the dialog.

fix red eyes p. 34

- For Pupil Size, enter no more than 50 % unless your want you subject to look as if he or she's just been to the eye doctor.
- For Darken Amount, 100 % would look unnaturally dark.
- Though the red-eye removal tool is a cross-hair cursor, and it lets you draw a selection rectangle, the tool works best if you just click once within a red pupil area. Only if that one click doesn't work should you try making a selection with the tool.

fix multiple flaws p. 36

- It's important to apply only one Auto correction from the Quick Fix tools. Try one, then if it's not what you want, click the Reset button and try something else. Applying more than one Auto correction quickly degrades the quality of your photo.

fine-tune Smart Fix p. 37

- The set of correction tools on the right side of the Quick Fix work area is divided into four sections. It's best to work in one section at a time; try a correction, then click the Cancel button if you want to try something else within the same section. Click the Commit button (or the Cancel button, if you decide not to make any change in that section) before moving on. If you've made slider adjustments in one section and then start adjusting sliders in a different section, Elements automatically commits the changes you made in the first section. The result may not be what you intended, in which case, you'll have to reset the photo and start all over again.

sharpen in Quick Fix p. 48

- Sharpening is truly an art. The amount of sharpening to apply depends on the type of photo, the subject matter and original intent for focus, as well as the final delivery medium. The amount of sharpening you need for images on the Web is different from the amount of sharpening you need for printed photos. Sharpening for a small photo in an album is different from sharpening for a large poster-sized print. If you want to move beyond the automated sharpening in Quick Fix mode, you'll need to use filters. You can access filters in both Quick Fix and Standard Edit mode. Choose

extra bits

sharpen in Quick Fix (cont.)

Filter > Sharpen to see a full list of sharpening filter choices. The Unsharp Mask filter is the standard professional sharpening tool. Experiment with its settings and your photos. But remember, it may take some time (or some expert advice from the many excellent books on Photoshop Elements of Photoshop) to learn how to get the best results using the sharpening filters.

4. creating albums with fixed layouts

Photoshop Elements 3.0 comes with an Album Creation wizard and templates for creating photo album pages in various styles. Some styles place photos inside a border, others are borderless. Borders can provide decorative frames, add drop shadows, or give digital photos the white edges of traditional prints. Styles with borders have fixed layouts. Borderless styles place photos in a default layout, but without frames, leaving you free to reposition the photos

The basics of working with photos and text in albums are the same with or without borders. The easiest styles to use have borders and a fixed layout. For your first project, try a fixed-border layout in a style designed to be printed on 8.5-by-11-inch paper on your home printer (these styles lack the yellow Order Online medallion). Once you've created a basic album, you'll be ready to tackle something more creative in Chapter 5.

The templates that shipped with Elements 3.0 use borders with an aspect ratio of 3:4 (or 4:3). The wizard crops photos that have any other aspect ratio to fit. To get the best framing for your photos, crop them to the 3:4 ratio yourself (see Chapter 3).

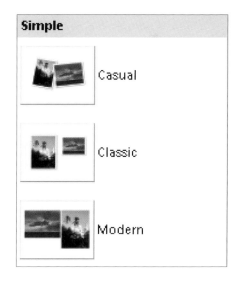

get new templates

Before working with the Album Creation wizard, update the templates.

1 To start the update process, open Organizer; choose Edit > Preferences > Services.

Adobe may use updates to correct template problems discovered since Elements shipped. Adobe will also use updates to add new styles.

2 Select Services in the Preferences dialog.

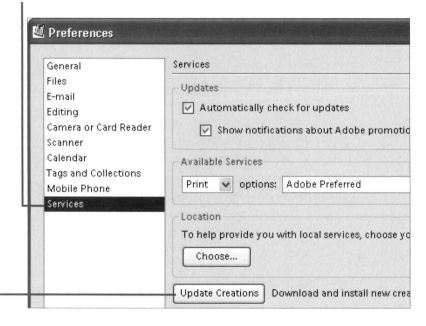

3 Click Update Creations.

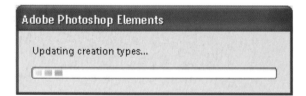

4 Elements connects to the Internet and downloads any new templates.

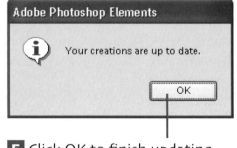

5 Click OK to finish updating.

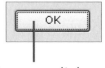

6 Click OK to close the Preferences dialog.

creating albums with fixed layouts

open creations wizard

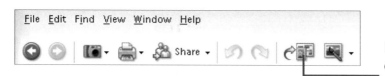

In Organizer, click the Create button in the shortcuts bar.

The Creation Setup wizard opens. It offers seven types of creative projects that you can make with your photos.

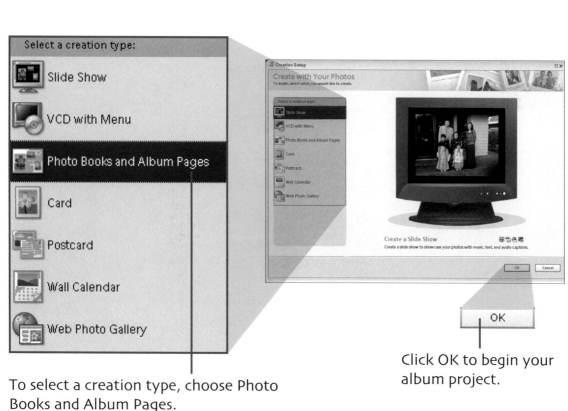

To select a creation type, choose Photo Books and Album Pages.

Click OK to begin your album project.

choose album style

The Album Creation wizard opens. In Step 1: Creation Set-up, you set parameters. For your first album, choose a style with borders that you can print on a home printer. For now, avoid the borderless styles (grouped under the heading Full Photo) and the styles designed to be ordered as books (the ones that include the word Book in their name and have yellow medallions that say Order Online).

Casual is a nice clean-looking style that's not too formal. Click the name to select it for this first album project.

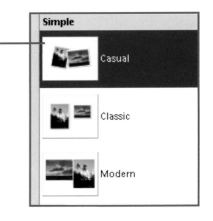

Check all of the Options. You can customize any item, except page numbers, as you lay out your album pages. Page numbers are the only items you can't change. You should know that for hardcover books, the page numbers are strange. Odd-numbers show up on left-hand pages, evens on the right. In professionally designed books, it's exactly the opposite. For home-printed, single-sided pages, however, the default page numbers look fine.

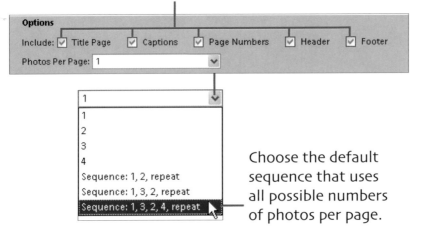

Choose the default sequence that uses all possible numbers of photos per page.

When you finish choosing album parameters, click Next Step.

choose photos

In Step 2: Arrange Your Photos, you bring photos into your album.

Click the Add photos button to start.

The radio buttons and check boxes in the Add Photos From section filter the images in your catalog. By default, this dialog displays the photos currently selected in Organizer's Photo Browser.

Scroll to see more images.

Back in Chapter 2, you set up some collections that hold just the photos you want for your album. Click the Collection radio button to access these photos.

From the Select menu, choose the first collection for your album, the one named TitlePage.

choose photos (cont.)

Click the check box to select your Title-page image.

Click Add Selected Photos to bring the checked images into your album.

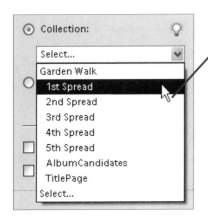

Next, select the collection named 1stSpread to bring those photos into the Add Photos dialog.

Click the check boxes to select the photos.

Repeat this selection process for the rest of the collections you set up.

When you've added all your photos, click OK to close the Add Photos dialog.

creating albums with fixed layouts

put photos in order

You can change the order of your images in Step 2: Arrange Your Photos.

1 Click the photo you want to move, then drag it to a new position. (To move several photos, [Ctrl]-click each one; if the photos are in a row, click the first one, then [Shift]-click the last one to select them all. Dragging one photo moves the whole selected group, even if the photos are not contiguous.)

2 The yellow bar highlights the new placement. Release the mouse.

3 The Album Creation wizard reorders the images and reassigns their pages.

put photos in order (cont.)

In Step 2: Arrange Your Photos, the Album Creation wizard lets you reuse photos without duplicating files. You can also remove photos from an Album here.

Let's repeat the Title photo on Page 1. (We're making a home-printed album, but for hardcover books, the wizard crops the Title photo to fit the die-cut square in the album cover. You might want to show off the full image as your first page.) Click the Title photo to select it.

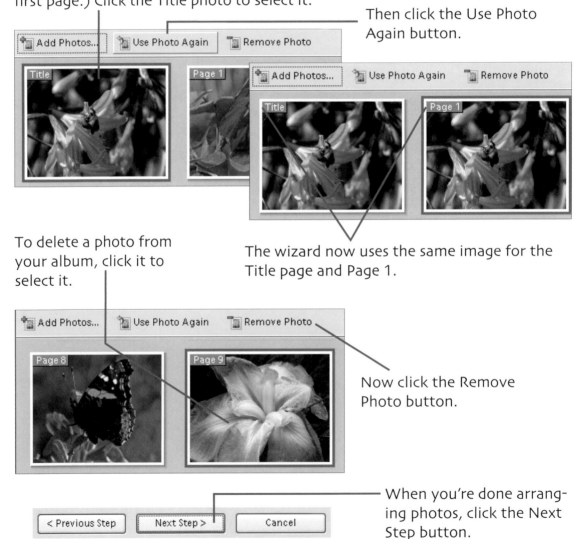

Then click the Use Photo Again button.

To delete a photo from your album, click it to select it.

The wizard now uses the same image for the Title page and Page 1.

Now click the Remove Photo button.

When you're done arranging photos, click the Next Step button.

creating albums with fixed layouts

fine-tune the layout

Step 3: Customize   ① Creation Set-up ② Arrange Your Photos **③ Customize** ④ Save

In Step 3: Customize, you fine-tune the layout. Album styles with borders aren't fully customizable, but you can enlarge what's in the frame and add text.

Page layouts vary according to album style, the number of photos per page, and the orientation of the images. The wizard places photos for you.

Before customizing, "flip" through your album to see how your layouts look.

To add, delete, or rearrange photos, click the Previous Step button to return to Step 2.

Click the Back button to move to the album's previous page.

Click the Forward button to move to the next album page.

< Previous Step

creating albums with fixed layouts

position photos

In a style with borders, the border always stays the same size, in the same spot on the page, and with the same aspect ratio (3:4). You can resize the image, to zoom in, then reposition the photo to determine what appears inside the frame.

Click a photo to select it and activate its selection rectangle. Place the pointer over a corner resize handle.

Drag the handle outward.

Release the handle to preview the image size; the dim area gets cropped. Drag the photo to move it.

Click outside the photo to deselect it and view the new cropping and enlargement.

creating albums with fixed layouts

add title text

1 Once you have all of the photos in place and sized as you want, you are ready to deal with the text elements of your layout. To return to the Title page, choose Title from the View Page menu.

2 A placeholder title appears automatically on the Title page. Click the title to activate its text box. Double-click the title to open a dialog for editing the title.

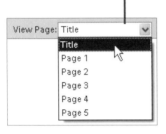

View Page: Title
- Title
- Page 1
- Page 2
- Page 3
- Page 4
- Page 5

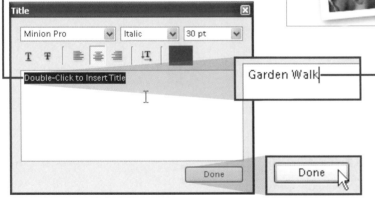

Double-Click to Insert Title

3 Drag, triple-click, or press [Ctrl]-[A] to select all the text in the Title dialog.

Title ☒

Minion Pro | Italic | 30 pt

Double-Click to Insert Title

Garden Walk|

4 Enter new text for the title.

Done | Done

5 Click the Done button to close the dialog.

6 The new title appears in the default font, style, size, and color. You'll learn to change these characteristics in Chapter 5.

Garden Walk

7 Click to go to Page 1.

edit headers & footers

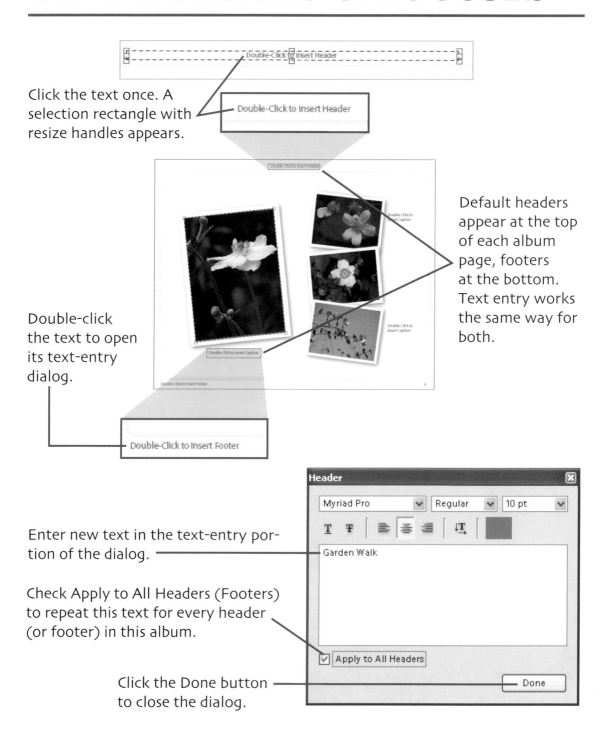

Click the text once. A selection rectangle with resize handles appears.

Double-Click to Insert Header

Default headers appear at the top of each album page, footers at the bottom. Text entry works the same way for both.

Double-click the text to open its text-entry dialog.

Double-Click to Insert Footer

Enter new text in the text-entry portion of the dialog.

Check Apply to All Headers (Footers) to repeat this text for every header (or footer) in this album.

Click the Done button to close the dialog.

Header

| Myriad Pro | Regular | 10 pt |

Garden Walk

☑ Apply to All Headers

Done

edit captions

Double-Click to Insert Caption

Snow berry bush

Photos without captions in Organizer get placeholder captions in your album.

A "missing" caption, usually means you once clicked that photo's caption in Organizer, but entered no text.

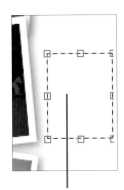

In Step 3 of the wizard, click in the area of any "missing" caption to activate its selection rectangle.

Photos that have captions in Organizer bring their captions with them when you import them into an album.

Double-click any caption to open its text-entry dialog.

Double-Click to Insert Caption

There is a tiny crab flower spider hidden in this blossom.

Snow berry bush

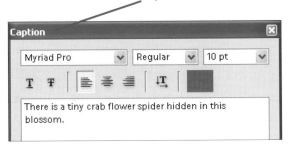

Caption

| Myriad Pro | Regular | 10 pt |

T T ≣ ≣ ≣ ↓T

There is a tiny crab flower spider hidden in this blossom.

check resolution

The Album Creation wizard warns you when you try to include photos whose resolution is too low in your album. Importing low-resolution images results in a warning in Step 2: Arrange Your Photos.

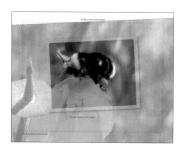

You can resize even a high-resolution image so much that you put it beyond the limits of best print quality. This 300-ppi photo has plenty of resolution at this album's default single-photo size, but going wild with enlarging will put it beyond the limits.

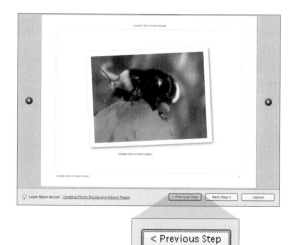

1 To see if your images have enough resolution after you have resized them in the album layout, click the Previous Step button to return to Step 2.

2 If you've enlarged a photo so that there's no longer enough resolution for best print quality, a warning dialog pops up every time you enter Step 2.

3 A warning triangle indicates problem photos. To insure best quality, go to Step 3 and reduce or reset the problem image (see extra bits page 71).

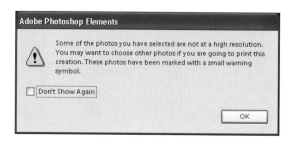

save and print

When you've finished positioning your photos and entering the text for headers, footers, and captions, it's time to save and print your album.

In Step 3, click the Next Step button to move to Step 4. (If starting from an earlier step, keep clicking Next Step until you reach Step 4.)

> < Previous Step   Next Step >

Step 4: Save (1) Creation Set-up (2) Arrange Your Photos (3) Customize **(4) Save** (5) Share

In the Step 4: Save page, enter a name for your album in the Creations Name field.

Or check the Use Title For Name check box.

Don't check the Show These Photos check box. (The main reason to do that would be to find album photos for editing, but editing photos after placing them in an album may corrupt the album.)

> You can now save your creation to edit it later.
>
> Creations Name:
> GardenWalkCasual
> ☐ Use Title for Name
>
> Your saved creation and all photos used in the creation will be included in the Organizer.
> ☐ Show these photos in my Photo Browser when finished.

Click the Save button to begin the process of saving your album. The wizard takes you automatically to Step 5.

> < Previous Step   Save >

Step 5: Share (1) Creation Set-up (2) Arrange Your Photos (3) Customize (4) Save **(5) Share**

> You can now share your creation in one or more of the following ways:
>
> 📄 Create a PDF...
> 🖨 Print...
> 📧 E-mail...
> 🛒 Order Online...

Step 5: Share offers options for printing and sharing your album. Skip these for now.

Click the Done button immediately (see extra bits, page 72, to learn why).

> < Previous Step   Done

creating albums with fixed layouts

save and print (cont.)

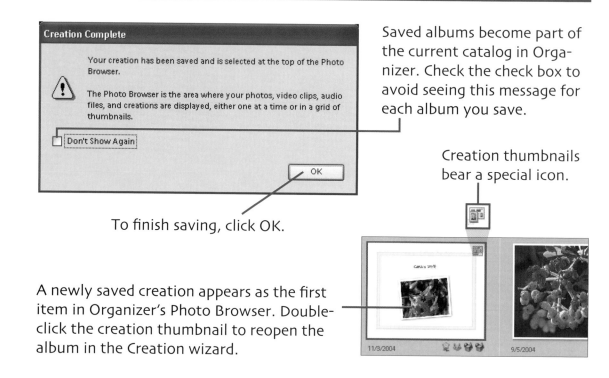

Saved albums become part of the current catalog in Organizer. Check the check box to avoid seeing this message for each album you save.

Creation thumbnails bear a special icon.

To finish saving, click OK.

A newly saved creation appears as the first item in Organizer's Photo Browser. Double-click the creation thumbnail to reopen the album in the Creation wizard.

When you open a saved album the Album Creation wizard takes you to Step 3. Click the Next Step button to move to Step 4.

To move on to Step 5, where you can print, click the Save button.

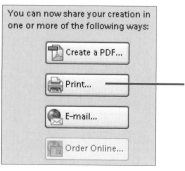

Click the Print button to print a test run on cheap paper or a final version on nice paper.

The dimensions of the album pages created by the Casual template measure 11 by 8.5 inches. In the settings for your printer, choose Landscape orientation for the paper. Choose a low print quality for test runs, high print quality for final prints.

creating albums with fixed layouts

extra bits

get new templates p. 56

- To update templates in Editor, choose Edit > Preferences > General. In the Services part of the Preferences dialog, check Automatically Check for Updates.

- Currently only one template style—No Borders—accepts photos in anything but the 3:4 (4:3) aspect ratio. The No Borders style must be printed on a local printer, not ordered as a photobook. Why might you want to work with other aspect ratios? Cropping to another aspect ratio may better frame a subject. A square crop, for example, might frame a face. Panoramic photos are a popular use of non-standard aspect ratios.

- Adobe plans to add templates that use aspect ratios other than 3:4 or 4:3. Be sure to keep checking for template updates.

choose photos p. 59

- Once you've brought photos into an album it's a good idea to save that work. Click the close icon for the Creation wizard; a dialog warns that the creation hasn't been saved. Go through all the save procedures outlined on pages 69 and 70. Just be sure to click the Done button to complete the save procedure. Then reopen your creation to continue editing it.

- Press Ctrl-A to check all the check boxes in the Add Photos dialog.

- Click in the gray area to uncheck any selected check boxes, or press Shift-Ctrl-A

fine-tune the layout p. 63

- If you set up your creation with a default series (for example, alternating pages of 1 and 2 photos), you can specify a new number of photos on a page by choosing the number from the Photos on This Page menu in Step 3. We'll do that in Chapter 5.

position photos p. 64

- If you don't like the resizing that you've done, click the Reset Photos button above the work area in Step 3 to return all photos on the page to their original size and position within their borders.

- When you resize within borders, dragging inward shrinks the image and leaves a wider border, which may look odd.

- Another way to deselect a photo or piece of text is to right-click it and choose deselect from the contextual menu.

extra bits

edit headers & footers p. 66

- Usually, it makes sense to click the Apply to All check box in the Header or Footer dialog on Page 1, even if you plan to change some on later pages. You can change individual headers or footers by double-clicking them and entering new text in the dialog.

- Be careful about clicking that box at later stages. The new header or footer overrides any previous header or footer text you entered.

edit captions p. 67

- What you type in an album caption has no effect on that photo's caption in Organizer.

- Don't make text changes until you've put your photos in order, chosen which pages they go on, and made any sizing changes. If you move a photo to a different page, you'll lose any caption text you've entered in the album.

- An advantage to creating captions in Organizer: they will be tied to the image and move with it.

save and print p. 69

- Resist the temptation to start sharing, printing, or making a PDF file until you've clicked the Done button. If you get caught up

in printing, for example, and close the wizard window before clicking the Done button, your album changes will not be saved.

- Many companies make glossy photo paper in 8.5-by-11-inch sheets suitable for use with your home color printer. Some sheets can even be printed on both sides. You can use a three-hole punch and place these sheets in notebooks or other types of binders. For starters, check out the following companies who list glossy photo paper in their product sections (usually under supplies and accessories): Canon (www.canon.com), Epson (www.epson.com), HP (www.hp.com), Kodak (www.kodak.com), and Strathmore (www.strathmoreartist.com). It's often possible to purchase glossy photo paper at discount office supply stores.

- In addition to paper that resembles photo prints, Strathmore makes 8.5-by-11-inch art papers, with various textures, that can be used on ink-jet printers and might dress up your album.

5. creating albums with flexible layouts

In the previous chapter you created an album in a simple fixed-layout style. To get more flexibility and exercise your creativity fully, you need to choose one of the Full Photo styles. When you choose one of these styles, the Album Creation wizard places your photos on the album pages without any borders. You can truly resize your photos (there's no frame to crop the enlarged image) and reposition photos on the album page.

One borderless style—No Borders—is designed for creating album pages that you can print on your home printer. At the time this book was being written, No Borders is the only style that allows you to work with photos that have an aspect ratio other than 3:4. For the future, Adobe plans to update templates to give you this freedom in the styles that create hardcover photobooks as well. For this project, we'll work with a style that gives you lots of creative license and that makes albums that can be printed as hardcover photobooks. (For more about updating templates and ordering photobooks, see Chapter 6.)

choose a flexible album

Open the Album Creation wizard, as described in Chapter 4.

Step 1: Creation Set-up

This time, in Step 1, choose No Borders Book as the album style.

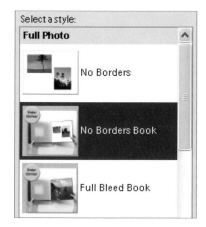

Check all of the options for title page and text elements. The wizard still sets page numbers oddly in this style, but the numbers on each page help you to position photos and text correctly. You can delete them before ordering the photobook.

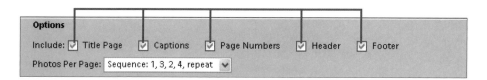

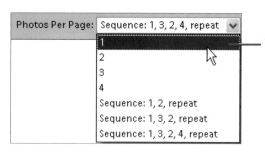

Choose 1 photo per page. It's easier to create a variety of multiple-image pages when no repeating series has been set up in advance.

Click Next Step. ──

Step 2: Arrange Your Photos

In Step 2, use the collections you've set up for your album to bring photos into the Album Creation wizard as described in Chapter 4.

customize title text

Step 3: Customize ① Creation Set-up ② Arrange Your Photos ③ Customize

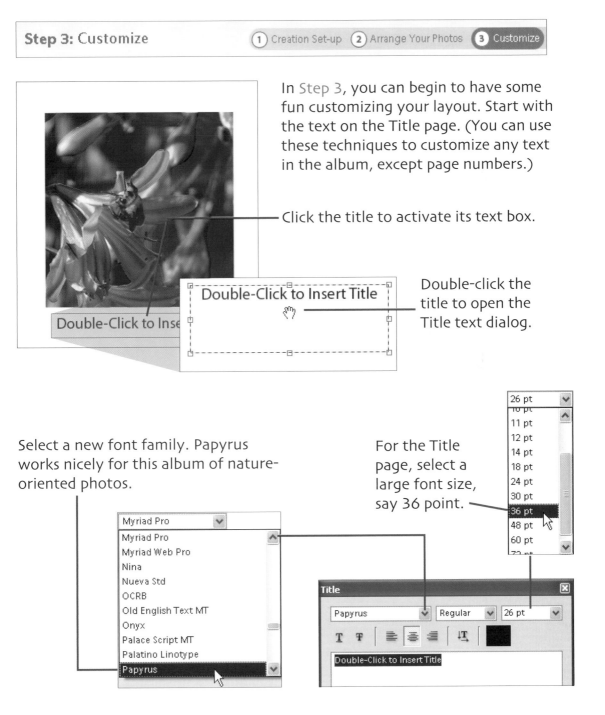

In Step 3, you can begin to have some fun customizing your layout. Start with the text on the Title page. (You can use these techniques to customize any text in the album, except page numbers.)

Click the title to activate its text box.

Double-Click to Insert Title

Double-click the title to open the Title text dialog.

Select a new font family. Papyrus works nicely for this album of nature-oriented photos.

For the Title page, select a large font size, say 36 point.

26 pt
10 pt
11 pt
12 pt
14 pt
18 pt
24 pt
30 pt
36 pt
48 pt
60 pt
72 pt

Myriad Pro

Myriad Pro
Myriad Web Pro
Nina
Nueva Std
OCRB
Old English Text MT
Onyx
Palace Script MT
Palatino Linotype
Papyrus

Title

Papyrus | Regular | 26 pt

T Ŧ | ≡ ≡ ≡ | ↕T |

Double-Click to Insert Title

creating albums with flexible layouts 75

customize title text (cont.)

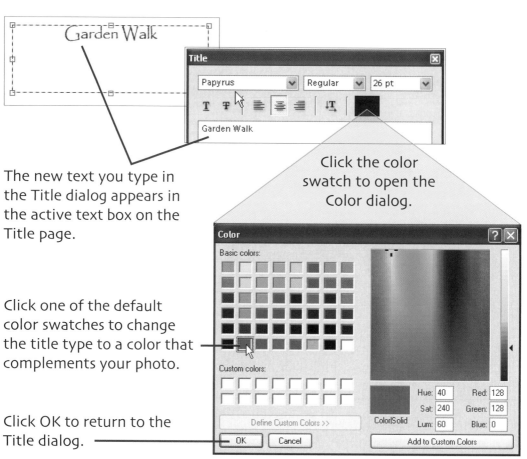

The new text you type in the Title dialog appears in the active text box on the Title page.

Click the color swatch to open the Color dialog.

Click one of the default color swatches to change the title type to a color that complements your photo.

Click OK to return to the Title dialog.

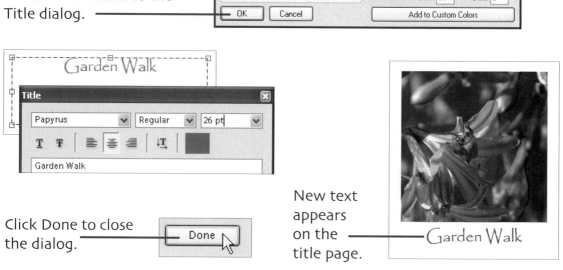

Click Done to close the dialog.

New text appears on the title page.

know the print area

The Full Photo album styles let you resize and reposition everything but the page number, but items that sit close to the edge of the page may disappear. A "page" in the Album Creation wizard measures 10.5 by 9 inches: the same dimensions as a photobook cover. Ofoto (the company that prints photobooks) trims the pages to fit inside the cover. The wizard doesn't explicitly define a safe area for photos and text, but you can visualize one yourself.

Imagine a rectangle bounded by the default header, footer, and page number. These items are sure to print; use them as guide to the safe-printing zone.

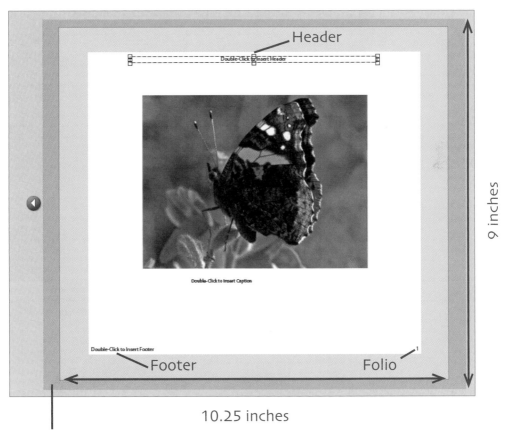

I've added orange highlighting to show the possible danger zone, but the wizard does not do that. You can't predict the final trim area precisely. Anything placed beyond the range of the default text elements runs the risk of getting chopped.

increase header size

Header text first appears on Page 1. In the No Borders Book style the default type is too small for my aging eyes. Let's choose something larger.

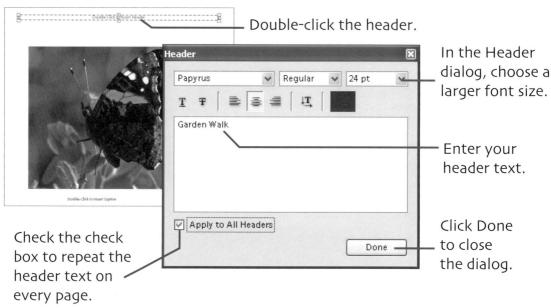

Double-click the header.

In the Header dialog, choose a larger font size.

Enter your header text.

Check the check box to repeat the header text on every page.

Click Done to close the dialog.

The header seems to disappear. The new font and larger size require a larger text box.

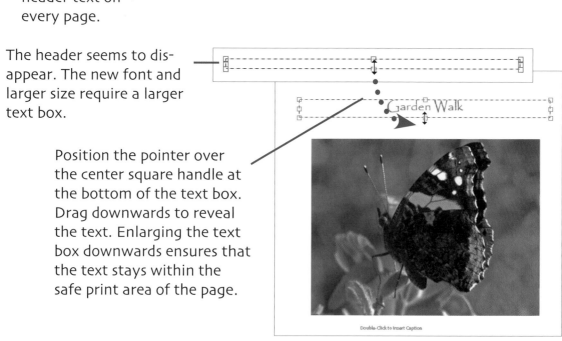

Position the pointer over the center square handle at the bottom of the text box. Drag downwards to reveal the text. Enlarging the text box downwards ensures that the text stays within the safe print area of the page.

creating albums with flexible layouts

increase footer size

1 Footers work the same way as headers. Double-click the footer to activate the text box and open the Footer dialog.

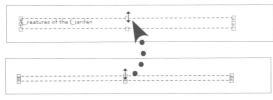

2 Choose your font and a size. For Papyrus, 14-point is easy to read but not overwhelming.

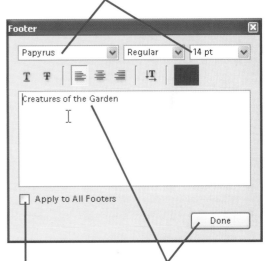

We'll use different footers on each page. Leave this box unchecked.

Enter footer text and click the Done button.

3 The new font is too big for the default text box. Drag the center handle upward to reveal the text. Drag upward to ensure that the footer stays in the safe-print zone.

4 Click any blank area of the page to deselect the text box. Now you can see the text without distraction.

adjust captions

Double-click the caption to activate its text box and open the Caption dialog.

Choose the font and size. Use one font family for headers, footers, and captions for a clean professional look.

Single-photo pages look nice with the caption centered against the photo. Click the center-text option.

Enter caption text. (If the photo has a caption in Organizer, that caption appears here. You can leave it alone, or modify it just for the album.)

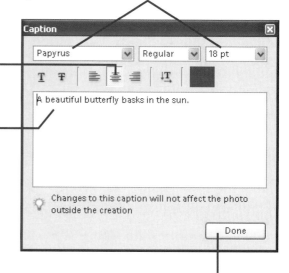

Caption

Papyrus | Regular | 18 pt

A beautiful butterfly basks in the sun.

Changes to this caption will not affect the photo outside the creation

Done

Click Done to close the dialog.

Drag the side handles of the text box to the right and to the left, aligning the box with the photo's edges. The text centers itself inside the text box.

Click any blank area of the page to deselect the text box.

Garden Walk

A beautiful butterfly basks in the sun.

lay out one photo

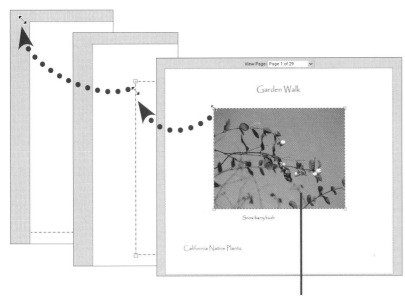

Single-photo pages look nice; the image is a good size. Still, you can increase the impact of some images by enlarging them. You can even make them so large, they run off the edge of the page, a technique called bleeding the image.

Click the photo to activate its handles. Drag the upper-left handle up and off the page into the gray area.

Some of the image will be trimmed at the edge and top.

Enlarging a photo this much creates a nice effect, making the image more dynamic, but leaving lots of white space for text.

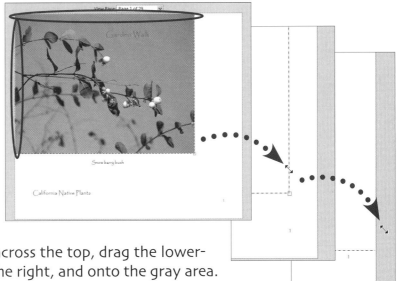

To bleed the image all across the top, drag the lower-right handle down, to the right, and onto the gray area.

lay out one photo (cont.)

Your photo is now large and dramatic, but it also covers all the text. You need to adjust the photo position and move or modify some text elements.

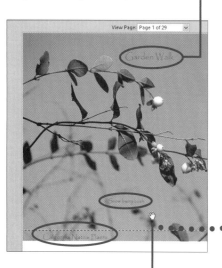

Position the pointer over the photo, away from any text. Drag the photo up.

Moving the photo up reveals the footer and page number.

It's usually best to delete the header when you push a photo to the top of the page. Double-click the header.

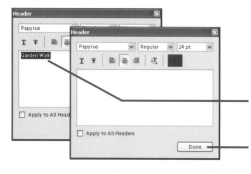

The Header dialog opens. Select the text and press Backspace or Delete.

Click the Done button to close the dialog.

The text box stays on the page, but it no longer displays text. Nothing will print.

82   **creating albums with flexible layouts**

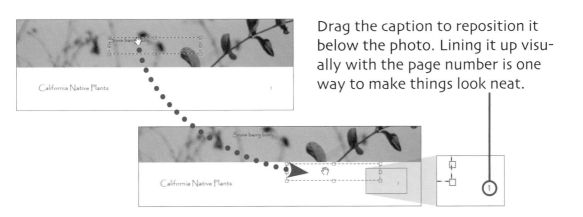

Drag the caption to reposition it below the photo. Lining it up visually with the page number is one way to make things look neat.

In the finished page the photo bleeds off the top and sides. All the crucial parts of the image fall inside the area bounded by the default header, footer, and page number. Whatever happens during trimming, this photo should still look OK.

creating albums with flexible layouts

lay out two photos

Click the next-page arrow to move to a page where you want two photos.

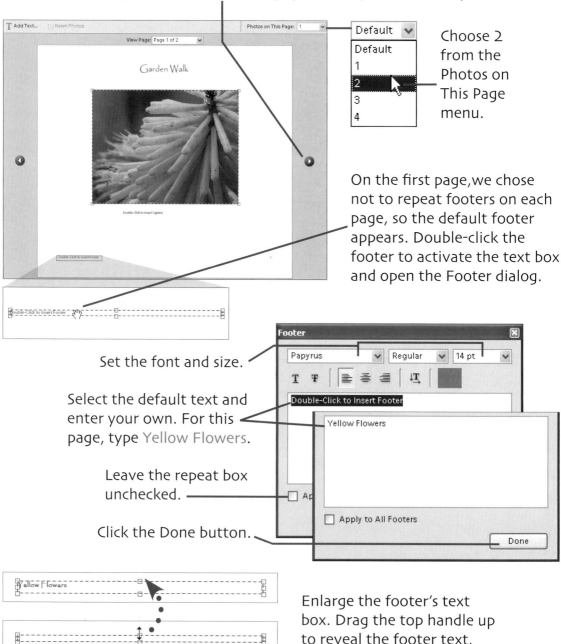

Choose 2 from the Photos on This Page menu.

On the first page, we chose not to repeat footers on each page, so the default footer appears. Double-click the footer to activate the text box and open the Footer dialog.

Set the font and size.

Select the default text and enter your own. For this page, type Yellow Flowers.

Leave the repeat box unchecked.

Click the Done button.

Enlarge the footer's text box. Drag the top handle up to reveal the footer text.

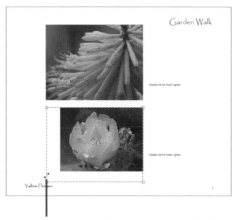

Move the header to make room for enlarging the photos. Click to select the header, but don't double-click. Press the → key to move the selected item 1-pixel to the right. Shift-→ moves it 10 pixels.

Push the header to the right; visually line up the header's right edge with the page number's right edge.

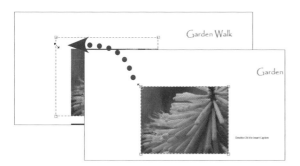

Drag the upper-left handle of the top photo outwards to enlarge the photo without running into the caption text box.

Drag the bottom photo's lower-left handle until it aligns (visually) with the top photo's left edge. The aspect ratio of these images is the same; enlarging them to the same width also makes them the same height.

creating albums with flexible layouts

lay out two photos (cont.)

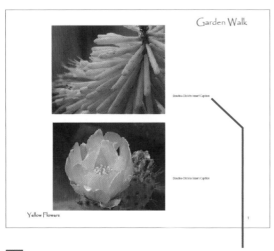

1 Double-click the top caption to open its Caption dialog.

4 You need to open up the text box to show all of the large caption. But the other caption is in the way.

2 Select the font, size, and color for your caption. Enter caption text. There's plenty of room to make a long caption to the right of the photos.

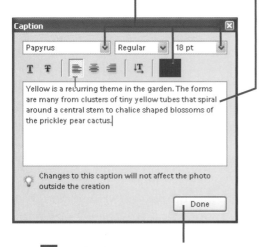

5 Drag that text box all the way off the page to delete it. Or drag it to a new position on the page.

3 Click the Done button to close the dialog.

6 Drag down to finish opening the caption text box.

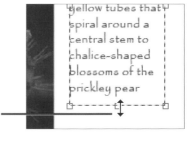

creating albums with flexible layouts

Layouts vary with the orientation of the photos involved. You've seen the layout for two landscape photos. Here are the other two-photo combinations.

You can always drag photos to a new position on the page.

If you just want to change the order in which the photos appear, however, it's better to return to Step 2 of the wizard and rearrange them there.

1 Click the Previous Step button.

3 Now click the Next Step button to return to Step 3 and the page you were on. The photo order has changed.

2 In Step 2, drag a photo to change the order. The yellow bar previews the new location.

creating albums with flexible layouts

lay out three photos

Click the next-page arrow to move to Page 3, where we'll lay out three photos.

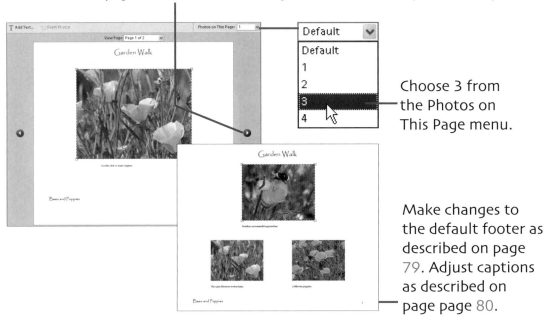

Choose 3 from the Photos on This Page menu.

Make changes to the default footer as described on page 79. Adjust captions as described on page page 80.

Use the objects on your page as alignment tools. Try putting the top photo's caption beside the photo instead of below it; line up the text with the photo.

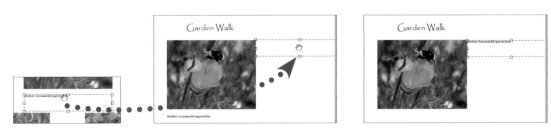

Click to select the caption.

Drag the caption to its new location. Position it so the selection marquee sits on the edge of the photo.

Use the arrow keys to move the caption away from the photo. A distance of 10 pixels looks good. Select the caption and press [Shift]-[→] once.

creating albums with flexible layouts

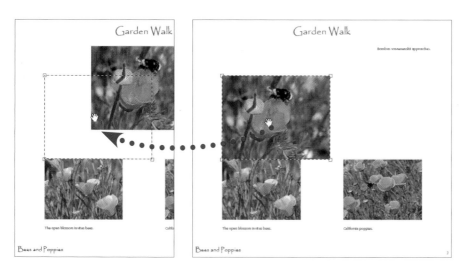

Use the same procedure to align photos. Drag the photo from the top of the page to sit right on top of the bottom-left photo.

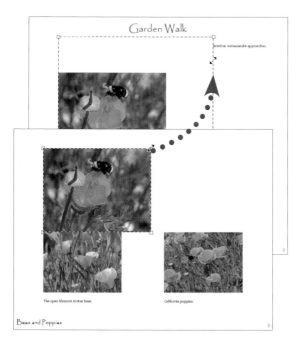

Drag the upper-right handle up and out until the edge of the photo's selection marquee meets the caption

You've enlarged the photo and preserved the original spacing on the right side of photo. Since you know that space is going to print safely, you can add display text there later.

lay out three photos (cont.)

With the photos lined up, try shrinking the smaller one even more. Click the photo to select it.

Drag the upper-right handle inward.

Repeat the process with the smaller photo on the right to match its size to the photo on the left visualy.

Drag the right-hand photo closer to the one on the left.

Select the caption and press ⬅ to move the caption to the left.

If you have trouble visually matching the photos when there's space between them, position one on top of the other, resize to match, then select one and use the arrow keys to position it.

creating albums with flexible layouts

You can add new text boxes to create display type. When you do, you may want to get rid of the individual captions because they look too cluttered.

Click the caption text to activate its text box. Drag the box completely off the page. Make sure that the resize handles no longer appear in the white area.

Click the Add Text button.

The Album Creation wizard puts new text boxes at the top of the page, right in the middle. Double-click the new text to open the Text dialog.

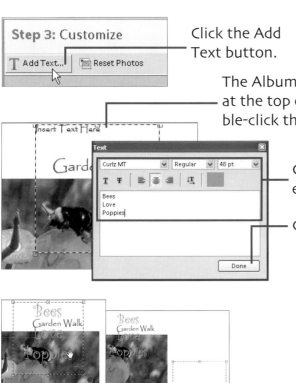

Choose the text attributes and enter your text.

Click Done to close the dialog.

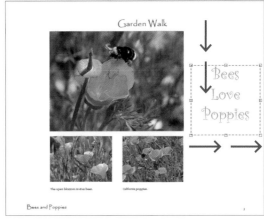

Drag the text box to the area where you want display text.

With the display text selected, use the arrow keys to position it.

creating albums with flexible layouts   **91**

lay out four photos

A four-photo page gives you lots of material to play with. Try different arrangements and sizes for your photos. To help line things up, you can create guidelines from text. You'll throw these guides away when you're done arranging.

Use the View Page menu to move to page 4 where we want to lay out four photos.

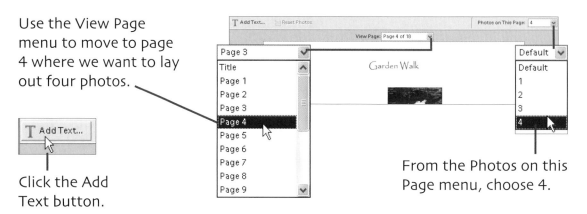

Click the Add Text button.

From the Photos on this Page menu, choose 4.

The Album Creation wizard places a text box on the page.

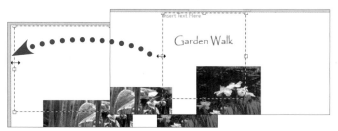

Drag the handle on the left side of the text box to the left edge of the page.

Drag the handle on the right side of the text box out to the right edge of the page.

Drag the bottom handle up to make a narrow box. Don't let the guideline text box overlap the header's box. Then double-click the text to open the Text dialog.

creating albums with flexible layouts

In the Text dialog, choose a sans serif font if you have one.

Choose a color that looks like a guide, say, bright green.

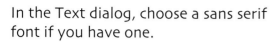

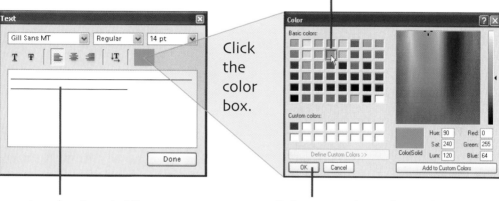

Click the color box.

To create a horizontal line, type underscore characters (Shift-–).

Click OK to close the Color dialog.

To create a vertical guide, select horizontal text.

Position the Text dialog so that you can see the text box and watch the line grow as you type each character.

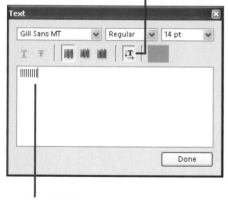

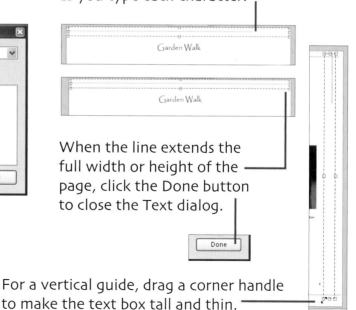

When the line extends the full width or height of the page, click the Done button to close the Text dialog.

Press Shift-\ to enter a series of pipe characters (|). You could also use lowercase l's (l).

For a vertical guide, drag a corner handle to make the text box tall and thin.

lay out four photos (cont.)

When you move and resize photos to make a more creative layout the captions can seem to clutter the page. To remove the captions, drag them off the page and into the gray area.

For variety on a four-photo page, balance three small photos against a large one.

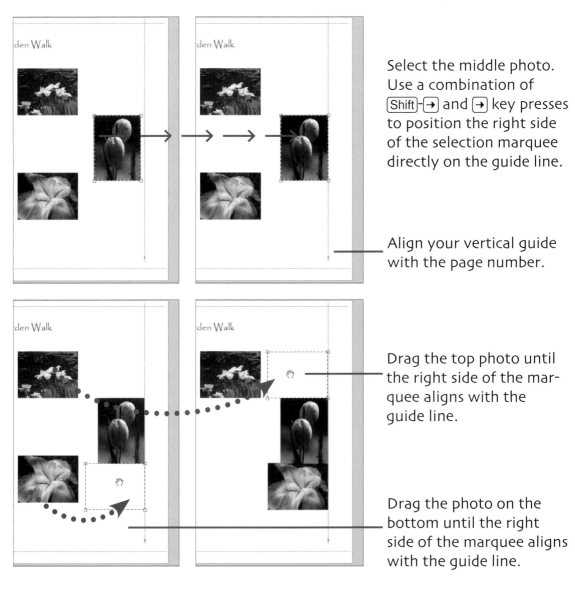

Select the middle photo. Use a combination of Shift-→ and → key presses to position the right side of the selection marquee directly on the guide line.

Align your vertical guide with the page number.

Drag the top photo until the right side of the marquee aligns with the guide line.

Drag the photo on the bottom until the right side of the marquee aligns with the guide line.

Select the top photo. Press [Shift]-[↑] three times to create space between the top and middle photos.

Select the bottom photo. Press [Shift]-[↓] three times to create the same space between the photos.

Place text guide lines at the top and bottom edges of the small-photo stack.

Drag the upper-right handle out-wards until it sits on your guide line to make the image even larger.

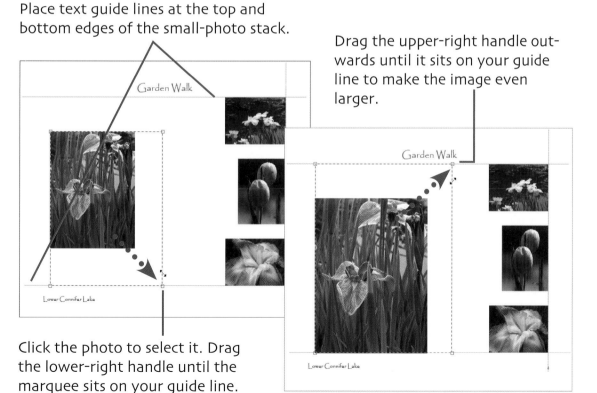

Click the photo to select it. Drag the lower-right handle until the marquee sits on your guide line.

lay out four photos (cont.)

 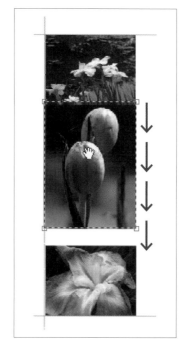 

Align the guide line with the left edge of the top and bottom photos. Select the middle photo and drag its upper-left handle. Align the left side of the marquee with the guide line.

With the middle photo selected, press the ⬇ key (or Shift-⬇ keys) to move the middle photo down. Line up its lower edge to meet the top edge of the photo on the bottom.

Keep track of the number of presses. Then use the ⬆ key (or Shift-⬆ keys) to move the photo back up half that number of key presses. This centers the photo in the available space.

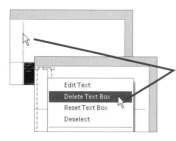

When you finish all alignments, you must remove any guides you created. These text elements will print in your album if you don't delete them. It's easiest to select the guide (instead of, say, the header) if you position the pointer over the guide near the edge of the page. Right-click the guide and choose Delete Text Box.

creating albums with flexible layouts

You can use additional text to create ornamental designs to accent your photos.

 Click the Add
Text button.

The new text appears at the top of your page. Double-click it to open its Text dialog.

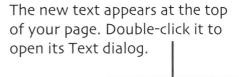

In the Text dialog, choose a pi font (one of the fonts that uses pictures instead of letters for each character).

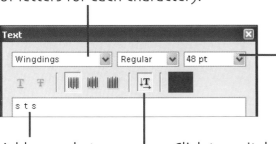

Increase the font size to make the ornaments bigger.

Add space between characters to separate ornamental elements.

Click to switch the orientation of your text from horizontal to vertical and vice versa.

 Click the Done button to close the Text dialog.

Use the aligning tricks you've learned to position the ornamental text. Don't go overboad adding doodads, but adding a little decoration is fun. Ornaments can tie images together, creating a theme for your book.

make blank pages

The Album Creation wizard always creates double-sided pages. But you can create one-sided pages by making a blank page. Why would you want to give up space for more photos? One reason to use a blank page is to prevent photos showing through on the opposite side of the page. This isn't a huge problem because Ofoto uses good quality paper. Still if the layouts differ on the front and back sides of a page, you can see shadows from the opposite side of the page. To prevent this, remove all of the photos and text elements from the page. (The exception here is the page number if you are using page numbers. The Album Creation wizard doesn't give you control over individual page numbers.)

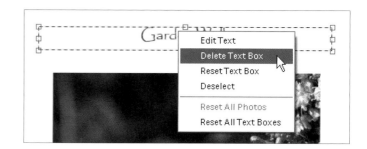

Right-click any text to access the contextual menu.

Choose Delete Text Box to remove it.

To remove photos, you must drag them off the page. (There's no contextual menu choice for it.) Drag the photo all the way off the white page area. Be sure that you no longer see the selection marquee and resize handles for the photo. The photo is still assigned to this page, but it won't print.

creating albums with flexible layouts

make text-only pages

Blank pages also give you room for lots of text. You can replicate the kind of text in columns that you find in books or magazines.

1 Click the Add Text button.

2 The wizard adds a new text box. Double-click the text to open its Text dialog.

3 Set options for your text. Select flush left for text alignment.

4 Enter the text you want to have in your first column.

5 Use 5 spaces for paragraph indents. (The Tab key won't work as it would in a text editor.)

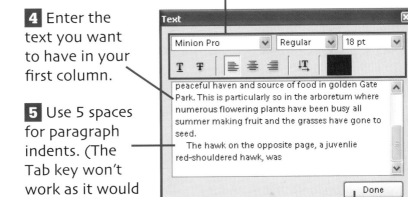

6 Click the done button to close the dialog.

8 Drag a corner handle to resize the text box and display all the text.

7 Drag the text to the left side of the page.

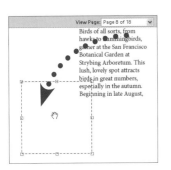

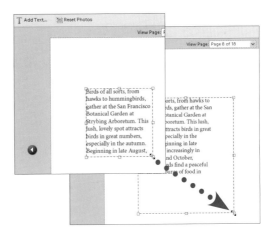

make text-only pages

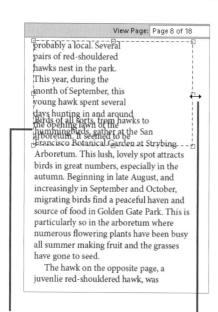

Create a second column. Move it to overlap the first, aligning both columns on the left. Drag one of the right-side resize handles to the right until the second column matches the first column's width.

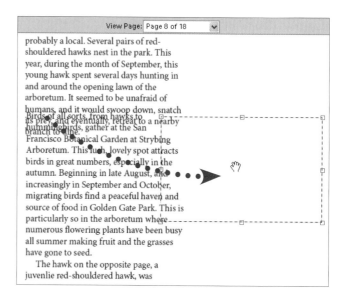

Drag the second column. Place it to the right of the first. Let the text overlap.

Using the ⬇ (or Shift - ⬇) keys, move the second column to align lines of text.

Press the ➡ (or Shift-➡) key to move the column to the right, keeping it aligned.

creating albums with flexible layouts

fix page numbers

The Album Creation wizard creates inappropriate footers and page numbers for a bound book. In a bound album, the title page—a right-hand page—is really the book's first page, but the wizard doesn't number it. The wizard starts numbering with 1 on the first left-hand page. Odd numbers wind up on left-hand pages, evens on the right. Footers always appear in the lower-left corner of a page, page numbers in the lower-right corner. In a professionally designed book, on left-hand pages the numbers are even and appear in the lower-left corner. You can't edit the default page numbers in the Album Creation wizard, but you can add your own as additional text. You must then remove the default numbers.

1 To fix page numbers and footers on left-hand pages, in Step 3, click the Add Text button. The Text dialog appears.

2 Choose a font family, size, and color. I like larger numbers; 24-point is huge, but it's easier to see in these examples.

Choose to align on the left. (For right-hand pages, choose align right.)

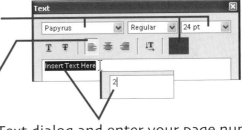

3 Select the default text in the Text dialog and enter your page number.

4 Click Done to close the dialog.

By default the wizard centers the additional text box at the top of the page.

5 Select the text and position the pointer over a corner resize handle. Drag to resize the box to show just the number.

fix page numbers (cont.)

6 Position the pointer over the text box; drag the box until it covers the default page number.

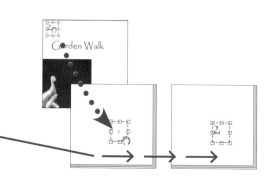

7 Click the box again to make sure it's selected, then use the arrow keys to align your number with the default number.

8 Press (Shift)-(←) or (←) to move your selected page number to align with the left side of the footer.

9 Now select the footer, press (Shift)-(→) and/or (→) to move the footer to align with the default page number.

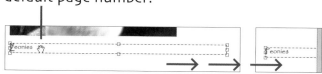

To fix page numbers and footers on right-hand pages, repeat Steps 1 through 7 of this task. The footer is already in the correct spot; you can skip Steps 8 and 9.

It's time to remove the default numbers. You must return to Step 1 of the wizard.

10 In the Step 3 page of the wizard, click Previous Step twice to return to the wizard's Step 1 page.

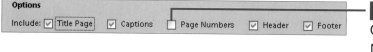

11 In Step 1, under Options, deselect the Page Numbers check box.

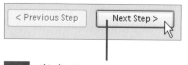

12 Click Next Step twice to return to the Step 3 page.

The default page numbers are gone, leaving your numbers and repositioned footers.

creating albums with flexible layouts

do a critical review

When you finish laying out your entire album, you should review your pages.

Select Title from the View Page menu to jump to the beginning of the album.

When you move to a new page the wizard selects a photo.

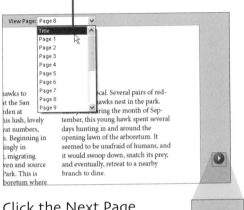

Click the Next Page arrow to view each page in turn.

Right-click the photo; choose Deselect to hide the distracting marquee.

Give each page a critical review. Use your editor's eye to check for spelling mistakes in text. Double-click any text with typos to reopen its text-entry dialog to correct your mistake.

do a critical review (cont.)

Check that alignment of photos is precise. Use any of the techniques from this chapter to fine-tune your layout.

If you find a page where you wish you could start the layout over, don't despair.

To restore photo defaults, click the Reset Photos button. Photos return to their default size and location on the page.

To restore default positions for text boxes (or photos), right-click anywhere on the page. Choose the items to restore from the contextual menu.

If you've deleted or moved any default text elements (headers, footers, photo captions), review those elements carefully. Moving back and forth between Step 3 and earlier steps (for example, to add more photos or change photo order in Step 2), sometimes restores those elements to their default positions. If you wanted to delete one of those elements, you may need to remove it again.

creating albums with flexible layouts

create PDF files

PDF files make excellent proofing tools. They allow you to see your pages unobstructed by the Album Creation wizard's interface. A really big plus is that you can view both pages of a spread simultaneously in a PDF. You can turn your album into a PDF in Step 5 of the Album Creation wizard. Be sure to save your album following the procedure outlined in Chapter 4: save and print (see pages 69 and 70) Then reopen your album and move to Step 5 of the wizard.

Step 5: Share   ① Creation Set-up ② Arrange Your Photos ③ Customize ④ Save ⑤ Share

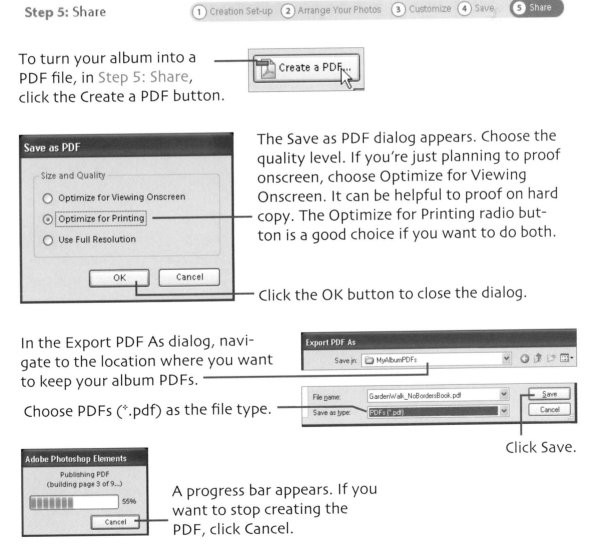

To turn your album into a PDF file, in Step 5: Share, click the Create a PDF button.

The Save as PDF dialog appears. Choose the quality level. If you're just planning to proof onscreen, choose Optimize for Viewing Onscreen. It can be helpful to proof on hard copy. The Optimize for Printing radio button is a good choice if you want to do both.

Click the OK button to close the dialog.

In the Export PDF As dialog, navigate to the location where you want to keep your album PDFs.

Choose PDFs (*.pdf) as the file type.

Click Save.

A progress bar appears. If you want to stop creating the PDF, click Cancel.

create PDF files (cont.)

To begin proofing right away, click Yes to open the PDF.

The PDF opens in Adobe Reader (when you installed Elements originally, it installed Reader 6.0 for you if you didn't already have it installed on your PC).

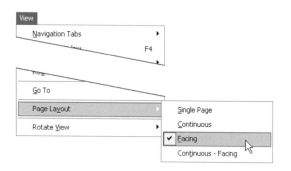

Choose View > Page Layout > Facing (or Continuous Facing) to see both pages of a spread at once. Viewing facing pages helps you judge how well the photos you selected go together and how your layout is working.

Reader's zoom tools let you view pages at various sizes.

Click the minus button to make pages smaller.

Click the plus button to make pages larger.

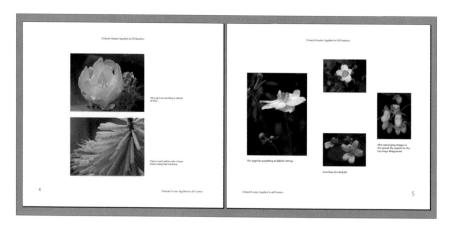

Now you see what an open album page looks like with the photos you've chosen for this spread.

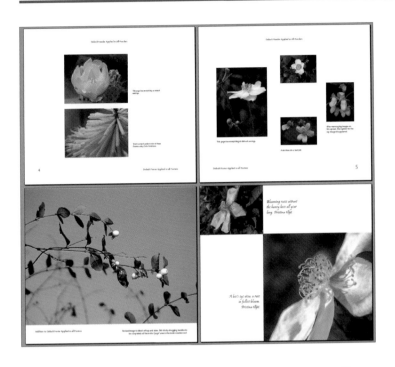

Zoom out more and you can see multiple spreads simultaneously.

Zoom out far enough and you can even see tiny thumbnails of the entire album to get a sense of the flow of images through the book.

A printed copy of an album makes a great proofing tool. Mark up the paper copy with corrections and any ideas for layout changes. You can print directly from the Album Creation wizard (as in Chapter 4) or print the PDF from Adobe Reader. Make corrections in Elements' Album Creation wizard then make a new PDF to proof. Repeat till you're satisfied with your album. Then order it (see Chapter 6).

creating albums with flexible layouts

extra bits

choose a flexible album p. 74

- Photos with white or light edges, say a light sky, look odd in albums that don't use borders. Your eye can't tell where the photo stops and the page begins. Use the graphics tools in Editor's Standard Edit mode to add a thin outline or border to such photos.

know the print area p. 77

- When deciding whether to go outside the imaginary box formed by the header, footer, and page number, consider the importance of the item you're placing in the unpredictable zone. Placing text boxes near the right or left edge of the page is especially risky.

adjust captions p. 80

- Page 1 is the first page that has captions, so it makes sense to learn about adjusting captions now. For the rest of your album, however, you should hold off entering captions until you're certain you like the order, position, and size of your photos for each page. Switching the photo order after creating captions and other text elements could force you to redo text changes.

lay out one photo p. 81

- If you like full-page photos that bleed off the page, check out the Full Bleed Book album style. In its default layout, single photos fill the page, bleeding on all sides.

- When a resized photo covers a text element, you can choose to leave the text element in place. (A header that winds up in a section of blue sky, might look OK, where a header in a tangle of branches might not). Text elements always print over photos. You might want to adjust the text color, make it lighter to print over a dark photo or vice versa so that it stands out more in print.

- If you want complete freedom in creating layouts, use Editor's Standard Edit mode tools to create a single file for each album page. Set the document size to 8.5 by 11 inches for print-it-yourself album pages; 10.25 by 9 inches for photobooks. Combine photos, text, and graphic elements any way you want. You might, for example, place a dozen small snapshots on a page, yearbook fashion. Then import those files as the "photos" for your album. The Full Bleed Book style, was created specifically to facilitate this type of layout.

creating albums with flexible layouts

lay out two photos p. 84

- Using the arrow keys to move objects in albums can be tricky. Even when the selection marquee appears around an item the Album Creation wizard may not realize that item is selected. If you press the arrow keys and your selected object doesn't move (you may see buttons and menus highlighting instead), the wizard isn't recognizing your selection. It's safest to click the object you want to move, pause, then click again before pressing the arrow keys.

lay out four photos p. 92

- When creating color text, you can make darker or lighter versions of default colors. Drag the slider (next to the color space) up for lighter colors, down for darker.

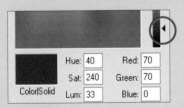

make text-only pages p. 99

- Album text boxes handle just one font and one size at a time. To combine text of different sizes (for a decorative capital, for example), use separate text boxes aligned to look like one paragraph. Click the Add Text button. In the Text dialog, choose a larger font size than in the paragraph; use the same font or a different one. Type the first letter of the paragraph and click Done. Resize the text box to fit closely around the letter. Double-click the paragraph where you want the large capital. In the Text dialog that opens, select the first letter of the paragraph and replace it with spaces to make room for the large capital; then click Done. Drag the large-letter text box over the paragraph. Position the text boxes so the large letter fits on the first line of the paragraph.

Birds of all sort, from hawks to hummingbirds, gather at the San Francisco Botanical Garden at Strybing Arboretum. This lush, lovely spot attracts birds in great numbers,

Birds of all sort, from hawks to hummingbirds, gather at the San Francisco Botanical Garden at Strybing Arboretum. This lush, lovely spot attracts birds in great numbers,

- To improve line breaks, double-click the text to open the Text dialog. Click between characters and type in a hyphen. Click the

extra bits

make text-only pages (cont.)

Done button. Resize the text box so the hyphen falls at the end of the line.

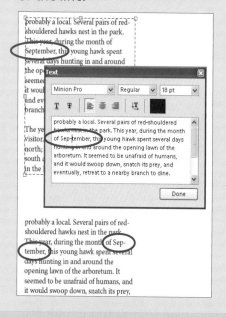

fix page numbers p. 101

- Most albums don't need numbered pages. You can simply remove the default page numbers. Skip task Steps 1 through 9; just follow Steps 10 through 12.

do a critical review p. 103

- No matter how carefully you edited your photos before creating your album, you're likely to see something else you'd like to fix when you start reviewing your album pages. Unfortunately, if you edit the photos that you've placed in the album, you risk corrupting the album and losing all your work. To avoid that problem, return to Step 2 in the Album Creation wizard. Select the photo you'd like to edit and click the Remove Photo button at the top of the work area. Click the Close icon to exit the wizard. A dialog opens asking if you want to save changes. Click the Yes button; the wizard saves your album. You can now open your photo in Editor and make any needed changes. Return to Organizer's Photo Browser; double-click the album thumbnail to open your album; the wizard takes you to Step 3. Click the Previous Step button to move back to Step 2. Click the Add Photos button to reimport the edited photo. The wizard puts the photo at the end of your album. You'll need to drag the photo back to its proper place in the work area. Then click the Next Step button to move on to Step 3, where you can review each page again. The corrected photo should appear in place in your layout just fine. If necessary, make any further adjustments to your layout.

6. ordering hardcover photobooks

Full Photo

No Borders

No Borders Book

Full Bleed Book

Order Online!

In September of 2004, Adobe Systems and Eastman Kodak teamed up to provide Elements users with new ways to share photos, both online and in print. This collaboration is officialy known as Adobe Photoshop Services, Provided by Ofoto. Ofoto is Kodak's online photo subsidiary. I'll be referring to it as Adobe Photoshop Services (APS) and Ofoto for the rest of this book.

One of the APS products you can order is a printed hardcover book starring your very own photos. Choose one of the album styles that bears a yellow Order Online medallion, to create an album that you can order as a hardcover book.

Album covers come in a variety of materials, the most expensive being leather. A window cut out of the front cover lets part of the first page show through. (The Book album styles help you place a photo directly below this window, so that the image shows through when the cover is closed.)

The hardcover books measure 10.25 by 9 inches. The interior pages are fairly heavy weight, archival quality, coated stock—that is, fairly thick paper with a low acid content (so it will last a long time) and a smooth glossy finish. The smallest photobook you can order contains 20 pages (10 sheets of paper, printed on both sides). Once you've filled those 20 pages, you can add more pages, two at a time, up to the maximum of 40 pages.

start the order process

To start the order process, in Step 5: Share of the Album Creation wizard, click the Order Online button.

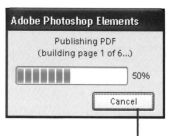

The wizard creates a Portable Document Format (PDF) file of your album. To stop the process click Cancel.

The first time you use Adobe Photoshop Services on your computer, whether to order prints, share photos online, or order an album, you'll see a Welcome page. If your first experience with APS is ordering an album, the Welcome page appears just after the wizard creates the PDF file.

Click the Sign In link to log in to an existing account (see page 114).

Enter your name, email address, and a password to start creating a new account (see page 113).

Welcome to Adobe Photoshop Services

Provided by Ofoto, A Kodak Company

Save 25% on a hardcover Photo Book!*

Adobe Photoshop Services, provided by Ofoto

SAVE 25%

It's easy to get creative with your photos. Sign up now to create a hardcover, high-quality Photo Book and we'll deliver it anywhere. Get 25% off a Photo Book with this coupon code: ADOBEBOOK25.

See offer details

Already a member? Sign in >>

Create Account

First Name *
Email Address *
Password * (6 character min)
Confirm Password *

☑ Remember my password
☑ Send me special offers and news from Ofoto and Kodak.
☑ Please send me information and promotions on Adobe products and services.
* ☐ I agree to use the Ofoto service in accordance with the Terms of Service.

set up your account

To order a photobook, you need an APS or Ofoto account. The first time you use APS, the Create Account fields appear on the Welcome page. You can also access the Create Account fields by clicking the Change link in Step 1 (see page 114).

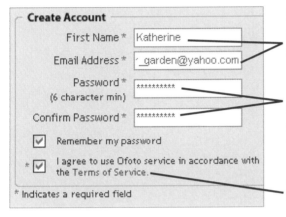

Enter your first name and the email address you want to use for this account.

Enter a password. It's safest to use one specifically for the APS account, not the same one you use for email. You must enter the password twice.

Click the Terms of Service link, read the terms, then check the check box.

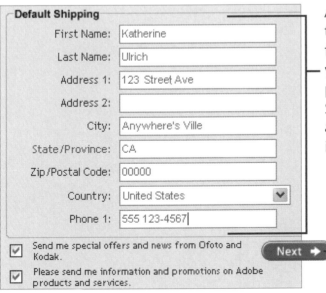

Assuming that you are going to be buying APS products for yourself most often, enter your name, address, and phone number in the Default Shipping area. You can easily add other shipping addresses in Step 2 (see page 116).

When you're done creating your account, click the Next button.

log in to your account

The Order Photobook wizard guides you through the ordering process.

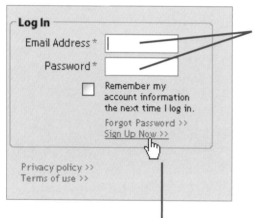

On the Step 1: Customize page, if you already have an APS or Ofoto account you just need to log in. Enter the email address and password you used to set up the account.

If you want to set up a new APS account, click the Sign Up Now link to go to the Create Accounts page (described on page 113).

Then click the Next button. APS verifies your account information and returns you to Step 1.

If you've already used Elements 3.0 to share photos online or order prints, you've already set up an APS account. If you chose to remember your password, the log-in segment doesn't appear in Step 1. Instead, the account holder's first name appears as the active account at the top of the page.

To change the account, click the Change link to go to the Create Account page.

step 1: customize

Order Photobook

Active Account: katherine Change >>

Step: ① Customize ② Recipients ③ Summary ④ Billing ⑤ Upload ⑥ Confirmation

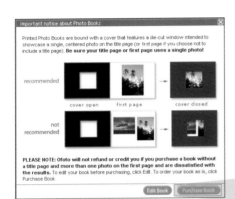

Before you start the actual order process, the wizard warns you about how the die-cut cover and title page work together. We've used a default title page to ensure that the image fits the window. Go ahead and click the Purchase Book button.

A thumbnail of a finished album cover changes color to show your selection. (To judge how this color goes with your peekaboo photo, see extra bits, page 121.)

1 Select a cover style. Black makes the peekaboo image on the title page pop. But for this nature-themed album, let's try Celadon linen.

3 To continue your order, click the Next button.

2 Enter the number of albums you want to order.

step 2: recipients

Order Photobook

Step: ① Customize **② Recipients** ③ Summary ④ Billing ⑤ Upload ⑥ Confirmation

Send books to the following people
(Use the checkboxes to indicate selections)

Address Book

Import Addresses >>   what is this? >>

Groups   Add New Group >>

People   Add New Address >>

☑ Katherine Ulrich 123 Street Ave ,San Francisco
(default address)

In Step 2: Recipients, you choose the address or addresses where APS will send the printed photobook.

Address Book

Import Addresses >>   what is this? >>

Groups   Add New Group >>

People   Add New Address >>

☑ Katherine Ulrich 123 Street Ave ,San Francisco ,CA
(default address)

☑ Maya Podruga 123 Ulitsa St. ,Townville ,CA ,00000

Check the check box for each address that should receive a copy of your album.

Click here to open a window where you can add a new recipient.

Add Address

Add New Address

First Name *	Maya
Last Name *	Podruga
Address 1 *	123 Ulitsa St.
Address 2	
City *	Townville
State/Province *	CA
Zip/Postal Code *	00000
Country *	United States
Phone 1 *	555-987-6543
Email	

* Indicates a required field

When you complete the new address, return to Step 2 by clicking the Next button in the Add Address window.

Next ➡

Click the Next button on the Step 2 page to move on to Step 3.

Next ➡

ordering hardcover photobooks

step 3: summary

Order Photobook

Step: ① Customize ② Recipients ③ Summary ④ Billing ⑤ Upload ⑥ Confirmation

In Step 3: Summary, you verify the details of your order, choose a shipping method, and apply any discounts you may have received from Adobe Photoshop Services or Ofoto.

APS offers shipping by U.S. mail and FedEx. Shipments originate from the West Coast. Choose your preferred shipping method from the drop-down menu.

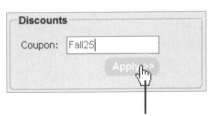

Enter any discount codes you have. You must click the Apply button to receive the credit. The Order Summary recalculates.

Click the Next button to continue the ordering process. ——

ordering hardcover photobooks   **117**

step 4: billing

Order Photobook

Step: ① Customize   ② Recipients   ③ Summary   **④ Billing**   ⑤ Upload   ⑥ Confirmation

In Step 4:Billing, you provide credit card information to pay for your order.

Select your credit card type.

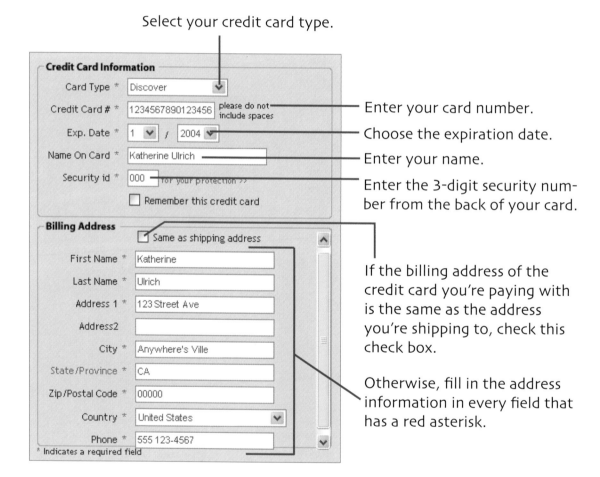

Enter your card number.

Choose the expiration date.

Enter your name.

Enter the 3-digit security number from the back of your card.

If the billing address of the credit card you're paying with is the same as the address you're shipping to, check this check box.

Otherwise, fill in the address information in every field that has a red asterisk.

Double-check all your billing information. Make any needed corrections. Then click the Place Order button to send your order request to APS/Ofoto.

ordering hardcover photobooks

step 5: upload

Order Photobook
Step: ① Customize ② Recipients ③ Summary ④ Billing ⑤ Upload ⑥ Confirmation

In Step 5: Upload, a progress bar tracks how much of your album has been sent to Adobe Photoshop Services/Ofoto. The file being uploaded is actually the PDF file of your album, not the individual images within it. Still, depending on how many pages and photos you've used in your album, the file can be large. If you are using a dial-up connection, you may want to carry out your order session when you have time to be online for a bit.

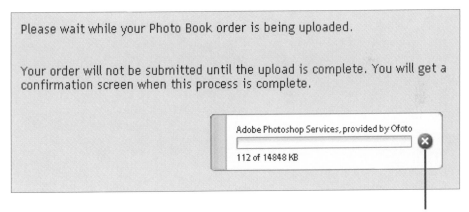

Please wait while your Photo Book order is being uploaded.

Your order will not be submitted until the upload is complete. You will get a confirmation screen when this process is complete.

Adobe Photoshop Services, provided by Ofoto

112 of 14848 KB

To cancel the upload process, click the Close button.

There is no Next button for this step. When the upload is finished you move directly to Step 6.

step 6: confirmation

The step numbers disappear from the top of the Order Photobook wizard, but this is Step 6: Confirmation. In addition to this summary of your completed order, you'll receive email letting you know that APS/Ofoto has received the order. You'll receive another email when the order ships.

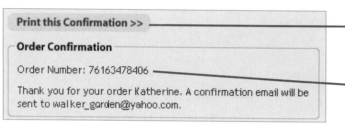

To print a copy of this confirmation screen, click the Print button.

You can use your order number to track your purchase at the Ofoto website.

To open a browser window showing the Ofoto website, click the active link. Once at the Ofoto site, you can enter your account and check the status of your order.

To exit the order process, click the Done button. The Order Photobook wizard closes, and you return to the Album Creation wizard at Step 5: Share.

extra bits

start the order process p. 112

- If your album contains fewer pages than the 20-page minimum-size album, the Order Photobook wizard warns you of that fact. You can stop the ordering process and return to the Album Creation wizard to edit your album.

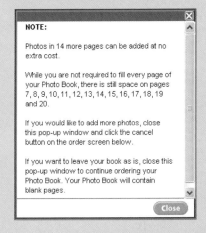

set up your account p. 113

- Sign up to learn about discounts and special offers by checking the Send Me Special Offers . . . check box below the Default Shipping section when you create your account. (Or you can Choose Edit > Preferences > Services and check the Show Notifications about Adobe Promotions check box in the Updates section.) In Organizer, click the Notifications icon to see any new APS offers.

step 1: customize p. 115

- After you pick a cover, position the Order Photobook window so that you can see the Album Creation window and Order Photobook window (with the title-page photo) simultaneously. If you've set both wizards to fill the screen (using the Maximize icon) you will need to restore the Order Photobook wizard to a resizable window (click the Restore icon in the upper-right corner of the window). You can get a rough idea of how the cover color goes with your title-page photo.

extra bits

step 3: summary p. 117

- Check the Ofoto web site (www.ofoto.com) to find any discounts or sales that are currently available.

- APS/Ofoto sometimes ships coupons with one finished order good for discounts on the next.

index

index

index

index

History view in properties window, 25
horizontal lines, 93
HP website, 72
hyphens, 109–110

i

ICC profile, 32
icons
  Adobe Gamma, 2
  binocular, 20
  collection, 22
  creation thumbnails, 70
  editing, 25
  Minimize, 43
  Notifications, 121
  pencil, 25
  photo categories, 16
  resizing, 25
  tag, 18, 25
  tagged photos, 18
  thumbnails, 25
  Tile Windows, 43
  version sets, 33
image editing
  Auto correction, 36–41, 48–49, 52
  Auto Smart Fix, 36–40, 53
  cleaning up photos, 46–47
  color cast, 41–42
  color correction, 36–45
  contrast adjustments, 38–40
  cropping photos, 30–31, 52, 64, 71
  exposure, 36–40
  fixing red eye, 34–35, 53
  General Fixes, 36
  harmonizing colors, 43–45

healing brush tool, 27, 46–47
interactive correction sliders, 39
lighting corrections, 36–40
multiple flaws, 36, 53
overview, 27
preview parameters, 29
Quick Fix. See Quick Fix mode
saving new version, 32–33
sharpening photos, 36, 48–49, 53–54
Smart Fix tool, 36–40, 53
Standard. See Standard Edit mode
undoing corrections, 36
images. See also files
  acquiring, 4
  adding to albums, 59–60, 71
  aligning, 92–97
  bleeding, 81–83, 108
  borders, 52, 55, 58, 64, 71, 108
  browsing for, 9
  captions. See captions
  categories. See categories
  cleaning up, 46–47
  collections of. See collections
  contiguous, 18
  cropping, 30–31, 52, 64, 71
  deleting. See deleting
  deselecting, 10, 71
  editing. See editing; image editing
  finding. See finding photos
  full-page, 81–83, 108
  icons for, 16

importing, 8–12
location, 9, 23
moving, 23
names, 10, 13, 15
noncontiguous, 12, 18
notes, 14–15, 25
numbered, 23, 32
opening, 28, 43
order, 19, 23, 61–62, 72, 87
organizing, 13–26
panoramic, 71
printed vs. on screen, 2
problems with, 68
properties, 15
range of, 12
rearranging, 23, 61, 64, 109
resolution, 30, 68
restoring defaults, 104
retouching. See image editing
reusing, 62
scanned, 4
selecting, 10, 12, 14, 24
selecting for albums, 59–60, 71
sequence, 19, 23, 61
sharpening, 36, 48–49, 53–54
size, 64, 68, 71, 81–82, 108
spreads, 24, 26
straightening, 31
tagged, 17–18
tiling, 43
title page, 60
uploading, 119
versions, 32–33, 50–51
viewing, 14, 23–24, 43, 50
working on copy of, 46

index

index

index

index

index

titles
    photo album, 69
    placeholder, 65
tonal adjustments, 36
Trash icon, 44
trimming photos. See
    cropping photos

Undo button, 45
Unsharp Mask filter, 54
Update Creations button, 56

version sets, 25, 33, 50–51
vertical guides, 93–94
video-card requirements for
    Elements, 2

warning triangle, 68
Watch folders, 8
website for Ofoto, 120
websites, 72, 120, 122
Welcome Screen, 5
windows, resizing, 43
work area, 43

z

zoom tools, 29, 46, 106–107

Visual QuickProject

Making a Movie
in *Premiere Elements*

JAN OZER

making a movie in premiere elements

Visual QuickProject Guide

by Jan Ozer

Peachpit
Press

Visual QuickProject Guide
Making a Movie in Premiere Elements
Jan Ozer

Peachpit Press

1249 Eighth Street
Berkeley, CA 94710
510/524-2178
800/283-9444
510/524-2221 (fax)

Find us on the World Wide Web at: www.peachpit.com
To report errors, please send a note to errata@peachpit.com
Peachpit Press is a division of Pearson Education

Editor: Suzie Lowey
Production: Lisa Brazieal
Compositor: Owen Wolfson
Cover design: The Visual Group with Aren Howell
Cover production: Aren Howell
Cover photo credit: Digital Vision
Interior design: Elizabeth Castro
Indexer: Rebecca Plunkett
Proofreader: Alison Kelley

Notice of Rights

Notice of Liability

Trademarks

ISBN 0-321-32120-0

Printed and bound in the United States of America

To Barbara, Whatley and
Eleanor Rose, the inspiration
for all my creative endeavors
(and the rightful consumers
of all their fruits)

Acknowledgements

Wow, another four-color book—a slice of family history in living color (and great gifts for friends and family).

Thanks to Nancy Davis for letting me write this book, and to Suzie Lowey for her light, yet effective editing touch. Thanks to moto-girl, Lisa Brazieal, for converting my prosaic page design into functional art, and to Owen Wolfson, compositor for this book.

I couldn't write books without the computers from Dell and Hewlett-Packard that I exclusively work on (and recommend highly) or the software from Adobe (InDesign, Illustrator, Premiere Elements and Photoshop Elements), Hyperionics (HyperSnap-DX), Microsoft (Word, Windows XP), and Ulead (PhotoImpact).

Once again, thanks to Pat Tracy for technical and other assistance.

contents

contents

contents

introduction

The Visual QuickProject Guide you're reading offers a unique way to learn new skills. Instead of drowning you in long text descriptions, this Visual QuickProject Guide uses color screen shots with clear, concise step-by-step instructions to show you how to complete a project in a matter of hours.

In this book, I'll be creating a movie and DVD from the video and digital pictures my wife and I shot of my eldest daughter's last birthday. You'll be working with your own video, which may be a birthday video, but could be video from a vacation, graduation, or any other occasion. Though the events may be different, the process of editing the video footage and digital pictures into a finished movie will be almost identical. Thus, you can apply the principles you learn here to your own movies—just replace "birthday movie" with the occasion of your choice.

We'll be working with Adobe's new video editor, Premiere Elements. Why Premiere Elements? Because for under $100, it offers an excellent suite of editing tools plus the ability to produce great looking DVDs.

what you will learn

You will learn to create a movie using Premiere Elements.

You'll start by capturing video from your DV camcorder using simple, VCR-like controls.

Premiere Elements stores all captured video in the Media window.

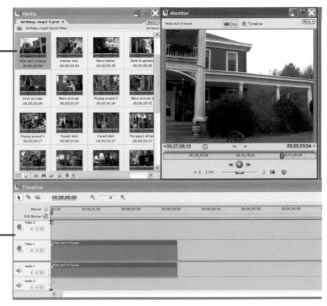

I'll show you how to drag your clips to the Timeline and arrange them in the proper order.

Transitions are visual effects that smooth the flow from one scene to another. Premiere Elements provides dozens to tickle your creativity; here I'm using the dissolve transition. I'll show you how and where to effectively use transitions and special effects.

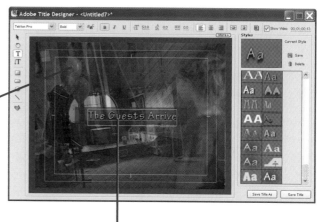

Titles help your viewers understand what's going on in the movie. I'll show you how to choose among Premiere Elements' extensive style options and how to change fonts and colors to your liking.

Sometimes your video will be too dark or too light, or perhaps a bit off tint. You'll learn how to adjust the brightness and contrast of your videos, as well as correct color imbalances.

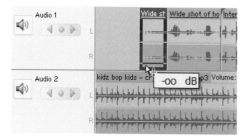

Premiere Elements makes it easy to add background music to your movies.

You'll learn how to add these audio elements and how to make them work smoothly with the audio captured with your camcorder.

what you will learn (cont.)

My wife is a digital camera fanatic, and I like adding her pictures to the movie, which is a snap in Premiere Elements. Here I'm creating a slide show from my wife's digital pictures with background music. You'll learn how to create a slide show and set options, such as picture and transition duration, to your liking, and even add pan and zoom effects.

Here's Premiere Elements' Timeline view, showing the digital pictures with transitions sitting atop the music track. Though we're using only two tracks here, Premiere Elements can add up to 99 video and audio tracks, sufficient for even the most complex projects. Though you probably won't use more than four tracks anytime soon, it's nice to know that Premiere Elements can grow with you.

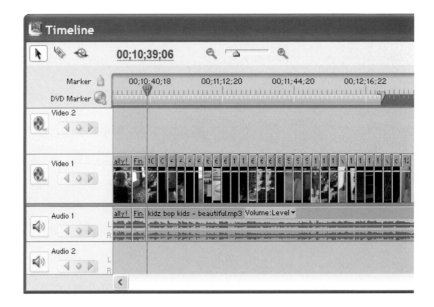

After completing your movie, you'll learn how to create DVDs that look great and allow your viewers to access specific scenes, just like DVDs from Hollywood.

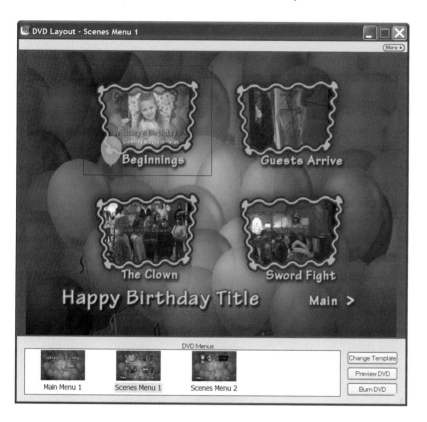

In addition to producing DVDs, you'll learn how to save a video file for viewing on your computer, create files for sharing via CD or over the Internet and how to send your movie back to your DV camera to archive the footage.

how this book works

The title of each section explains what is covered on that page.

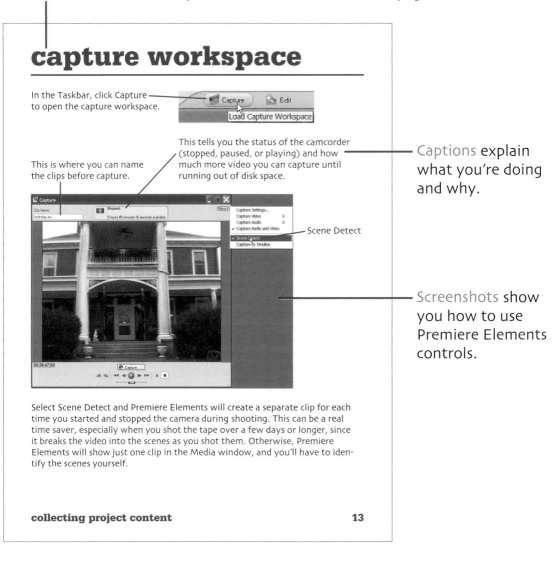

capture workspace

In the Taskbar, click Capture to open the capture workspace.

This is where you can name the clips before capture.

This tells you the status of the camcorder (stopped, paused, or playing) and how much more video you can capture until running out of disk space.

Scene Detect

Captions explain what you're doing and why.

Screenshots show you how to use Premiere Elements controls.

Select Scene Detect and Premiere Elements will create a separate clip for each time you started and stopped the camera during shooting. This can be a real time saver, especially when you shot the tape over a few days or longer, since it breaks the video into the scenes as you shot them. Otherwise, Premiere Elements will show just one clip in the Media window, and you'll have to identify the scenes yourself.

collecting project content 13

The extra bits section at the end of each chapter contains tips and tricks that you might like to know, but which aren't absolutely necessary for creating a movie.

The heading for each group of tips matches the section title.

The page number next to the heading makes it easy to find the section the tips belong to.

extra bits

capture workspace p. 13

- I typically don't select Capture to Timeline, which automatically inserts all captured video into the Timeline. Instead, I prefer to add my video to the project one clip at a time from the Media window.

capture dv p. 16

- You can change the name of any imported asset in the Media window by right clicking the image and choosing rename. This does not change the name of the corresponding file on your hard disk.

import pictures p. 18

- Premiere Elements can import images up to 4000x4000 pixels in .bmp, .eps, .ico, .gif, .jpeg, .jpg, .pdd, .pdf, .png, .psd, and .tiff formats.
- Right click any image on the Premiere Elements Timeline and choose Edit Original, and Premiere Elements opens that image within your default image editor. Any edits made and saved to the image are automatically applied to the image in Premiere Elements.

import audio p. 19

- Premiere Elements can import .aiff, .avi, .mov, .mp3, .wav, and .wma audio files. The only noteworthy omission is files produced with RealNetworks technology, which usually have the .rn extension.
- Premiere Elements can't rip tracks from a CD. A good free alternative is Microsoft's Windows Media Player, but make sure you disable copy protection before ripping.
- Premiere Elements can't record narrations directly, though you can import narrations recorded in another program. One very simple narration tool is Windows Sound Recorder, which is available on all Windows systems by clicking Start > Programs > Accessories > Entertainment > Sound Recorder.

import video p. 19

- Premiere Elements can import .avi, .mov, .mpeg, .mpe, .mpg, and .wmv video files and animated GIF files

20   **collecting project content**

tools you will need

Here's what you need to complete the project in this book:

At least 20 GB of free disk space for each hour-long project and a DVD-Recordable drive for producing recordable DVDs.

An Intel® Pentium® III 800MHz or AMD Athlon XP processor, Microsoft® Windows® XP Professional, Home Edition, or Media Center Edition with Service Pack 1, 256MB of RAM, 1.2GB of available hard-disk space for installation, 1024x768 16-bit (XGA) display, Microsoft DirectX 9 compatible sound and display drivers, DV/i.LINK/FireWire/IEEE 1394 interface to connect a Digital 8 or DV camcorder.

If you produce lots of movies, you'll run out of disk space quickly. If you think you may not have enough space, consider adding another drive to your computer; contact your local computer dealer to find out how.

A digital camcorder with miniDV tapes for shooting video footage and transferring video to and from the computer.

You'll also need some interesting video to work with and some digital photographs and songs.

(Used with permission of Sony Electronics, Inc.)

A FireWire cable to connect the camcorder to the computer.

Blank DVD-Recordable discs (to produce a DVD).

Premiere Elements installed.

Either a DVD player connected to a TV set or a DVD-ROM drive with DVD player software for your computer.

video production terms

To make your work in Premiere Elements easier, I've defined some of the key terms you'll encounter as you build your movie and DVD. We'll be using these terms throughout this book.

- **Video:** The footage you shoot with your camcorder. It includes both images and audio.

- **Movie:** The final result that Premiere Elements produces when you've finished editing and are ready to share your production.

- **Capture:** The process of transferring video from your camera to your computer.

- **Import:** The process of inserting an audio, video, or picture file already on your hard drive into Premiere Elements.

- **Render:** The process Premiere Elements goes through in producing a movie.

- **Video clip:** Video captured or imported into Premiere Elements. Video clips include the audio originally shot with the video.

- **Audio clip:** Separate audio files (usually music) imported into Premiere Elements.

- **Picture:** A still image you shoot with your digital camera and import into Premiere Elements.

- **Project:** The file where Premiere Elements stores your work while you're working on a movie. The project file references the video clips, audio clips, and pictures (often collectively referred to as content or assets) you're including in your movie, but Premiere Elements doesn't actually copy them into the project file. This keeps the project file small, but it also means that you must be sure not to delete the captured files until after you produce your final movie.

the next step

While this Visual QuickProject Guide will give you an excellent start, there's a lot more to learn about the art of movie making and working with Premiere Elements. If you're curious, check out *Premiere Elements for Windows: Visual QuickStart Guide*, also published by Peachpit Press.

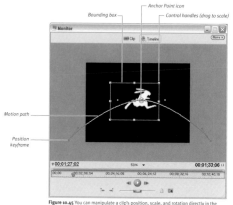

The Visual QuickStart Guide features clear examples, concise step-by-step instructions, and lots of helpful tips. It covers every aspect of shooting and capturing video and editing and producing compelling, fun-to-watch movies.

1. welcome to premiere elements

Premiere Elements is easy to learn, and for the most part, you can use it without having to fiddle with its options or do any elaborate set up. But just as with any new tool you use, it's a good idea to take a quick look around to familiarize yourself with the basic operations. That's what you'll do in this chapter. Then you'll be ready to jump right in and start bringing your video footage into Premiere Elements and begin making movies.

Hold off on launching Premiere Elements while we take a quick tour of its main windows. Then we'll launch the program, select startup options and set all necessary project options.

Premiere Elements in all its glory.

Producing family videos is fun and rewarding (plus you get to make sure that you're included).

Here's me with Whatley, whose birthday party video will be your model throughout this book.

premiere elements tour

In Premiere Elements, you work through your project using the Taskbar buttons on the upper right. When you choose a button, Premiere Elements automatically arranges the interface to facilitate that activity.

This is the Media window. When you choose a task, Premiere Elements automatically displays the appropriate content in the Media window. For example, in Effects mode, as shown at right, the Media window displays all audio and video effects.

No matter what mode you're in, you can always view your captured and imported content by clicking the tab on the extreme left.

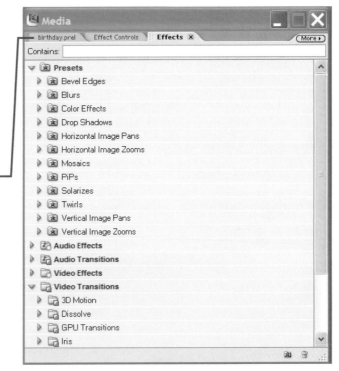

This is the Monitor window, which displays content from the Timeline and Media Window.

Click Clip to display content in the Media Window.

Click Timeline to display content in the Timeline.

The controls on the bottom of the Monitor window change depending upon whether you've selected Clip or Timeline. I'll describe the Clip-related controls in Chapter 2 and the Timeline controls in Chapter 3.

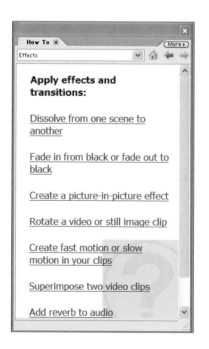

This is the How To palette which displays task-specific direction. Here, in Effects mode, the palette displays tips on how to create a number of video effects. When you select another mode, the palette displays tasks specific to that mode.

premiere elements tour

This is the Timeline window, where you'll build your production. A timeline is a longitudinal view with separate tracks for the various video and audio elements you'll add to your movie.

Specifically, you'll add visual content (video, still images, and titles) to video tracks, and audio content (audio captured when you shot your video, background music, and narration) to audio tracks. Not that you'll ever need anywhere near this many, but Premiere Elements can support up to 99 audio and video tracks.

Timeline tools —

Video tracks —

Audio tracks —

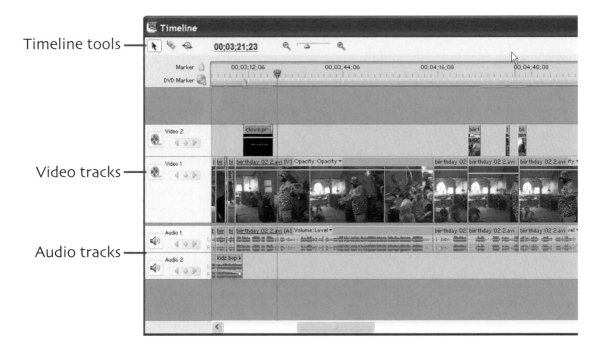

As mentioned previously, Premiere Elements customizes its interface for each Taskbar activity, revealing the relevent controls and aligning the windows into the optimal position. This is called a workspace. Click on a button in the Taskbar, and Premiere Elements automatically opens the designated workspace.

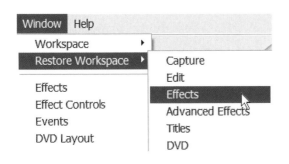

Premiere Elements lets you customize each workspace as desired, so you can resize and move the various windows around to your liking.

If the interface gets too cluttered, however, you can also revert to the factory installed configuration by choosing Restore Workspace and the desired workspace.

start your project

Now that you know the basics, let's get started by launching Premiere Elements.

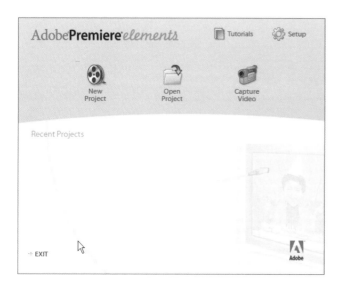

This is the first screen you'll see whenever you launch Premiere Elements. If this isn't your first project, you'll see previous projects listed under Recent Projects, which you can click to open.

If you have previous projects that aren't listed, you can find them by clicking Open Projects.

For now, click Setup on the top right of the screen to select project options.

Choose NTSC in the United States and Canada and PAL in most other locations. Choose the standard project unless you shot in 16:9 format with your camcorder. If you did shoot in 16:9 mode, click Widescreen.

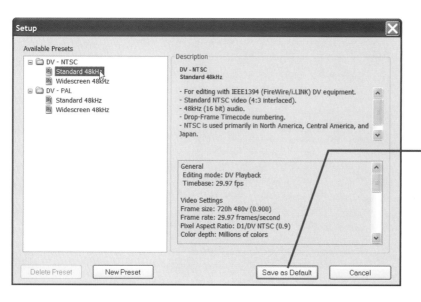

Click Save as Default to return to the opening screen. Premiere Elements will use these settings for all future projects until you change them.

Next click New Project. As you can see, Premiere Elements forces you to save your project before you start editing. As we'll see in Setting Project Defaults, by default, Premiere Elements stores captured and all temporary files (files produced behind the scenes during production) in the same folder as your project file, which makes the location of that file an important decision.

Start by naming your project.　　　　　　　　　　　　　Click Browse...

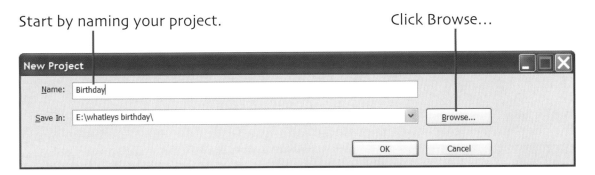

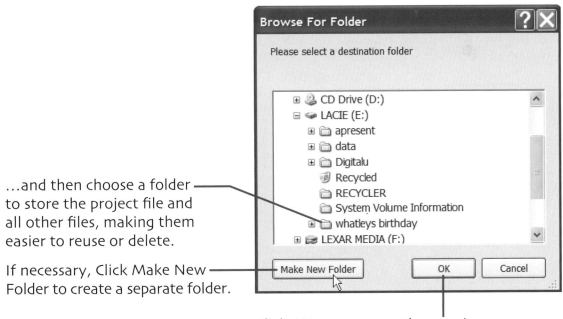

...and then choose a folder to store the project file and all other files, making them easier to reuse or delete.

If necessary, Click Make New Folder to create a separate folder.

Click OK to return to the opening screen, then OK again to enter Premiere Elements.

setting project defaults

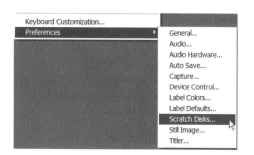

Premiere Elements offers a boatload of preference settings accessed by choosing Edit > Preferences. In most instances, the default settings will do, but there are several settings to be aware of before starting your first project.

These preferences are not project specific and will remain in place until you change them.

Make sure that all Scratch Disks are set "Same as Project" which will place these files in the same folder as the project file.

Now let's look at some other preferences. Click Auto Save.

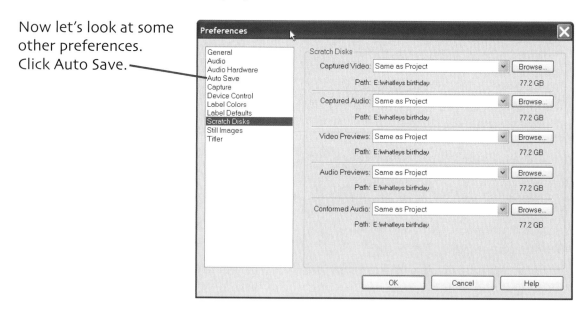

Make sure that Automatically Save Projects is selected and change the duration to 10 minutes; the default 20 is too long for me.

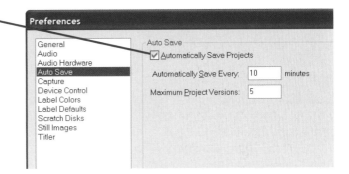

If you don't save the project in the interim, Premiere Elements will store the designated number of project versions in the Auto Save folder, which you can restore by selecting them just as you would a normal project file. The default of 5 is fine here.

Note that Premiere Elements stores your Auto Save folder in the same folder as your project file.

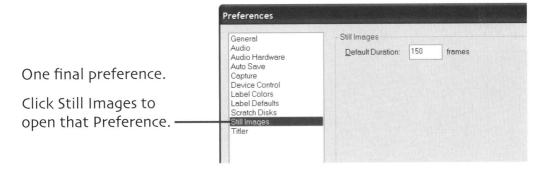

One final preference.

Click Still Images to open that Preference.

Since we're working in NTSC, there are 30 frames per second (25 in PAL), so the default 150 frames value for still image duration translates to five seconds. Use the default setting for now; you'll learn about choosing a different duration in Chapter 3.

extra bits

Premiere Elements Tour p. 2

- Premiere Elements has one workspace that you can't reach via a button on the Taskbar. Specifically, you have to open the Advanced Effects workspace by choosing Workspace > Advanced Effects from the main menu. More on that in Arrange Effects Workspace on page 64.

start your project p. 6

- Note that Premiere Elements offers several useful tutorials accessed by clicking the tutorial button on the opening screen.

set preferences p. 8

- Changing the Still Image Default Duration affects pictures inserted after you make the change (not those previously inserted into the project).

2. collecting project content

I like collecting all of my audio and video clips and pictures—the project assets, or content—before I start serious editing, and that's what you'll do here. You'll set up and capture—or transfer—video from a DV camera, and import audio files and digital photos. You'll also learn to manage these collections in Premiere Elements' Collections pane.

I'm assuming that you've already shot your video and that you may have some digital photographs and music files already stored on your computer that you want to use to create a slide show to include with your video footage. You'll be getting these assets into Premiere Elements in this chapter and then working with them to create your project in the rest of this book.

Premiere Elements stores all content in the Media window. ————

In Organize Media Window, you'll learn how to organize your content into folders that help reduce clutter and make your project assets easier to find.

This folder contains digital pictures you can use to build a slide show. ——

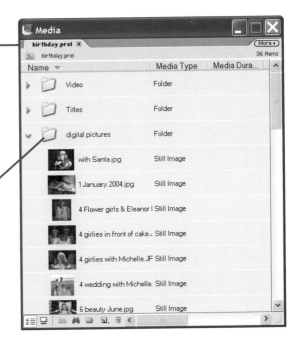

set up for dv capture

Find the DV output port on your DV camera. It's usually marked DV, as shown here. Briefly, DV is the format used to store video on the camcorder. During capture, DV video is transferred from camcorder to computer via a FireWire cable. FireWire is a common standard for linking computers and peripherals, and is also also known as IEEE1394 and iLink.

Not this one—it's for analog audio-video you watch on your TV.

Not this one—LANC is a little-used standard for controlling your camera with external devices.

Not this one—it's the universal serial bus (USB) port used to send still pictures to the computer.

4-pin to 6-pin DV cable. This end goes into your camera.

6-pin FireWire port on the computer. You can connect the cable to any FireWire port on the bracket.

This end goes into the DV card in your computer. Note that some laptops have 4-pin ports, like the DV camera shown here, instead of 6-pin ports. If this is the case for your computer, make sure you buy a 4-pin to 4-pin DV cable.

Plug in your camcorder and set it to VTR—which stands for Video Tape Recorder—(shown) or Play mode.

collecting project content

capture workspace

In the Taskbar, click Capture to open the capture workspace.

This is where you can name the clips before capture.

This tells you the status of the camcorder (stopped, paused, or playing) and how much more video you can capture until running out of disk space.

Scene Detect

Select Scene Detect and Premiere Elements will create a separate clip for each time you started and stopped the camera during shooting. This can be a real time saver, especially when you shot the tape over a few days or longer, since it breaks the video into the scenes as you shot them. Otherwise, Premiere Elements will show just one clip in the Media window, and you'll have to identify the scenes yourself.

capture workspace

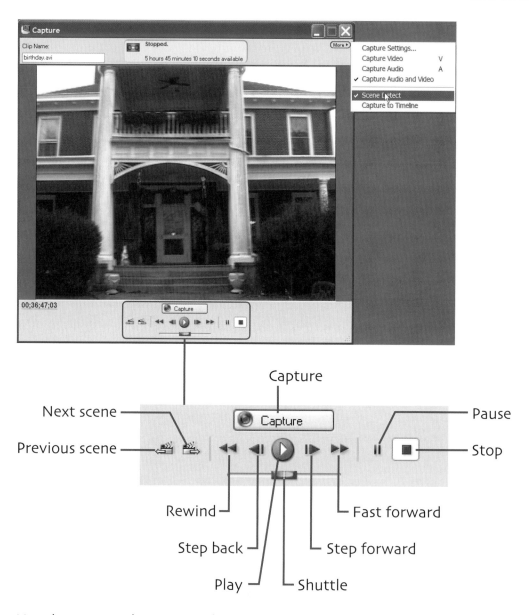

Use these controls to move the video to the desired starting point for your capture. The Shuttle is a real time saver; drag it to the left to rewind, or the right to fast forward. Notice that the camcorder's speed increases as you drag the shuttle further from the middle.

capture dv

Now that you know the lay of the land, let's capture your video.

Name your captured files (or accept the default, which is the project name).

If your project has multiple source tapes, always use a different name for each tape; otherwise, the automatic numbering system Premiere Elements uses for the captured scenes can get very confusing.

Use these controls to move to the desired starting point of the video in your camcorder, which should always be two to three seconds before the start of the target scene on your camcorder.

Click Capture to start capturing.

Once you click capture, Premiere Elements automatically rolls the tape (you don't have to press Play first) and changes the Capture button to a Stop Capture button, which does exactly what you'd expect. Wait until two or three seconds after you see the last frame you'd like to capture to make sure you captured all the frames you need.

capture dv (cont.)

If you don't manually stop capturing, Premiere Elements will automatically stop when it reaches the end of the video on the tape. This means that you don't have to stick around to stop the capture process; you can start capturing and then walk away.

Premiere Element inserts the video into the Media window, separated into automatically numbered separate scenes. Note that each scene is a separate file on your hard disk.

As you can see, I took my own advice and labeled one captured tape "birthday" and the other "clown." This makes finding the desired clips much, much easier.

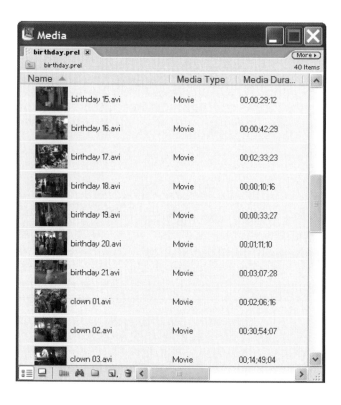

organize media window

If your project only contains a few video files, organizing the Media window isn't important. Since this project includes multiple videos, still images, background music, narration and several titles, which all are stored in the Media window, organization is essential to avoid wasting time looking for project assets.

For projects like these, I always store my audio, video, still images and titles in separate folders. Here's how to create the folders and drag your content into them.

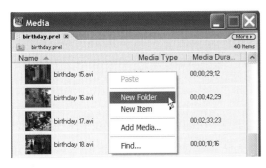

Click the Media window, then right click and choose New Folder.

Here's the new folder. Type the desired name.

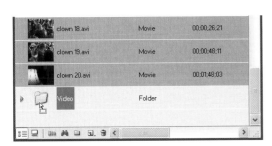

Now drag all content into the new folder.

All videos are now in the video folder. Click the triangle beside the folder icon to open and close the folder.

import pictures

Go ahead and create folders for all types of media you plan to include in your project. That way they'll be ready when you start importing other content.

Here's what my Media window looks like now; I'm ready to start importing digital pictures.

Assuming you are too, right click the Digital pictures folder, and choose Add Media.

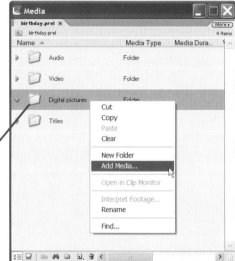

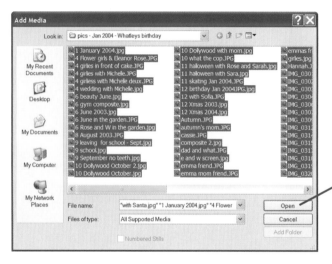

Navigate to the folder that contains your digital pictures and select all that you want to import.

Then click Open.

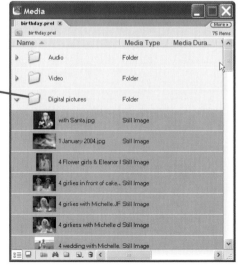

Premiere Elements imports the images into the Digital pictures folder.

collecting project content

import audio and video

Importing audio and video is identical to adding pictures, as I'll demonstrate by adding some audio files.

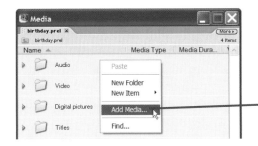

Right click the target folder and choose Add Media.

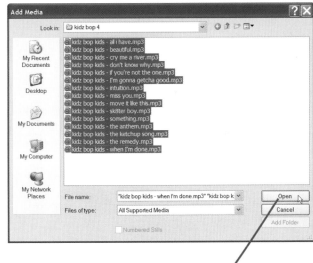

Navigate to the folder that contains your media files and select all that you want to import.

Then click Open.

Here's the imported audio. I find that the best strategy for finding audio that your audience will like is to use their CDs. Kidz Bop Kids is a CD that my daughter listens to frequently when she's playing. Since she's my primary audience, it was an obvious safe choice.

collecting project content   **19**

extra bits

capture workspace p. 13

- I typically don't select Capture to Timeline, which automatically inserts all captured video into the Timeline. Instead, I prefer to add my video to the project one clip at a time from the Media window.

capture dv p. 16

- You can change the name of any imported asset in the Media window by right clicking the image and choosing rename. This does not change the name of the corresponding file on your hard disk.

import pictures p. 18

- Premiere Elements can import images up to 4000x4000 pixels in .bmp, .eps, .ico, .gif, .jpeg, .jpg, .pdd, .pdf, .png, .psd, and .tiff formats.

- Right click any image on the Premiere Elements Timeline and choose Edit Original, and Premiere Elements opens that image within your default image editor. Any edits made and saved to the image are automatically applied to the image in Premiere Elements.

import audio p. 19

- Premiere Elements can import .aiff, .avi, .mov, .mp3, .wav, and .wma audio files. The only noteworthy omission is files produced with RealNetworks technology, which usually have the .rn extension.

- Premiere Elements can't rip tracks from a CD. A good free alternative is Microsoft's Windows Media Player, but make sure you disable copy protection before ripping.

- Premiere Elements can't record narrations directly, though you can import narrations recorded in another program. One very simple narration tool is Windows Sound Recorder, which is available on all Windows systems by clicking Start > Programs > Accessories > Entertainment > Sound Recorder.

import video p. 19

- Premiere Elements can import .avi, .mov, .mpeg, .mpe, .mpg, and .wmv video files and animated GIF files

collecting project content

3. assembling your clips

When creating a birthday or other similar video, I try to accomplish two things. First, I try to tell a story, with a beginning, middle, and end. This helps keep the viewer's attention. Second, I try to chronicle the event, primarily by making sure I include all key shots inherent to the occasion, like a shot of everyone singing "Happy Birthday," and all key participants, typically family and important friends. Then I chop off the rest, aggressively and relentlessly, to keep the movie as short as possible. With Premiere Elements, you'll do part of this work in the Monitor window and part on the Timeline.

If you captured with Scene Detect enabled, as described in Chapter 2, you're probably staring at a bunch of video clips in the Media Window: one for each time you started and stopped recording on your DV camera. Having these clips broken out is helpful, but to provide the necessary pace, you'll usually have to cut additional frames from these clips before using them in the final movie.

This is the Media Window in Icon view, which shows a thumbnail of the first frame of each captured video clip to help jog your memory of the contents.

Double click any icon and Premiere Elements will open the clip in the Monitor window, shown on the following page.

Icon view

List view

21

review your clips

After capture, you should play each clip to see how the video looks and to refamiliarize yourself with exactly what you shot. Then you can start shaping the raw captured clips into a polished video production.

When you double click a clip in the Media window Premiere Elements automatically enters Clip view with your clip open. This view contains a different set of tools than Timeline view, discussed in on page 34.

You can tell which view you're in by noticing which button is depressed atop the Monitor and change views by clicking the other button.

Premiere Elements offers several ways to move through your clip in the Monitor. Start by dragging the Current Time Indicator slider through the clip, and then use the arrow keys on your keyboard to locate exact frames.

Then try the shuttle. Notice how it increases speed as you drag it away from the center, which can be very useful with longer clips.

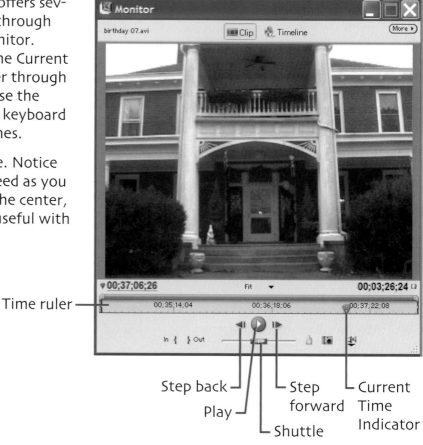

Time ruler

Step back
Play
Step forward
Shuttle
Current Time Indicator

rename your clips

After playing the clip in the monitor, rename the clip so you can find it later during editing.

Click the file name and Premiere Elements makes the text active.

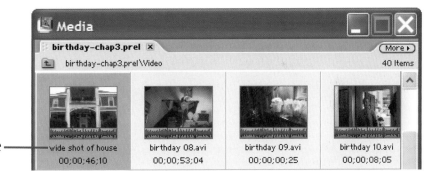

Type the new name and press Enter.

delete unneeded clips

If you know you won't use a clip in the production, remove it from the Media window to reduce clutter.

Select the clip or clips. ——

Right click.

Choose Clear. ——

tell the story

Before you start assembling your clips, plan the visual flow of your movie to tell your story. That will make it easier to identify which clips to add to the project, and which to leave out. Here are the key scenes I'll include in the birthday movie.

Wide shot of house

I start with a shot of the house—technically called an establishing shot, because it establishes the location in the viewer's mind.

Interior shot

Since the party is taking place indoors, I add a few interior shots to provide more visual context.

First arrivals

Folks are coming! I try to find shots of all key friends and relatives as they arrive.

The gang's all here

Next come shots of pre-entertainment meeting and greeting (multiple shots of key guests).

Enter the clown

The clown arrives and performs.

Balloon fight 1

The entertainment concludes with balloon swords and helmets for all, creating general havoc (multiple clips of key guests).

tell the story (cont.)

Time for cake

That lasts until it's time for the cake. The crowd comes down the stairs.

Happy Birthday S...

Everyone sings "Happy Birthday."

Eat! Eat!

Then everyone starts chowing down.

Finally! Presents

Finally it's time to open presents (multiple clips of key guests).

Parting shots

Then it's time for hugs and air kisses (multiple clips of key guests).

meet the timeline

By now, you've reviewed your captured video, deleted the clips you won't use, and renamed those that you will. Now let's look at the Timeline, which is the palette upon which you'll create your video.

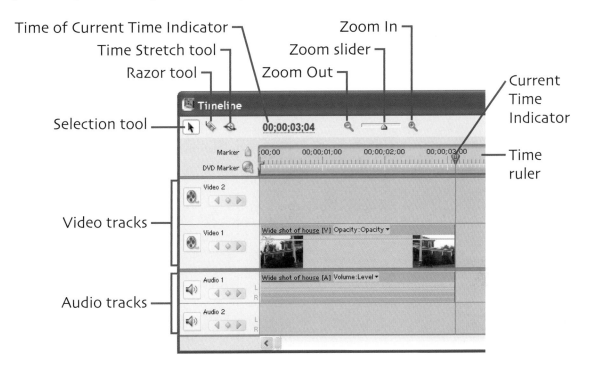

The Timeline can look intimidating, but it's actually pretty logical. As you add video, Premiere Elements displays the files on the Timeline, with the size of each clip determined by its duration, about three seconds for the clip in the Timeline above. As you add more video and still images to the project, Premiere Elements simply adds their durations to the Timeline, extending the project to the right.

Premiere Elements inserts video to the Video tracks and the associated audio to the Audio tracks. For simple projects, like that we're building here, you'll insert video and still images on Video 1 and titles on Video 2. Audio captured with the video will typically go on Audio 1, with background music and narration (if any) on Audio 2.

set in/out points

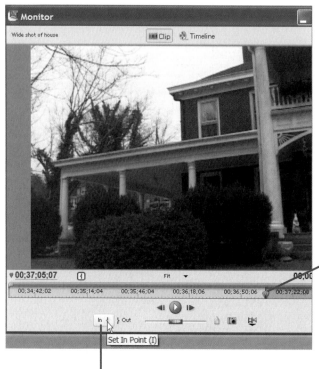

Suppose one of your captured clips is thirty seconds long, but you only want to include five seconds from the clip in the movie. Using the Set In Point/Set Out Point controls, you essentially tell Premiere Elements to start here (Set In Point) and stop there (Set Out Point).

Then you can drag only the video between those two points into the project. Here's how.

Drag the Current Time Indicator to the start of the frames you want to include in the project.

Click Set In Point.

Drag the Current Time Indicator to the end of the frames you want to include in the project.

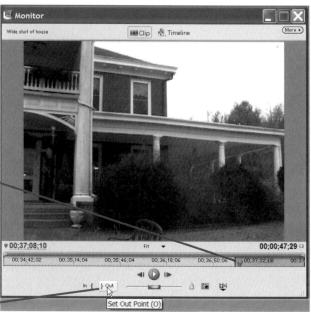

Click Set Out Point.

assembling your clips

drag clip to the timeline

Then drag the clip from the Monitor to Video 1 and release.

Premiere Elements adds the video between the In and Out points to Video 1 and the audio to Audio 1. If you subsequently move the clip, Premiere Elements will keep the audio and video tracks "linked" to maintain synchronization unless and until you "unlink" the two tracks.

split clips on timeline

You can set In and Out points multiple times within a single captured clip, and Premiere Elements will save the settings for each scene inserted into the Time-line. However, if there are many separate scenes within one long capture file that you wish to include in your movie, it's faster to drag the clip to the Timeline, split it into separate scenes there, and remove unwanted frames by trimming on the Timeline.

For example, there are two scenes I'd like to include from the first captured clip; one the wide shot of the house, the second a shot taken while walking up the path to the front door.

Click the clip in the Media Window.

Hold down the mouse button and drag the clip to the desired location.

Release the mouse button.

Premiere Elements inserts the video into Video 1 and the audio into Audio 1.

Now split the clip into two parts. While watching the Monitor, drag the Current Time Indicator to where you want to split the clip.

Click the Razor tool.

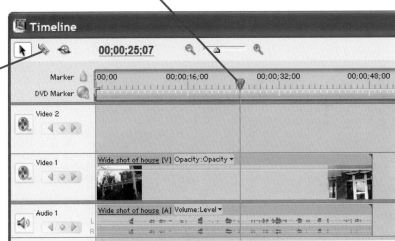

Hover the razor icon over the Current Time Indicator and click the left mouse button.

Premiere Elements splits the clip into two clips, here and here.

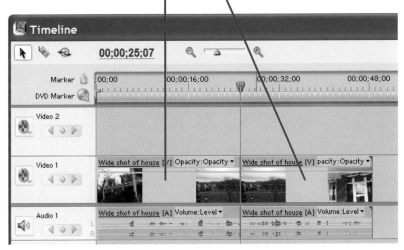

trim on the timeline

After splitting your clip, click the Selection arrow button on the top left of the timeline to restore the cursor to the Selection tool. If necessary, click the Zoom In button to zoom into the Timeline.

Zoom In

Selection Tool

Click the clip to make it active.

Hover your pointer over the edge of the clip until the Trim cursor appears.

Click the mouse button.

When trimming the beginning of the first clip, drag to the right and watch the Monitor until the first frame you want to appear in the Movie appears.

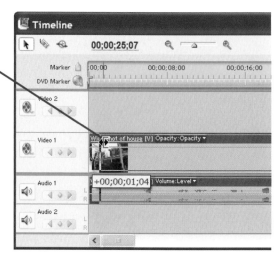

Premiere Elements removes the frames at the start of the clip and shifts all subsequent clips to the left to close the gap. You can reverse the trim immediately by clicking Undo or at any time by dragging the edge back out.

assembling your clips

trim between clips

We just trimmed the first video in the project, during which Premiere Elements displayed the normal Monitor display. However, when you trim between clips, Premiere Elements displays the Trim Monitor, which shows the last frame from the first clip on the left, and the first frame of the second clip on the right. This makes it easy to set up the ideal flow from clip to clip.

Last frame first clip

First frame second clip

To display the Trim monitor, I'll trim the frames from the end of the first clip. Note that you don't have to do anything special to make the Trim Monitor appear, you just have to trim between clips.

Same basic procedure as before:

Hover your mouse over the edge you wish to trim.

Wait for the Trim cursor to appear.

While watching the Trim Monitor, click and drag the edge of the clip to the left until you reach the desired position.

When trimming from the end of a clip, wait until the last frame you want to remain in the movie appears in the Trim Monitor.

preview your movie

Let's play the movie to see how it's flowing so far. This gives us a chance to get familiar with the Monitor in Timeline view.

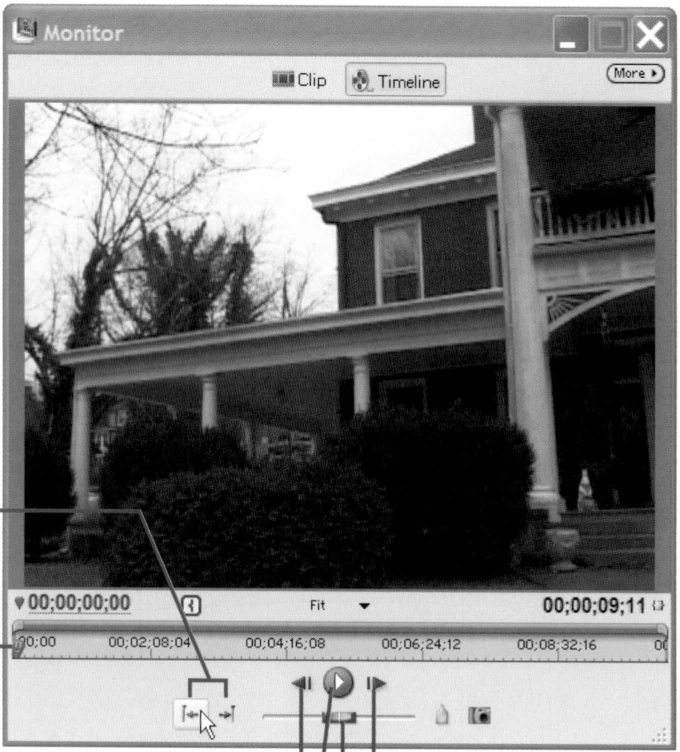
Monitor
Clip
Timeline
More
00;00;00;00
Fit
00;00;09;11
00;02;08;04
00;04;16;08
00;06;24;12
00;08;32;16
Click the Go To Previous Edit Point or Go To Next Edit Point icons until you get to the clip you want to preview.
Current Time Indicator
Step back
Step forward
Play
Shuttle

Use these buttons to control playback.

After Premiere Elements plays the selected clip, it will play subsequent clips until you pause playback or it reaches the end of the project.

Note that you can also use the spacebar on your keyboard to start and pause playback—definitely one of the most useful keyboard shortcuts in the program.

save your project

Like what you just saw? Great, now save the project to make sure you don't lose it.

From the Premiere Elements main menu, choose File > Save.

Since you named your project when you first started, Premiere Elements will simply save the file.

To save a copy of the project and then work on the new project, click Save As, name the file, and click Save.

To save a copy of the project and continue working on the original project, click Save a Copy, name the file, and click Save.

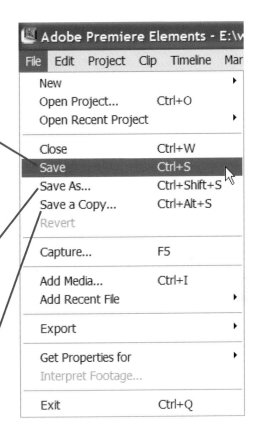

add clips between clips

One of Premiere Elements' best features is the ability to add clips anywhere in the project, not just at the end. For example, in my movie, I will show clips of people arriving at the party, and then, in the next scene, meeting and greeting before the entertainment started.

When shooting the video, however, these scenes were intermixed; some folks arrived, then mingled, then more arrivals, then more mingling. During editing, I'll group all the arrival shots first, then the meeting and greeting shots. This means that I'll have to insert some clips in between others already on the Timeline. Here's how it's done.

Set the In and Out points as normal.

Click and drag the clip to the desired location between clips and release.

If you release the cursor in the middle of a clip, Premiere Elements will split the clip on the Timeline and insert the new clip, which is generally not what you want. To help make sure you're between two clips, the cursor "snaps" to the intersection of the clips.

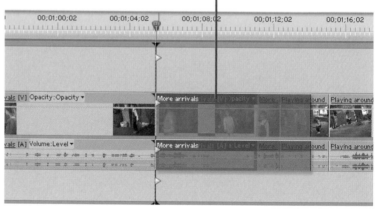

assembling your clips

arrange clips

Here I inserted the clip "More arrivals" between "First arrivals" and "Even more arrivals." Note that after inserting the clip, Premiere Elements automatically pushed back all clips located after the insertion point.

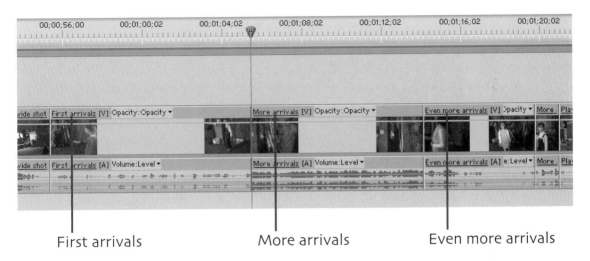

First arrivals   More arrivals   Even more arrivals

If you don't like the current clip order, you can click and drag the clip to the new location.

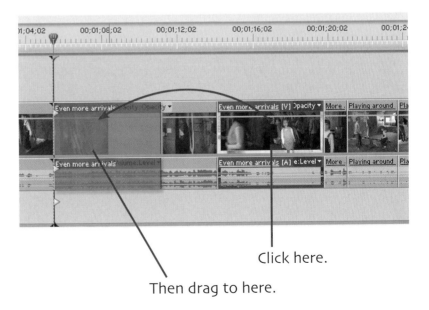

Click here.

Then drag to here.

ripple delete

Yikes! Premiere Elements left a huge gap in the Timeline after the move. Let's close it up with the Ripple Delete command.

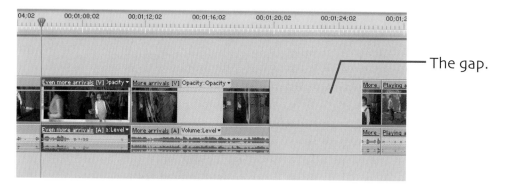

—— The gap.

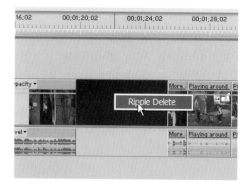

Click the gap.

Right click.

Choose Ripple Delete.

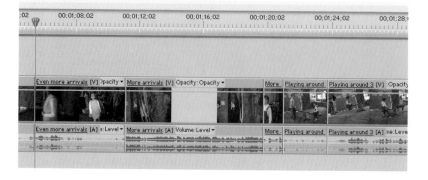

Gap gone.

assembling your clips

insert music files

Now you'll start the slide show component of the movie. Here you'll add a music file to the Timeline and then your pictures. Movie Maker will convert this content to video when rendering the final movie. You'll use the still pictures and a music file that you imported in Chapter 2.

You can add a slideshow anywhere in the production, though I usually add mine to the end, after all the trimmed video clips.

Click and open the folder that contains your music files.

Click the desired song and hold down the mouse button.

Drag the song to the Audio 1 track.

Release the mouse button.

Premiere Elements inserts the song into the Audio 1 track.

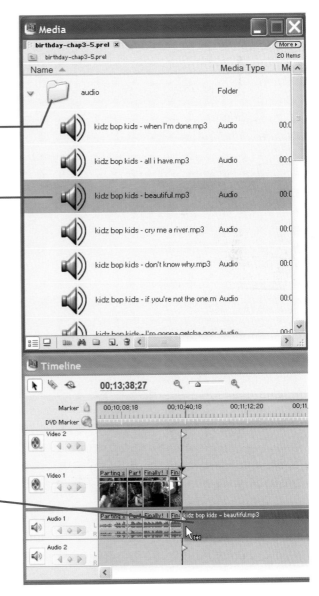

add a picture

You can add one or more pictures to your production simply by dragging them to the Timeline. Here's how.

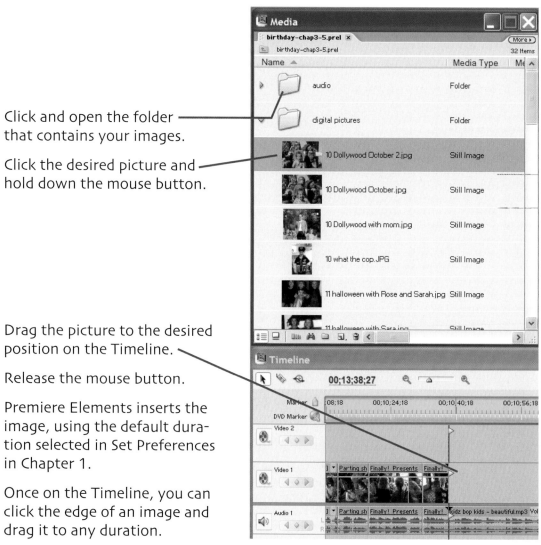

Click and open the folder that contains your images.

Click the desired picture and hold down the mouse button.

Drag the picture to the desired position on the Timeline.

Release the mouse button.

Premiere Elements inserts the image, using the default duration selected in Set Preferences in Chapter 1.

Once on the Timeline, you can click the edge of an image and drag it to any duration.

assembling your clips

create a slideshow

Dragging works fine for single images here and there, but Premiere Elements has a great feature for easily creating slide-shows, complete with transitions, in just a couple of clicks. Start by switching to Icon view and arranging your pictures in the desired order.

Select the images to include in your slide show. As with most Windows programs, you can press and hold down the shift key and select sequential images, or press and hold down the Ctrl key and select random images.

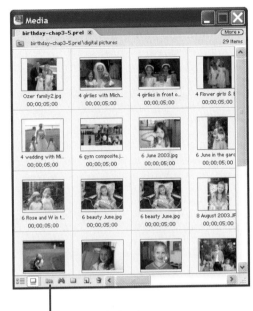

Click Create Slideshow.

If you pre-sorted your images, use Sort Order for Ordering.

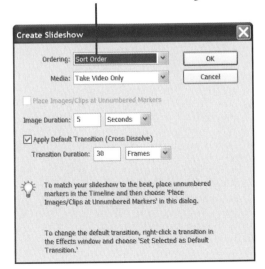

If you select your images in the desired order, use the other option, Selection Order (not shown).

When selecting digital images, your only Media option is "Take Video Only" since there is no audio. This changes if you use this tool to create slides from videos, which is beyond the scope of this book.

The default values of five seconds per image and 30 frames (one second) per transition are good starting points. Try a shorter image duration if your music is fast-paced. For slower music, you can extend image duration, especially when adding pan and zoom effects as discussed in Add Motion to Images in Chapter 5.

preview the slideshow

Premiere Elements built the slide show. Since your music file is already on the Timeline, you can preview after adding the pictures. Click Undo if you don't like the result, and immediately experiment with new picture and transition durations.

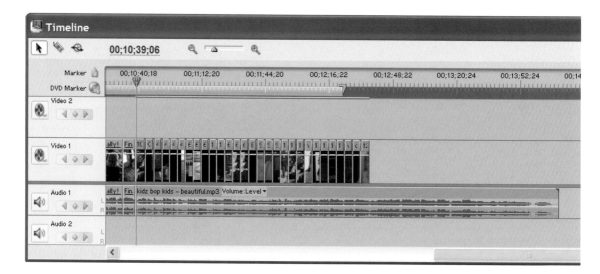

Note that the song is longer than the slide show, which is OK. In Chapter 6, you'll add a title before the slideshow, and at least one title ("The End") after the slideshow. These will consume some of the extra music, and you'll delete the rest and fade to silence in Chapter 7.

assembling your clips

edit your images

Here's a close-up look of the slideshow, complete with transitions. However, as I preview the slide show, I see that one image has red-eye issues. If you have this or similar problems, you can fix them in your default image editor. Mine is Photoshop Elements.

To edit an image, select it.

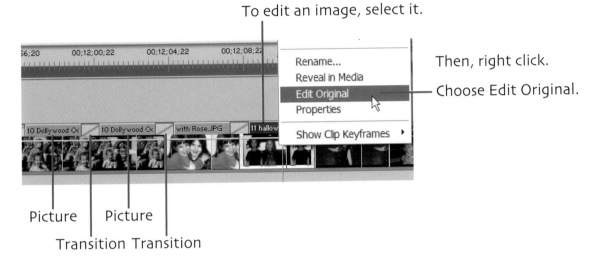

Then, right click.

Choose Edit Original.

Picture   Picture

Transition Transition

Photoshop Elements opens with the file inserted.

I've fixed one eye (on the right) and have one to go. Photoshop Elements' Red Eye Removal tool fixes red-eye issues, and there are a host of tools that can fix other common problems quickly and easily.

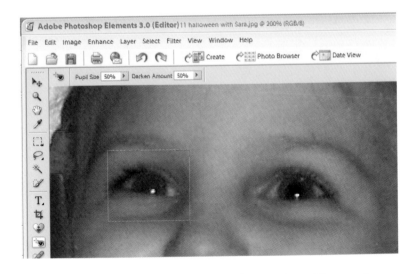

Then save the file as normal and Premiere Elements automatically imports the updated file.

extra bits

delete your clips p. 24

- Deleting clips from the Media window (or the Timeline for that matter) doesn't delete the clip from your hard drive.

tell the story p. 25

- Obviously, you can't include clips in your projects that you haven't first shot with your video camera. When I shoot an event, be it a wedding, concert, birthday, or family outing, I make a short list of required shots for that event before I leave for the shoot. It's typically pretty easy to formulate the list if you think about it in advance, but if you try to get all the shots without planning, you're bound to miss one or two.

meet the timeline p. 27

- You can add more video and audio tracks to the Timeline by right clicking on the Video 1 or Audio 1 track labels, all the way to the left.

set in/out points p. 28

- Some clips, like the Happy Birthday Song clip in my birthday video, must be long enough to cover the entire scene. Most other clips, however, such as those shot just to make sure that all relevant friends and family make it into the video, should be as short as possible, under 5 seconds if possible. These will feel pretty choppy when you initially preview them, but everything will fall into place when you add background music to these clips in Chapter 7.

trim between clips p. 32

- In the next chapter, you'll learn about transitions, which are visual effects that help smooth the move from one clip to the next. If you plan to use transitions between clips, consider the transition duration when trimming your clips. For example, a 30-frame dissolve transition creates a 1-second overlap between the two clips. When trimming, be sure that any critical action or audio in the first clip ends at least half a second from the end of the clip, and that any critical action or audio in the second clip starts at least half a second into that clip. Similarly, if you fade in from black (an effect discussed in Chapter 5), the first half-second of the clip will be partially obscured by the fade-in effect. When trimming, be sure that any critical action or audio starts after that half-second. Ditto at the end of a clip if you plan to fade to black at the clip's end.

save your project p. 35

- The project file doesn't contain the video, audio, and digital picture files that make up the project; it simply contains references to them. This keeps the project files small, but it means that you can't delete those files until after you've rendered your final movie.

ripple delete p. 38

- If you click a clip and press Delete on your keyboard, Premiere Elements deletes the clip, and shifts all subsequent clips to the left to close the gap, which is the same result you get if you right click and choose Ripple Delete.

- To leave a space in the Timeline where you deleted a clip, right click and choose Clear.

- To delete only the audio or video portion of a clip, right click and choose Unlink Audio and Video. Then you can delete either track without deleting the other.

4. inserting transitions

Transitions are audio and visual effects used to smooth the flow from clip to clip. For example, in movies, you may have noticed the screen fade to black at the end of one scene and then fade back in at the start of the next. You may have also noticed that the audio followed suit, growing quieter during the fade to black and then welling up as the picture faded back in. These are transitions.

Note that you don't have to insert a transition between each clip in a project. If you don't insert a transition, the second clip starts playing immediately after the first clip ends, which is commonly called a cut transition.

Premiere Elements offers a great mix of transitions in the Effects tab, separated into useful categories like Dissolves and Page Peels.

That said, like many things in movie making, less is more when it comes to using trans-tions. Here, knowing which transitions to use, and when, is key to using transitions effectively

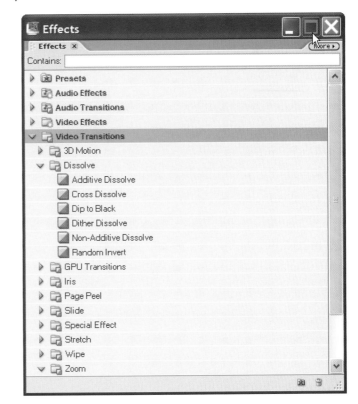

explore transitions

In the Taskbar on the top right of Premiere Elements, click Effects to load the Effects Workspace.

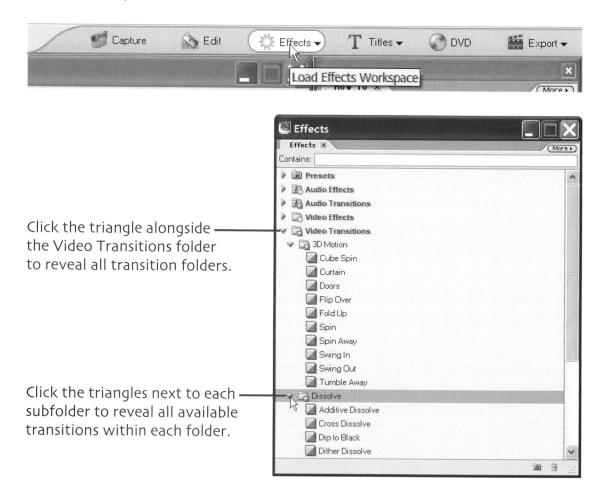

Click the triangle alongside the Video Transitions folder to reveal all transition folders.

Click the triangles next to each subfolder to reveal all available transitions within each folder.

Unfortunately, there's no easy way to preview transitions without actually applying them. So without further ado, let's apply your first transition.

insert a cross dissolve

I want to smooth the scene change from a view of the party room to the arrival of the first guests. This is a minor change, so I'll try a subtle cross dissolve transition, which blends frames from the two video clips.

Find a similar spot in your project, where you're moving from one scene to another, making sure the change is equally minor. Before applying the transition, have the intersection of the last clip from the first scene and the first clip from the second scene in view.

Open the Dissolve folder in the Effects panel and select the Cross Dissolve transition.

Hold down the mouse button and drag the transition to the intersection of the two clips.

Release the mouse button.

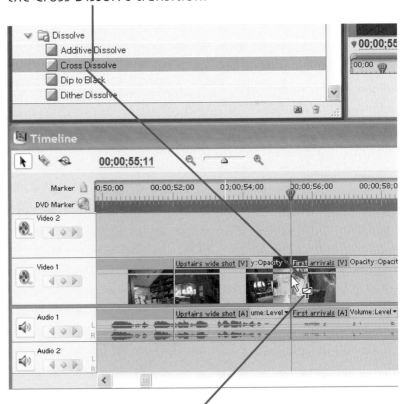

Note the small icon that looks like a two-headed top at the intersection of the two clips where I dragged the transition. If you see a different icon, or get an error message when you release the mouse button, see Transitions In-Depth on page 57.

insert a cross dissolve

Premiere Elements inserts the
transition on the Video 1 track.

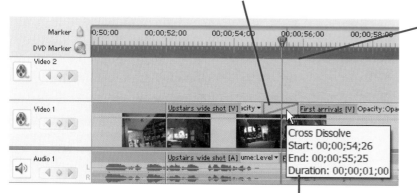

This red bar tells
you that Premiere
Elements may need
to render the transi-
tion to preview it at
full frame rate. More
on this in Render
Your Transition on
page 52.

Note the information window Premiere Elements displays when you hover your mouse over any content in
the Timeline. This is the easiest way to identify which
transition you inserted and its duration.

preview your transition

Now preview your transition to be sure it works the way you want it to.

Drag the Current Time Indicator
to a position before the transition.

Transition

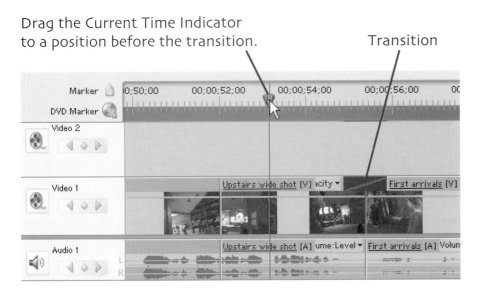

Click the Play button (or press
the space bar on your keyboard)
to start the preview.

Premiere Elements plays
through the transition and
beyond to subsequent clips.

Most computers can play the
Cross Dissolve transition at
full frame rate without first
rendering. If yours can't, or
if you applied a more complicated effect that doesn't play
smoothly, see Render Your
Transition, later.

render your transition

Suppose your preview of the transition wasn't smooth, either because you're working on a slower computer or applied a complex transition. Let's render the transtion so it plays smoothly.

Double click the
Work Area ruler.

Premiere Elements displays the
Work Area bar.

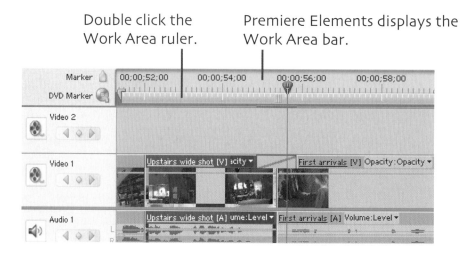

Grab and pull the handles of the Work Area bar until they cover the red line designating the unrendered transition. This defines the Work Area that Premiere Elements will render.

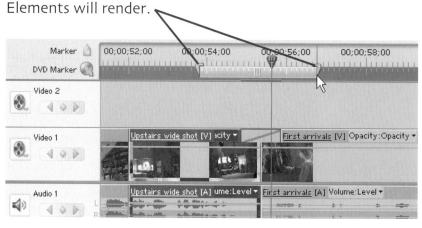

After rendering your transition, Premiere Elements plays the selected work area. It's good practice to overlap the work area before and after the transition as shown in the figure so you can preview your transition in the context of the video surrounding it.

In Premiere Elements main menu choose Timeline > Render Work Area, or click Enter on your keyboard, to render the transition.

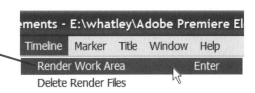

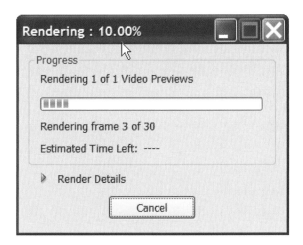

Premiere Elements renders the work area, and displays this message.

Then preview as normal, and playback should be perfect!

change duration

Preview your new transition. Mine flashes by a bit too quickly, so I'm going to make it longer. Two seconds sounds about right. Try a 2-second duration for your transition, too.

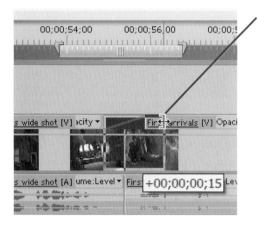

Hover the cursor over the right edge of the transition until the trim cursor appears.

Hold down the mouse button and drag the edge of transition to the right, watching the information window until you've added 15 frames (+00;00;00;15) to the transition.

Release the mouse.

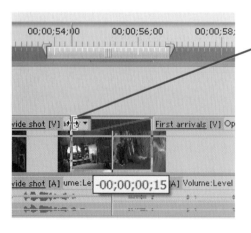

Now let's get the other side.

Hover the cursor over the left edge of the transition until the trim cursor appears.

Watching the information window, hold down the mouse button and drag until you've extended the transition 15 frames (-00;00;00;15) to the left.

Release the mouse.

Now preview again. If playback is choppy, it's because you need to render again, as noted by the re-appearance of the now familiar red bar.

change transition

Come to think of it, this dissolve is looking a bit plain. My movie is a birthday party, so perhaps I should liven it up a bit.

I'll try this Sphere transition. Same drill as before.

Click the new transition.

Hold down the mouse button and drag the transition to the intersection of the two clips, and drag onto the existing transition.

Release the mouse button.

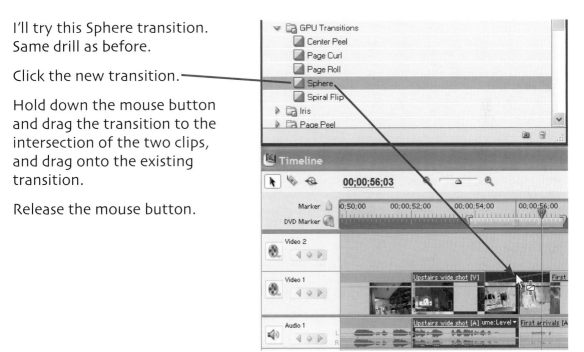

Premiere Elements replaces the Cross Dissolve transition with the Sphere. Note the reappearance of the red line. On my computer, I'll definitely have to render to see this complicated transition play smoothly.

fade audio out and in

You just inserted a video transition. Now you'll work on the audio. You'll apply a Crossfade audio transition that fades out the audio on the clip before the transition—from 100% volume to 0%—and fades it back in on the clip after the transition—from 0% volume to 100%.

Since Premiere Elements stores audio transitions in the Effects folder, just like video transitions, applying audio effects is very similar.

Click the triangle beside the Audio Transitions folder.

Click the triangle beside the Crossfade folder.

Select the Constant Power effect.

Hold down the mouse button and drag the transition to the intersection of the two clips.

Release the mouse button.

Again, if you see a different icon than the two headed top, or get an error message when you release the mouse button, see Transitions In-Depth, later.

Note that you can adjust the duration of audio transitions using the same technique described earlier for video transitions; just click and drag either edge.

transitions in-depth

Knowing how Premiere Elements handles transitions will help you use transitions effectively and understand some of the limitations that Premiere Elements applies during operation. Here's the skinny.

Premiere Elements creates transitions using handles, or frames trimmed from the beginning and end of the clip when setting in and out points or trimming on the Timeline. For example, when creating a cross dissolve transition between two clips, Premiere Elements uses frames trimmed from the end of first clip to blend ahead into the second clip, and frames trimmed from the beginning of the second clip to blend back into the first clip. Problems arise when you don't have any trimmed frames for Premiere Elements to work with.

Let's look at several scenarios using two clips from another project, the lady (my wife) and the tiger.

Scenario 1 - No Handles: Here neither clip has been trimmed at all.

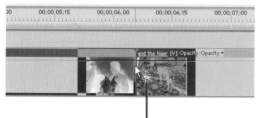

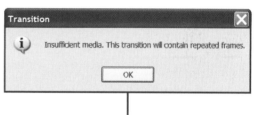

Drag a transition between the two clips and Premiere Elements displays the familiar two headed top.

And also this message when you release the mouse.

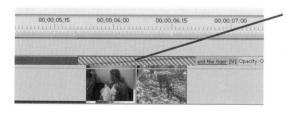

These stripes tell you that the transition contains duplicate frames, which degrades appearance. If possible, trim both clips by at least 15 frames so Premiere Elements can produce the transition with video frames, which will look much smoother.

transitions in-depth (cont.)

Scenario 2 - Love Handles: Here I've trimmed the video of the love of my life, so that video has handles. When I drag the transition between the two clips, Premiere Elements displays the one-sided icon shown below: This icon tells you that Premiere Elements will create a single-sided transition, using frames from the trimmed video of my wife to extend into the tiger video, as shown below.

The single-sided transition only extends into one clip.

While a transition that extends over both clips (a double-sided transition) may look a bit more symmetrical, few viewers will ever notice the difference, so if this is where you end up, that's OK.

As you probably would guess, had I trimmed the tiger video, and not that of my wife, the icon would point in the other direction and the one-sided transition would extend over the first video, not the second.

Scenario 3 - Dual Handles: Here I've trimmed both videos so both have handles. Accordingly, Premiere Elements lets me choose between a double-sided transition (shown below) or a single-sided transition on either side.

The simple answer is to go double-sided and place the transition in the middle. However, as you get more advanced as an editor, you may want to experiment with single-sided transitions and see which looks best to you.

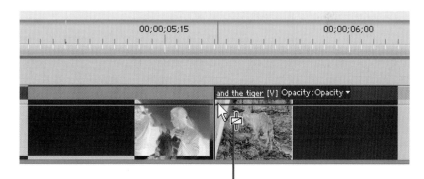

This two-headed top icon...

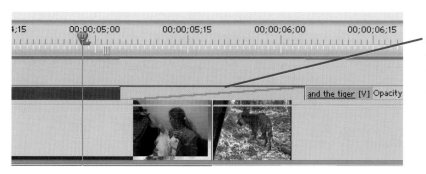

...produces a double-sided transition, which is generally your best choice.

extra bits

insert a cross dissolve p. 49

- Note that you can insert transitions on any track and on single clips, not just between clips. For example, I almost always apply a cross dissolve transition to dissolve into and out of titles.

- Premiere Elements offers several types of dissolves, including the Dip to Black dissolve that fades briefly to black, which is a great effect to use for major scene changes in your movie.

render your transition p. 52

- If you need to drag the Work area bar to render a different region on the timeline, you can either grab it on the three faint lines in the center of the bar, or press Alt on your keyboard and grab it anywhere.

- When you render your transition, Premiere Elements produces the effect and saves the result as a file on disk. After rendering, the red line turns to green.

- Get familiar with these rendering skills, since you'll often use them when applying effects.

5. applying special effects

Special effects are filters that change the appearance of video either to fix under-lying problems or to enhance the video artistically. In both roles, they can help make your video much more watchable.

For example, if your video is too dark, perhaps because the lighting was inadequate during shooting, you can use effects to brighten it up before your viewers see it. In addition, you can use artistic special effects to change the pace and appearance of your video to help retain the viewer's interest.

Make no mistake, however; overusing special effects will likely have the reverse impact, like throwing too many different spices into a casserole. However, as you'll see, a dash here and a pinch there really helps make your movie more pal-atable to your viewers.

Use Premiere Element's effects to adjust color, contrast and brightness.

Or to change your color movie to old style black and white.

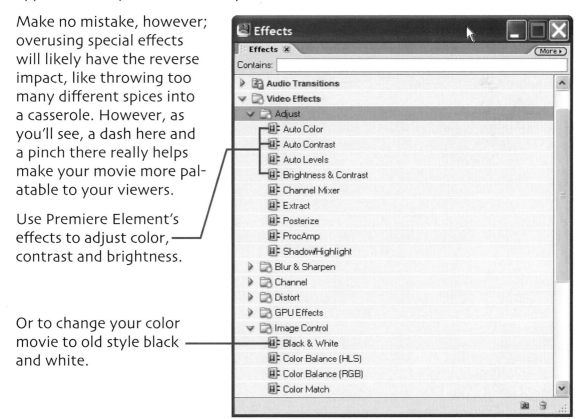

explore effects

In the taskbar on the top right of Premiere Elements, click Effects to load the Effects Workspace.

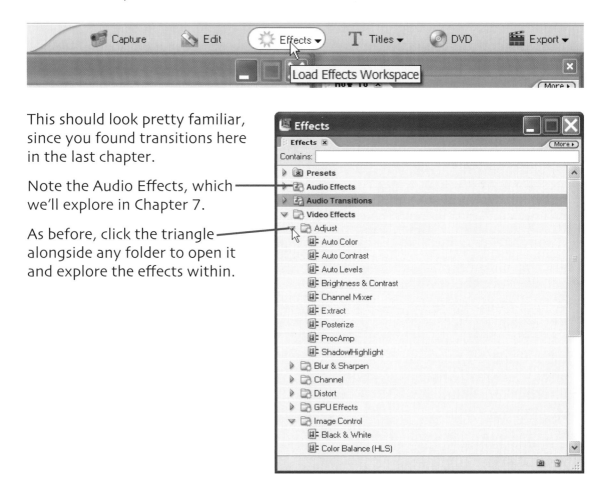

This should look pretty familiar, since you found transitions here in the last chapter.

Note the Audio Effects, which we'll explore in Chapter 7.

As before, click the triangle alongside any folder to open it and explore the effects within.

fade video in and out

I start most movies by fading in, and fade out at the end, which are generally considered effects. However, with Premiere Elements, you fade in or out by applying the dissolve transition to the beginning or end of a clip.

Click the triangle beside the Video Transitions folder.

Click the triangle next to the Dissolve folder.

Click and drag the Cross Dissolve transition to the first clip in the Timeline.

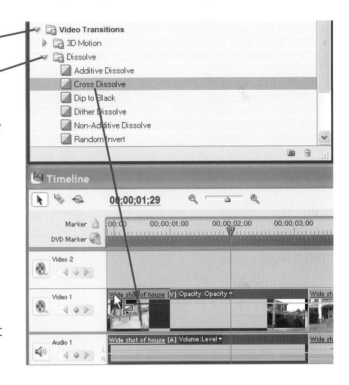

Release your mouse button.

Premiere Elements will fade that clip in from black.

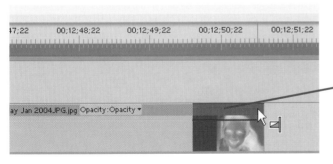

Use the same technique to apply a dissolve transition to the last clip on the Timeline, and Premiere Elements will fade that clip to black.

To extend the duration of either the fade in or fade out effect, click and drag the edge to the desired duration.

effects workspace

To apply and configure effects, you'll have to open the Effect Controls palette, which you haven't seen yet. To minimize clutter in your working space, you should arrange your effects workspace so you can see your content, Effects and Effect Controls tabs, all at the same time. Here's how, assuming that you're already in Effects Mode.

Media window   Effects window

Click and drag the Effects window to the right so you can see the Project tab in the Media window below.

Click and drag the Effects tab from the Effects window over to the Media window tab bar and release.

Media window   Effects tab
tab bar

Premiere Elements combines the two windows into one tab-selectable window.

Now let's add the Effect Controls window.

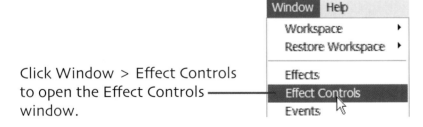

Click Window > Effect Controls to open the Effect Controls window.

Click and drag the Effect Controls tab from the Effect Controls window over the Media window tab bar and release.

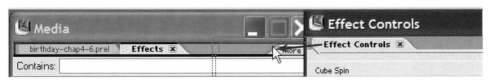

Effect Controls tab   Media window tab bar

This configuration makes it simple to switch back and forth between the Effects tab, where you choose your effects, and the Effect Controls tab, where you configure the effects.

This workspace configuration will appear when you click on the Effects button unless you return to the original configuration by clicking Window > Restore Workspace > Effects.

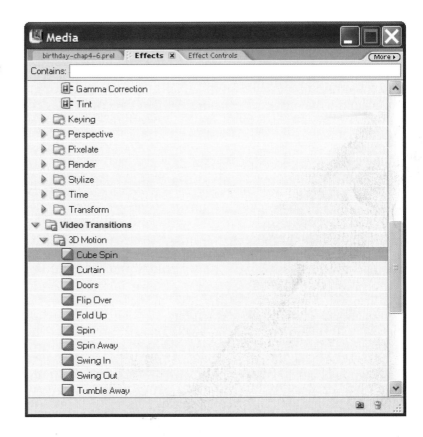

applying special effects

color correct video

One of Premiere Elements' strongest features is color correction, which can improve video shot with improper white balancing and fix other problems. Fortunately for me, the birthday video doesn't have color issues, so I'll switch to another source to show you this feature. Notice the blue color cast on the video below. Find a clip with similar color problems and work along.

You apply all effects the same way.

Select the Auto Color effect in the Adjust folder.

Hold down the mouse button and drag it to the target clip.

Release the mouse button.

Here's the result, a vast improvement!

I typically accept the automatic results that Premiere Element produces, since they're usually excellent.

You should do the same, so we'll hold off looking at the Effect Controls window until we go back to the birthday project and adjust color and brightness.

applying special effects

brighten a video clip

Since we often shoot in less than ideal conditions--either dark rooms or bright sunlight—having to adjust video brightness and contrast is pretty common. Fortunately, Premiere Elements has an excellent Brightness & Contrast adjustment. Find a clip that's either too dark or too light and let's give it a try.

Click the Brightness & Contrast effect and drag it onto a clip that needs brighness or contrast adjustments.

Then click the Effect Controls tab.

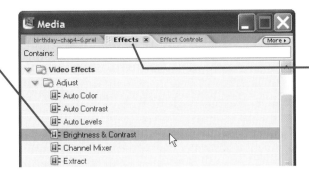

Click the triangle next to the control to open the configuration options.

Adjust Brightness and Contrast by clicking and dragging the number to the left or right.

Or click the triangle beside the option to adjust the slider bar beneath.

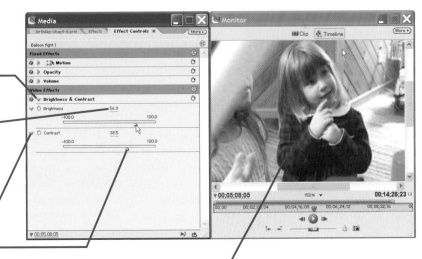

Premiere Elements will preview the adjustments in the Monitor window, assisting your customization options.

When you're done, just move on to your next edit, Premiere Elements saves your adjustments in real time.

common effect tasks

After applying an effect, you can guage its effectiveness by toggling it on and off, which will enable and disable the effect in the Monitor window.

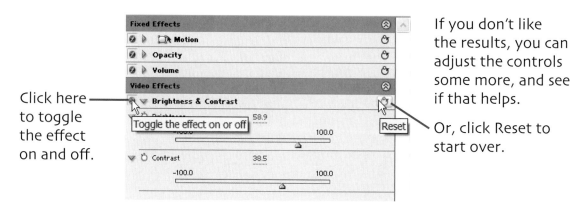

Click here to toggle the effect on and off.

If you don't like the results, you can adjust the controls some more, and see if that helps.

Or, click Reset to start over.

You may decide to simply delete the effect. Here's how.

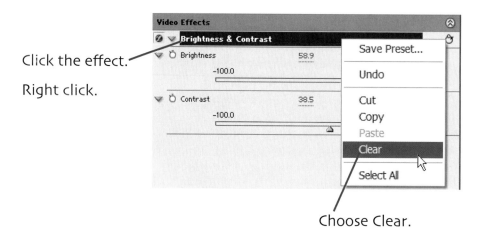

Click the effect.

Right click.

Choose Clear.

save a preset

Most of the time, when you have to color correct or adjust the brightness of one clip in a project, you have to adjust several others as well. Premiere Elements simplifies this process by allowing you to save a preset, which is essentially the effect and the customized parameters.

Here's how to save the brightness and contrast parameters you just applied to your video.

Right click the effect.

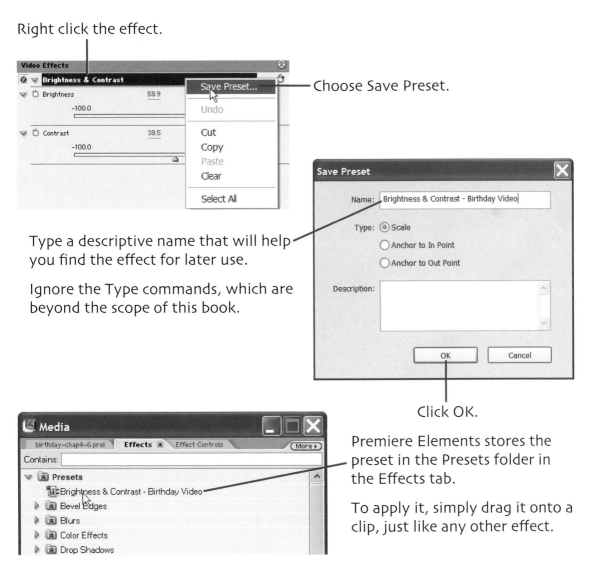

Choose Save Preset.

Type a descriptive name that will help you find the effect for later use.

Ignore the Type commands, which are beyond the scope of this book.

Click OK.

Premiere Elements stores the preset in the Presets folder in the Effects tab.

To apply it, simply drag it onto a clip, just like any other effect.

change playback speed

I use this effect a lot, generally to increase playback speed, but sometimes to slow it down as well. In my movie, I have a sequence of guests walking down the stairs to eat that was just begging to be sped up, since folks walking at double speed (especially to eat cake) looks pretty funny. Find a sequence in your movie where there's a lot of action and try the same thing. When you preview, the audio will probably sound funny as well, as it will when sped up or slowed down, but you'll learn how to mute a clip in Chapter 7.

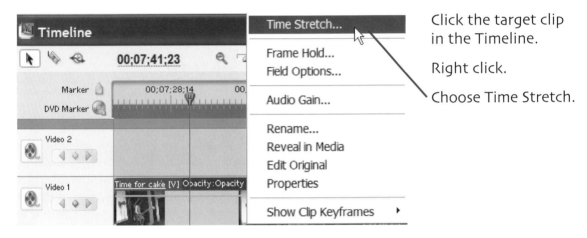

Click the target clip in the Timeline.

Right click.

Choose Time Stretch.

Enter the desired speed.

I choose 200%, which doubles the speed, while 50% would create a slow motion effect at half speed.

I'll be muting this clip, so I don't check Maintain Audio Pitch. Give this a try if you're keeping your audio, but be sure to listen to the audio to make sure it's not too distorted.

Click OK when you're done.

applying special effects

As you learned last chapter, the red line in the Work Area bar indicates that Premiere Elements needs to render the effect to play at full speed. Use the procedure described in Render Your Transition in Chapter 4 to render the effect.

The red line means rendering may be necessary for full speed playback.

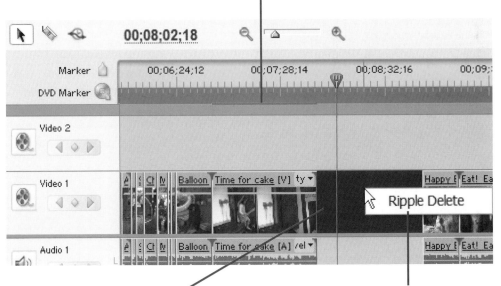

When you double the speed of a clip, you cut its duration in half, which is why there's a gap behind the clip I just speeded up.

To delete the gap, right click and choose Ripple Delete.

adjust image size

When you add a digital picture to a project, Premiere Elements displays the complete image, without scaling which prevents distortion.

For example, Premiere Elements inserted this picture in its entirety, placing black bars on the sides to completely fill the picture.

What I'd like to do is zoom into my daughters and eliminate the black bars. If you have any pictures you'd like to adjust in your project, work with me.

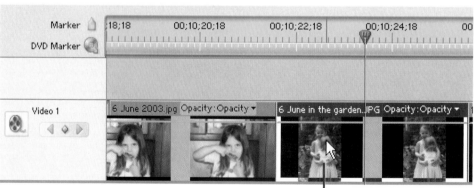

Double click the image in the Timeline to make it active.

Now make the adjustments to the image. Click the Effect Controls tab.

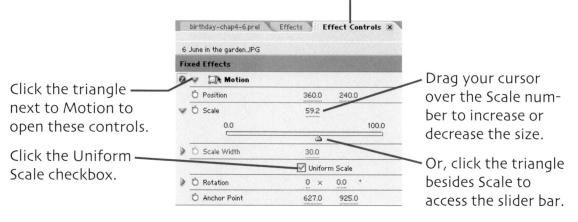

Click the triangle next to Motion to open these controls.

Click the Uniform Scale checkbox.

Drag your cursor over the Scale number to increase or decrease the size.

Or, click the triangle besides Scale to access the slider bar.

Now let's move the image around to get the best framing.

Click the image in the Monitor window to make it active.

Hold down your mouse button, and drag the image to the desired location (if necessary).

It will probably take several Scale and positioning adjustments to get it right, so experiment until you get the result you want.

add motion to images

Once you've learned to adjust image size, adding motion to your images is a snap. Basically, you choose a starting position, then choose an ending position. To do this, you'll use keyframes, or the beginning and end points for the motion effect.

I'll add motion to this image, starting here and then zooming in for a close up.

As before, start by double clicking the image in the Timeline to make it active.

Click the Effect Controls tab.

Click Show/Hide Timeline View to open the Effects Timeline.

Drag the Effect Current Time Indicator all the way to the left (to the beginning of the clip).

Adjust Scale and Position paramers to your start position.

Click the small clock next to Position and Scale. This sets a key frame at the start of the clip.

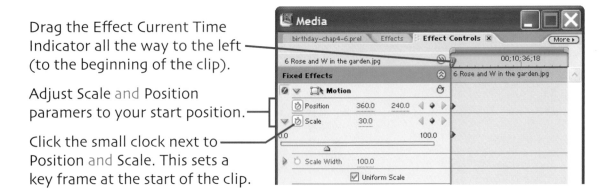

Drag the Effect Current Time Indicator all the way to the right (to the end of the clip).

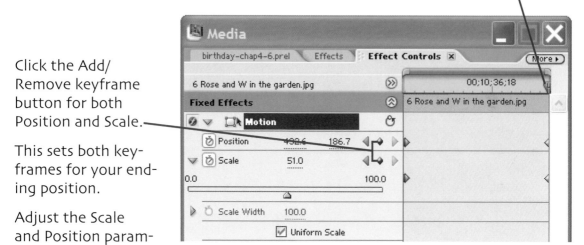

Click the Add/ Remove keyframe button for both Position and Scale.

This sets both keyframes for your ending position.

Adjust the Scale and Position parameters to your ending position.

When Premiere Elements renders your final movie, it will produce all frames required to move from the position at the first keyframe, shown on the previous page, to the position of the final keyframe, shown in this figure.

Adding motion is a great way to make your pictures more interesting to watch (just ask Ken Burns, who produced several prime time shows using these techniques).

extra bits

explore effects p. 62

- Premiere Elements has a great effect called ShadowHighlight that can help fix video shot with a backlight (like a window or spotlight).

- As you probably guessed, we barely scratched the surface of Premiere Elements' Effect Capabilities. There are many, many other effects which you apply and configure just like those you worked with in this chapter.

- The best approach for applying artistic effects is to match the effects (or lack of effects) with the movie or scene. For example, I apply lots of effects to the Meeting and Greeting scene in this movie, which is backed by some pretty wild music, to create a music video-like effect. Beyond that one scene, I speed up one clip to double speed, and that's it for artistic effects.

add motion to images p. 74

- Premiere Elements has some presets that can add motion to images in the Vertical Image Pans and Vertical Image Zooms folders in the Presets folder. Though easy to apply (just click and drag), they never quite give me the result I really want. That's why it's better to learn how to create them yourself.

- You can apply multiple keyframes to a single image for more complicated moving effects, and apply keyframes to most Premiere Elements effects. This adds tremendous design flexibility to the program.

applying special effects

6. creating titles

Titles are text-based frames that can appear full screen on a video track or super-imposed over video clips or digital pictures. I generally use titles in at least three places in my video productions.

First, I open each movie with a title so the viewer knows what he or she will be watching. I also usually insert titles at scene changes, primarily to let the viewer know what's coming and that the movie is, in fact, moving along. Finally, I close most projects with closing credits.

Premiere Elements includes some amazing templates that make it simple to add high quality titles to your movie. If you prefer to design from scratch, you'll be delighted with the styles and tools included with the Title Designer.

Either way, there's nothing like a great title to begin a movie.

create an opening title

Let's start by adding an opening title to your project.

Drag the Current Time Indicator to the beginning of the timeline.

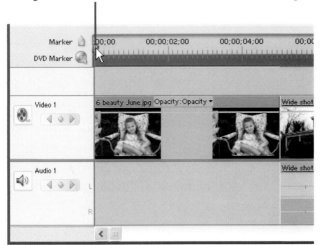

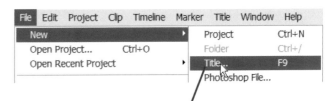

From the Premiere Elements main menu, choose File > New > Title.

Premiere Elements opens the Title Designer displaying the video at the Current Time Indicator. I wanted my opening title to combine a picture of my daughter and a Premiere Elements Template, so before creating the title, I dragged an image to the start of the timeline.

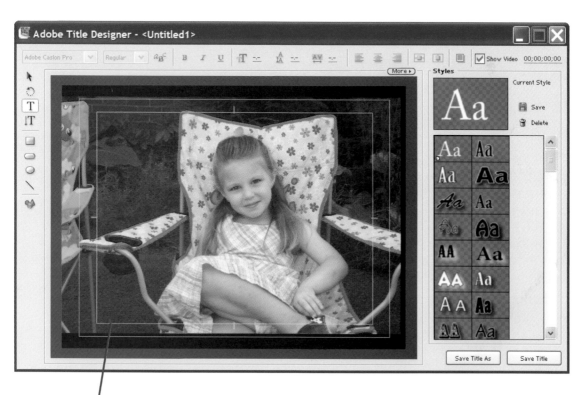

The inner box is the "Title Safe" zone, reflecting the fact that TV sets cut off the outer edges of the screen during display. When creating DVDs to watch on a TV set, make sure your titles are inside this zone, otherwise they may not be completely viewable. Since computers show the entire video window, edges and all, you can ignore the Title Safe zone when producing a movie strictly for computer playback.

The outer box is called Action Safe, which you can ignore when creating your titles.

creating titles

choose a template

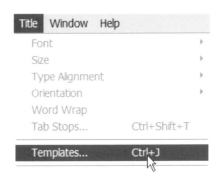

Click Title > Templates to open the Templates window.

Click the triangles on the left to open folders and subfolders. Note that each menu group has multiple titles you can use in different places in your movie.

Many templates also have corresponding DVD templates so you can produce a consistent look throughout your production. See Chapter 8, Creating DVDs, for further information.

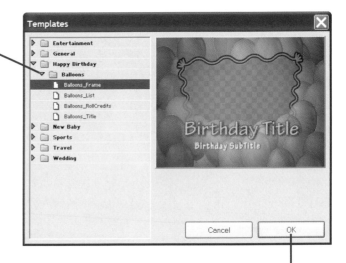

Choose the desired template and click OK.

Premiere Elements inserts the template into the new title.

This is an "overlay" title because the title displays over a still image or video in the background.

customize a template

Now let's customize the template for Whatley.

Click and drag your cursor over the text you wish to edit.

Ruh Roh, Scooby Doo. my text is too large which is why Birthday is truncated.

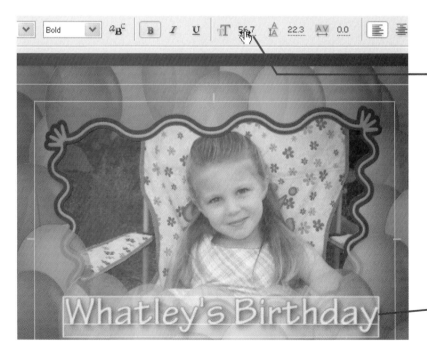

With the text still highlighted, click the font size and drag it to the left to make it smaller (as required here) or to the right to make it larger.

Now the title is safely within the Title Safe zone.

save your title

You'll probably have to drag your text around after resizing to make it fit better within the title. Click this cursor to drag your text.

If you decide to get creative, click here to rotate your text.

Click here to create new text for your title.

Click here to make your new text vertical.

When finished customizing your title, click Save Title.

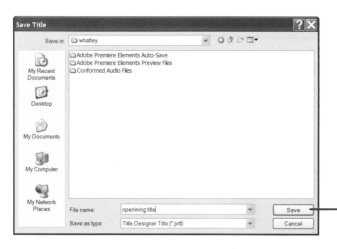

Premiere Elements defaults to the folder where you saved your project file, which is fine.

Name your title something recognizable like "opening title" so you can easily find it later in the Media window.

Then click Save.

Premiere Elements closes the Save Title window and returns to the Title Designer. You can start working on another title, or click the X in the upper right to close the window and return to editing.

Let's create some additional titles, then drag them into the project.

create a custom title

I like Premiere Elements opening title template, but prefer a different look for the titles I'll use between scenes. If you want to create your own titles too, follow along.

The initial steps are the same; move the Current Time Indicator to the target position on the timeline, then open the Title Designer. Let's take it from there.

When creating overlay titles, I usually create a translucent background box behind the text so that it's easy to read over the background video.

To start, click the Rectangle tool on the top left of the Title Designer.

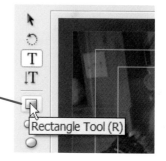

Click and draw the rectangle in the middle of the screen.

White doesn't work for me; to customize the color, right click and choose color properties.

Lots of options here, but let's keep it simple. Dark gray backgrounds make text easy to read, irrespective of the video behind it.

Choose gray by dragging this circle to the desired color.

Or, if you're mathematically minded, you can click and enter 50 for the R, G, and B values.

However you get there, click OK to accept the color.

set opacity

Now make the background translucent with the opacity control.

Click the (now dark gray) rectangle.

Right click and choose Transform > Opacity.

Type a value of 65% and click OK.

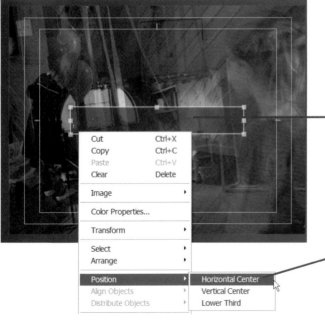

Here's our title background, ready for text.

To precisely set positioning within the frame, right click the rectangle and choose Position, then the desired positioning. To set this title's position, I chose both Horizontal and Vertical Center.

choose a text style

Now choose a style and insert the title text. Note that I chose the same style used in the opening title template so my titles look consistent.

Click the Type Tool.   Click the desired style.

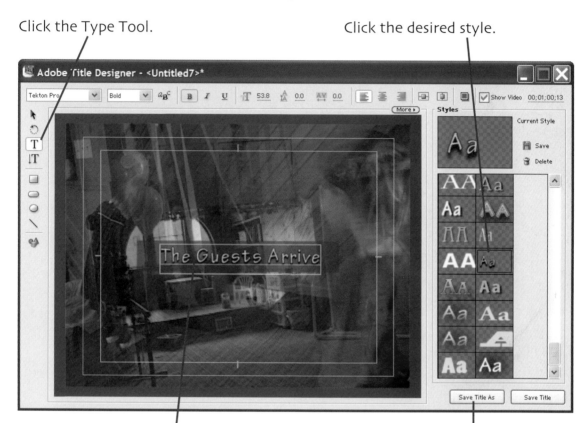

Click in background rectangle and type the desired text.

Click Save to save the title. To produce multiple titles using the common background, type the desired text, use Save As to save the title under a different name, then repeat as necessary.

create closing credits

Closing credits add a nice professional touch to your movie. You know the drill by this point, move the Current Time Indicator to the desired title position, open the Title Designer, then click Title > Templates.

Here's the template I want use. You choose yours.

Click OK after making your selection.

Add your own closing credits.

Then click More and choose Roll and Crawl options.

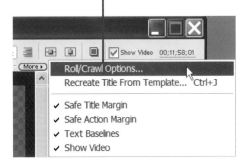

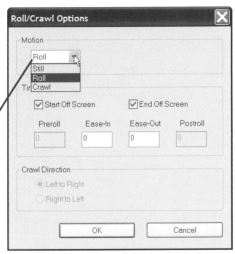

Choose Roll for your title, and accept all other defaults.

Click OK to return to the Title Designer and then save the title as usual.

insert titles

Premiere Elements stores all saved titles in the Media window.

To insert the title, select it in the Media window.

Then drag it to the target position.

Drag overlay titles, like this opening title, to the track above the background video or still image. Usually, this is Video 2.

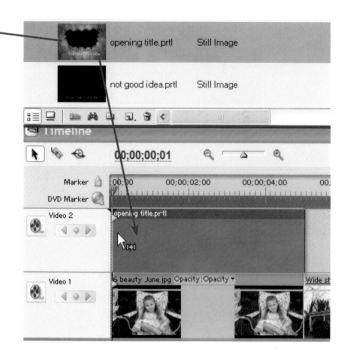

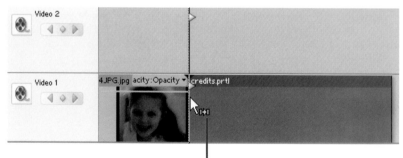

In contrast, drag full screen titles, like our credits title, to Video 1.

common title tasks

Inserted titles have the same duration as still images—here five seconds.

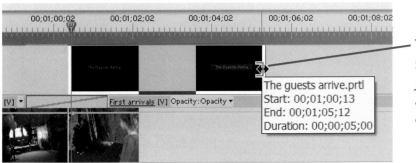

To lengthen or shorten your title, just grab an edge and pull to the desired duration.

The guests arrive.prtl
Start: 00;01;00;13
End: 00;01;05;12
Duration: 00;00;05;00

I usually insert a dissolve transition before and after all titles.

To insert a dissolve, open the effects window.

Click the Cross Dissolve effect.

Drag it down to the edge of the title.

Repeat as necessary.

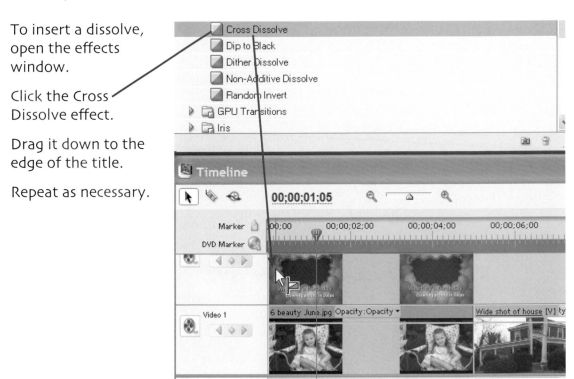

To preview your titles, see the instructions at Render Your Transitions, on page 52.

creating titles

extra bits

choose a text style p. 85

- Text styles included in title templates are also in the style library. If you use a template for some titles, and build others from scratch, you can use the same font style and maintian consistency by choosing it from the style library.

create closing credits p. 86

- You can set the speed of the closing credits and other scrolling titles by adjusting title duration on the timeline. Making the title shorter will speed the credits up; making it longer will slow them down.

7. using audio

Adding background music that your audience enjoys is the easiest way to help them enjoy watching your movies; worst case, if they don't like what they're seeing, their toes will be tapping.

Premiere Elements makes it easy to add background music to your projects. Then, you can either mute the audio captured with the camcorder so that your viewers can hear only the music, or mix the two tracks so the audience can hear both. In my project I'll do both.

This 11-minute project has five background music tracks (including the one inserted beneath the slide show). That's about right in my book (and this is my book).

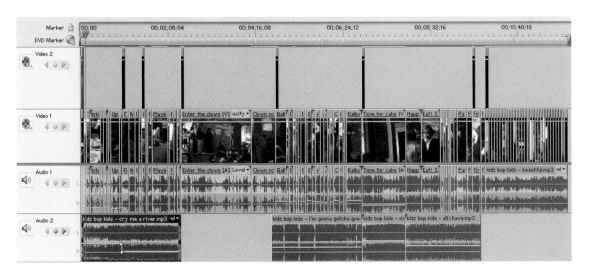

add background music

Let's start by inserting some background music into the project. Find some music appropriate for your project and import it into the Media window as described in Chapter 2.

In the Media window, click the audio track.

Drag the audio clip to track Audio 2.

Release your mouse button.

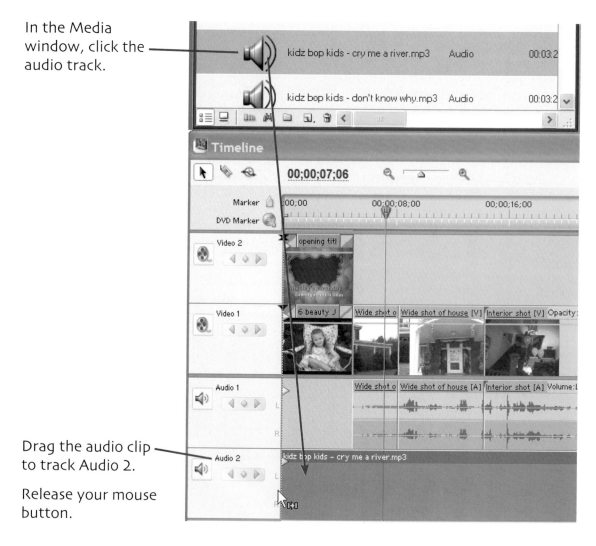

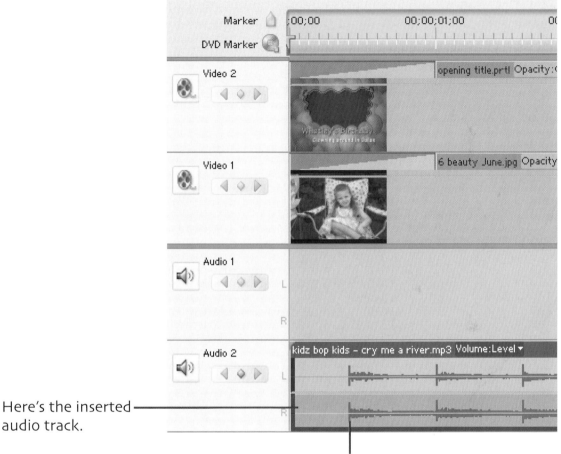

Here's the inserted audio track.

The flat line at the start of the audio track indicates that it's silent there. The silence is less than a second long, but to make the music start right away, the silence needs to be trimmed off.

trim audio clips

You trim audio clips like any other content: you simply grab an edge and drag it to the desired length.

Click the clip on the Timeline to select it.

Hover the mouse over the edge until the trim cursor appears.

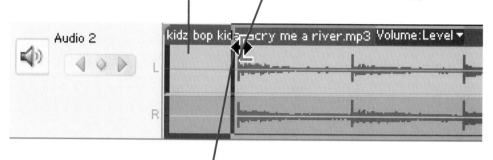

Click the mouse button and drag to the right (or left if you're trimming the end of the clip).

Release the mouse at the desired location.

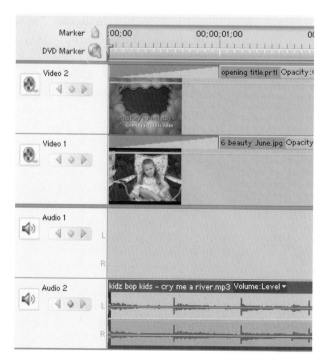

Premiere Elements automatically "snaps" the audio track back so that there's no gap left from the trim. If you ever get an undesired gap on the audio track, click the gap, right click and choose Ripple Delete, and Premiere Elements will delete the gap.

using audio

the big picture

Here's a big-picture view of how I want the background music to integrate with the audio from the camcorder during the opening scenes of the movie.

Each track displays a waveform, which is a graphical representation of the audio file.

A small waveform indicates low volume.

A larger waveform indicates higher volume.

A mix of high and low volumes often indicates someone talking.

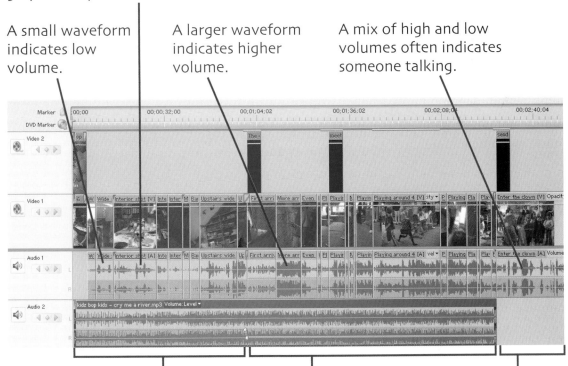

These are my outdoor and indoor establishing shots, which give the viewer the lay of the land. Here I want to turn off the audio on the Audio 1 track (captured with the video) and solely use the background music track.

Here guests are arriving. Now I want to hear the conversation with the music track much lower in the background.

Now the clown starts performing, so I want no music at all so the audience can hear the show.

Your project will likely have scenes with similar characteristics: some where you want just the background music, some where you want just the audio that is part of your video, and some where you want a mix of both. Follow along to see how to make this happen.

mute audio 1

Find a clip or clips in your project that you want to mute (turn down the audio to 0%). I'm muting the Audio 1 track for all clips in the opening scene of my movie.

Click the clip you want to mute.

Right click.

Choose Show Clip Keyframes > Volume > Level.

Hover your mouse over the Volume graph until you see the double-arrow cursor.

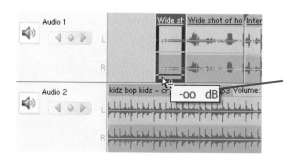

Drag the Volume Graph down until you see the— infinity sign, indicating zero volume.

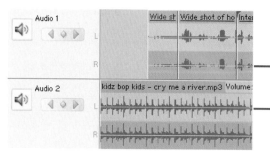

All the clips on Audio 1 (from the camcorder) are muted.

While the background music clip is at full volume.

normalize audio 1

In the next scene, I'll mix the conversation on Audio 1 with the music on Audio 2. This involves two steps.

First, I will normalize the audio on all relevant clips on Audio 1. If the clips are too low, this increases their audio volume to the maximum level possible without introducing distortion. If the audio is too loud, it reduces volume to minimize distortion.

After normalizing Audio 1, I'll adjust the volume of Audio 2 so I can comfortably hear both the conversations and the background music.

Find a captured clip with audio you wish to include in your movie.

Click the clip.

Right click and choose Audio Gain.

Click Normalize in the Clip Gain window.

Premiere Elements computes the normalization level (here 4.7 decibels).

Click OK. Repeat as necessary on other clips.

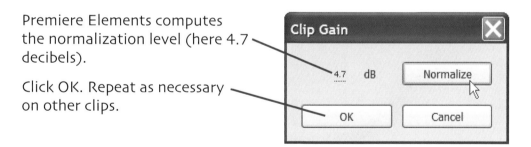

adjust the volume

After normalization, we can't increase the volume on Audio 1 without distorting the audio, so to mix Audio 1 and Audio 2, we'll reduce the volume in Audio 2. However, I want to reduce the volume at the start of scene 2 (where guests arrive), not during the earlier establishing shots. Here's how we'll get that done.

Drag the Current Time Indicator to where you need lower volume.

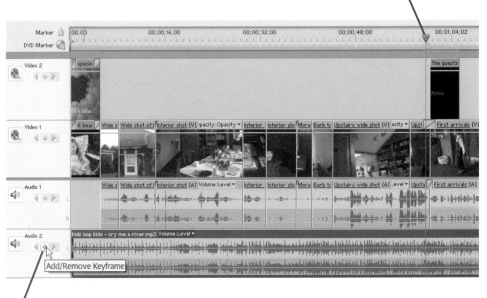

Click Add/Remove Keyframe.

Then move the Current Time Indicator a second or so backwards and click Add/Remove Keyframe again.

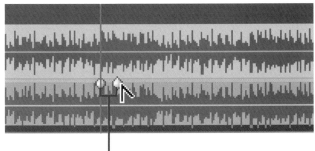

Your Audio 2 track should have two keyframes.

Click and drag the second keyframe down to the desired volume (-10 decibels is usually a good starting point).

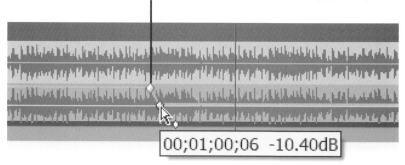

00;01;00;06 -10.40dB

Preview and adjust as necessary.

To raise audio volume later in the Timeline, create two additional keyframes and drag the second keyframe higher.

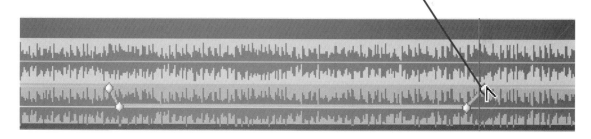

add audio effects

Premiere Elements has a useful library of audio effects, including a balance effect that controls the respective volumes of the left and right audio channels and the DeNoiser, which removes noise from audio clips converted from analog sources.

See Effects Workspace on page 64 to learn how to set up your interface as shown in this screen.

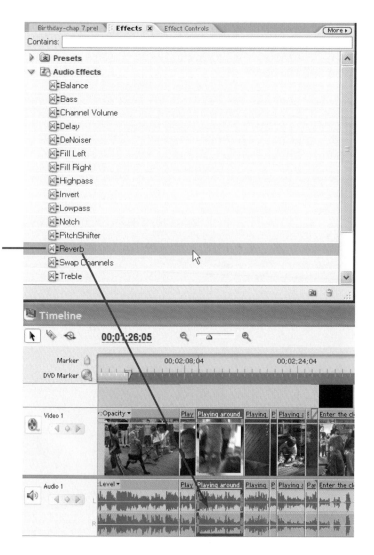

To add an effect...

...drag the effect onto the target audio track.

Release your mouse button.

fade audio

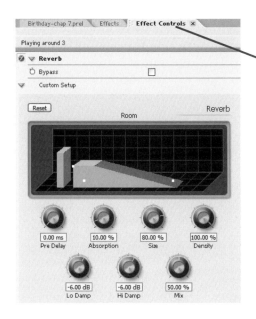

Customize your audio effects by clicking the Effect Controls tab.

Here I'm tinkering with the Reverb effect that makes a clip sound like it was recorded in an auditorium or other setup.

I always fade my audio in at the start of each movie, and fade out at the end.

If you'd like to do the same, open the Audio transitions folder in the Effects panel, then the Crossfade folder.

Then click and drag the Constant Power effect to the start and end of the audio track.

extra bits

add background music p. 92

- I use Windows Media Player to copy audio tracks from a CD-ROM so I can include them in a movie. It's very simple to use, but if you want step-by-step guidance, see Microsoft Windows Movie Maker 2: Visual QuickStart Guide from Peachpit Press for details.

normalize audio 1 p. 97

- There's no reason to normalize tracks you've ripped from CD or other professionally sourced music tracks because they're normalized during production.

8. creating dvds

One of Premiere Elements strongest features is the ability to quickly and easily produce DVDs that look great and are easy for your viewers to navigate. As you'll see, you can choose a template that matches the titles that you inserted, providing professional quality consistency.

You can also create Hollywood-like scene selection menus that let your viewers jump directly to the scene they'd like to see. You'll need a DVD recorder and the appropriate recordable media, of course, but if you're ready to burn, baby burn, let's get going.

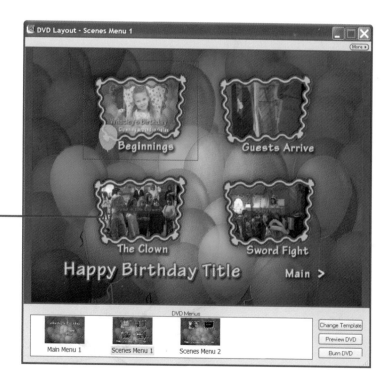

Here's one of those great looking menus I was talking about.

Want to see the clown's act? Just click The Clown button and you go directly there.

Once you set a scene marker, which we'll do next, Premiere Elements builds these scene menus automatically.

insert scene markers

Scene markers allow your viewers to jump directly to marked scenes. For example, I'll insert markers at the start of the movie, when guests start arriving, when the clown starts performing and the year in review slide show, among other scenes, so my viewers and I can quickly access them.

Think about scenes in your movie you want viewers to be able to directly jump to and work with me.

Move the Current Time Indicator to the target location. Right click.

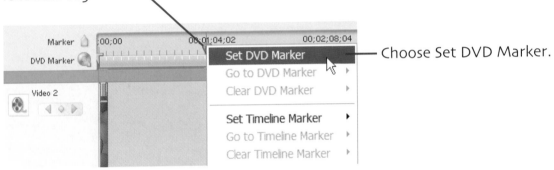

Choose Set DVD Marker.

Type the desired name. Keep it short to avoid overlapping buttons in the DVD menu.

Select your marker type. I'm going with Scene Marker; see Extra Bits at the end of this chapter for an explanation of the other choices.

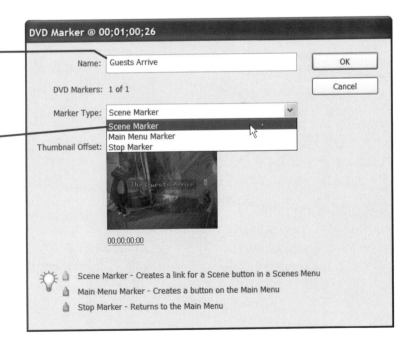

customize thumbnail

Each scene menu contains button frames with a video thumbnail. Premiere Elements uses the first frame of the scene by default, but sometimes that's not the best choice. Here's how you change the thumbnail to a new frame:

Hover your cursor over the thumbnail timecode until a hand and double arrow appear.

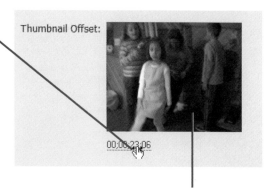

Thumbnail Offset:

00;00;23;06

Drag the double arrow to the right until the frame you'd like to use appears. This is Whatley's best friend Sarah. Let's give her her own thumbnail.

Click OK in the DVD Maker window (see previous page) to set the marker.

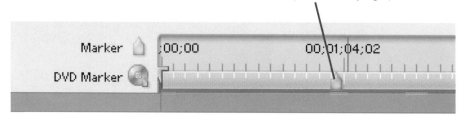

Marker ⬜ ;00;00   00;01;04;02

DVD Marker 🔵

Note that you can move the marker by clicking and dragging it, or open the DVD Marker window to change the name or thumbnail image by double clicking the marker.

You can delete the marker by right clicking and choosing Clear DVD Marker.

Set DVD Marker
Go to DVD Marker ▸
Clear DVD Marker ▸
Set Timeline Marker ▸
Go to Timeline Marker ▸
Clear Timeline Marker ▸

choose a template

All Premiere Elements menus come from templates.
Let's choose one for your DVD.

In the taskbar on the top right of
the Premiere Elements screen, click
DVD to load the DVD Workspace.

Here's the DVD
Layout window.

This shows the first
menu that DVD viewers
will see, which always
has at least two
buttons.

The Play Movie button
plays the movie from
start to finish.

The Scene Selection
button takes the viewer
to the scene selection
menus.

Most Premiere Elements templates produce Scene menus with four scenes per
menu. Because I inserted six scene markers, Premiere Elements automatically
created two scene menus (Scene Menu 1 and 2). The program also automatically
creates all links between menus.

creating dvds

I'm not crazy about this menu, so I'm going to change the template. On the bottom right of the DVD Layout window, click Change Template (see previous page).

Click here to create a DVD without menus. Called an Auto-play DVD, upon loading, it simply starts playing the movie, no muss, no fuss.

I prefer a menu for my productions, so I'll click here.

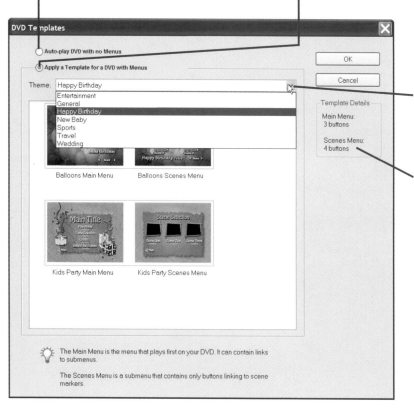

Click the drop down box to view Premiere Elements' templates.

Click the Template you like and Premiere Elements describes it here.

Click OK (on the top right) after making your selection.

customize your menus

This template matches some of the titles I inserted into the video, which is good, but the text title is too long.

Double click the title text to open the Change Text dialog.

You can only type new text, you can't change font, font size, or color.

Click the other menus here to review them.

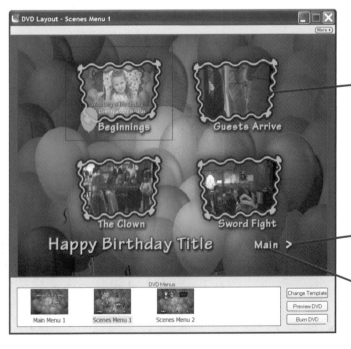

Here is Scenes Menu 1.

If you need to adjust the button title or thumbnail, double click the thumbnail and Premiere Elements will open the DVD Marker menu shown on Page 104.

Here's what your viewer will click to jump to Scenes Menu 2.

And they'll click here to return to the main menu.

creating dvds

preview your dvd

After finalizing your menus, preview your production before recording the DVD. Check that you've spelled all of your buttons correctly, that your capitalization is consistent between buttons and that your chapter markers are at the desired location.

To get started, click Preview DVD in the bottom right of the DVD Layout window.

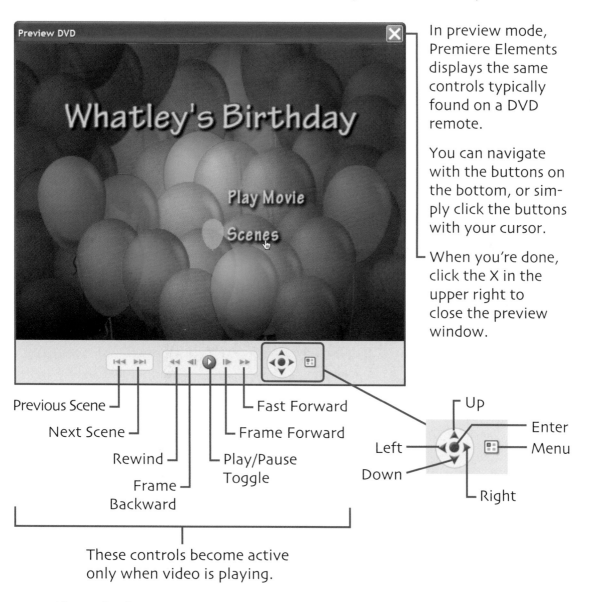

In preview mode, Premiere Elements displays the same controls typically found on a DVD remote.

You can navigate with the buttons on the bottom, or simply click the buttons with your cursor.

When you're done, click the X in the upper right to close the preview window.

Previous Scene

Next Scene

Rewind

Frame Backward

Play/Pause Toggle

Frame Forward

Fast Forward

Up

Enter

Left

Menu

Down

Right

These controls become active only when video is playing.

record your disc

Now let's burn the DVD. Click Burn DVD on the bottom right of the DVD Layout menu.

Check the Disc radio button.

Type the Disc Name.

If you have multiple burners, select the target burner.

Enter the desired number of copies.

Click the Fit Contents checkbox.

Check the appropriate TV standard.

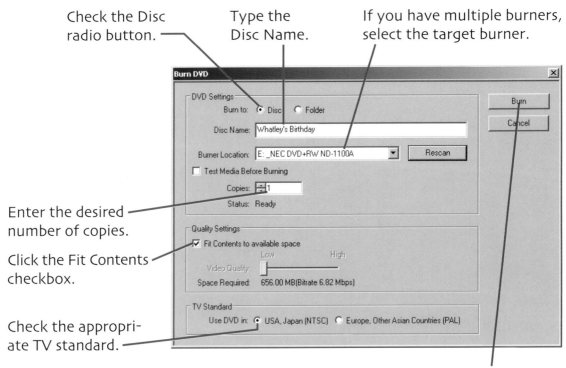

After selecting all options, click Burn.

Premiere Elements displays the Burn DVD Progress status screen.

Burn time relates to project length and speed of your computer, but longer projects can easily take a few hours.

After successfully recording the disc, Premiere Elements will eject the disc and display Export Completed in the Burn DVD Progress screen.

extra bits

insert scene markers p. 104

- Main Menu Markers place a text link directly on the main menu. Stop Markers stop video playback at that location and return the viewer to the main menu.

- Note that you can add scene markers at any time, before or after choosing a template, and Premiere Elements will automatically update all necessary menus.

record your disc p. 110

- If your button labels are too long, they will overlap and Premiere Elements will open an error window to this effect before burning. To locate the overlapping buttons, click More in the upper right of the DVD Layout window and choose Show Overlapping Menu Buttons.

- Premiere Elements should work with most DVD-recorders, but if it doesn't work with yours, burn the project to a folder, then use software that came with your recorder to record the project to a disc.

- Theoretically, you can produce DVDs with any amount of video, but quality may suffer if you go beyond 80-90 minutes.

9. that's a wrap

In addition to building a DVD, you may want to produce a digital file to play from your hard disk, burn to a CD-ROM to send to a friend or loved one, or post to a web site for downloading. You may also want to produce a file to import into another program for further editing or DVD production. You'll probably also want to record your project back to tape, just to save an archival copy.

To accomplish all these tasks, Premiere Elements can produce a range of output formats including QuickTime, Windows Media, MPEG, and AVI. Fortunately, Premiere Elements makes all of these operations simple, typically with presets like those shown above. No confusing parameters to learn, just click and go.

Let's start by writing your project back to tape. Then we'll explore some of Premiere Elements' other rendering capabilities.

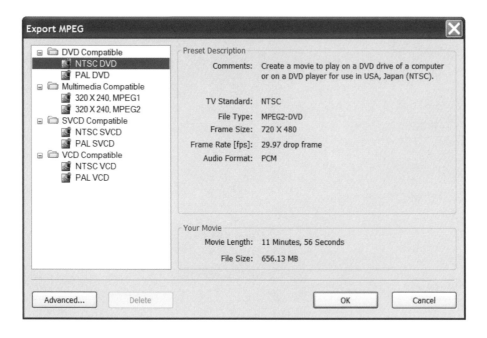

export to tape

All of my video projects start life on DV tape, and end up there as well, since DV tapes are an economical medium to archive the edited version of my movies. Once on DV tape, I can also easily dub a copy to VHS tape for viewers who don't have DVD players or a computer.

To start, go back to Set Up for DV Capture on page 12 and get your DV camera connected in VTR/VCR mode with a DV tape cued to where you wish to start recording. We'll be overwriting any content on the tape, so get a new tape, use an old tape you don't mind overwriting, or cue a tape with sufficient capacity beyond any content you wish to save.

Click Export in the Premiere Elements Taskbar.

Choose To Tape.

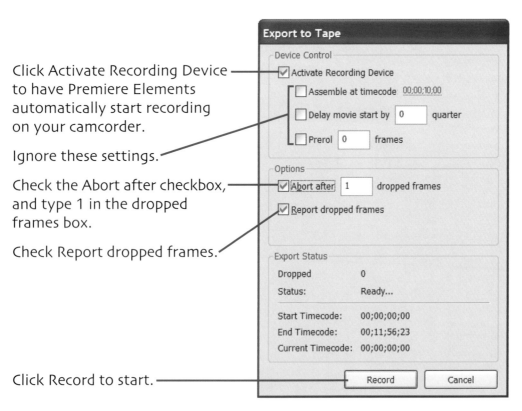

Click Activate Recording Device to have Premiere Elements automatically start recording on your camcorder.

Ignore these settings.

Check the Abort after checkbox, and type 1 in the dropped frames box.

Check Report dropped frames.

Click Record to start.

Before writing to tape, Premiere Elements will render any sections of the timeline as necessary and display this dialog.

Writing to tape is very demanding, and any performance hiccups will produce dropped frames that end the process. Accordingly, it's best not to use the computer for other tasks when writing back to tape.

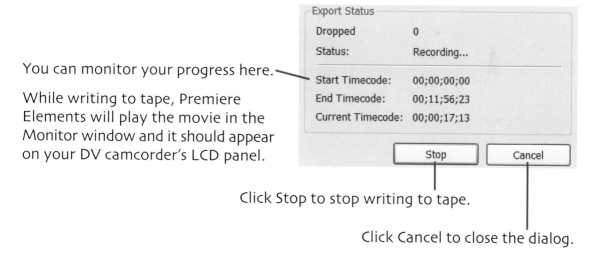

You can monitor your progress here.

While writing to tape, Premiere Elements will play the movie in the Monitor window and it should appear on your DV camcorder's LCD panel.

Click Stop to stop writing to tape.

Click Cancel to close the dialog.

create an mpeg file

If you're trying to produce a DVD with Premiere Elements, you're in the wrong place; go back to Chapter 8. Here, you'll produce MPEG files for including in other programs, especially those that can produce VideoCD and SuperVideoCD discs, which Premiere Elements can't.

The two MPEG Multimedia presets are also your best choice for producing files to play back from your hard drive, or to burn to CD-ROM to send to someone else.

To start, click Export.

Then choose MPEG.

Premiere Elements displays the encoding parameters here.

Click the appropriate preset for your intended use.

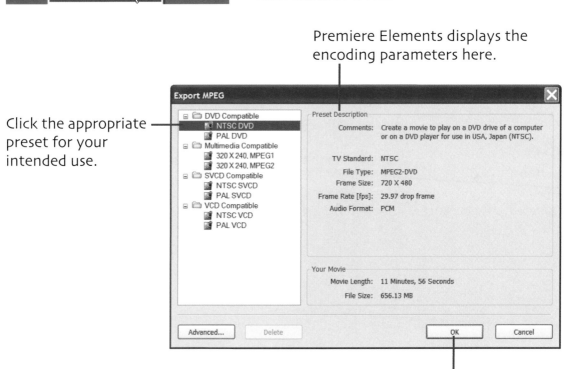

Click OK to start encoding.

that's a wrap

create a quicktime file

QuickTime files are your best option for files to be played on Macintosh computers. Though the files will play on Windows computers as well, viewers on Windows computers may need to download the free QuickTime Player from www.quicktime.com.

QuickTime files work best when they're very large, like movie trailers you may have downloaded from the Internet. Generally, at the Broadband, Dial-up, and Wireless targets shown below, you'll get higher quality results faster creating Windows Media files, rather than QuickTime files. But if your heart is set on a QuickTime file, then here's how to do it.

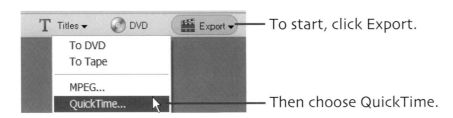 ———— To start, click Export.

———— Then choose QuickTime.

Premiere Elements displays the
encoding parameters here.

Click the appropriate
preset for your
intended use.

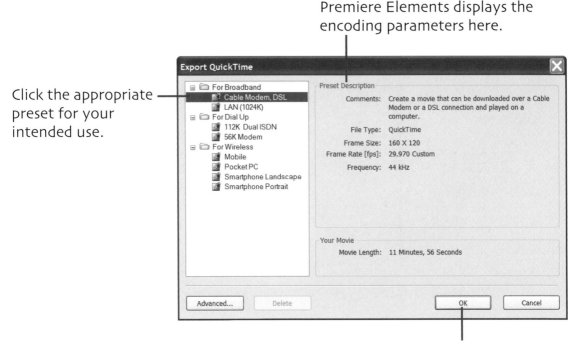

Click OK to start encoding.

create a wmv file

The Windows Media format is very popular for producing files to upload to Web sites or for sharing with other users of the Windows operating system. Typically, when produced for the same target, Windows Media produces larger resolution video (like 320x240 rather than 160x120) that looks better than QuickTime.

Recently, Microsoft released Macintosh players so even Macintosh owners can play Windows Media files. For this reason, Windows Media is my "go-to" compression technology for Broadband, Dial-up, and Wireless applications.

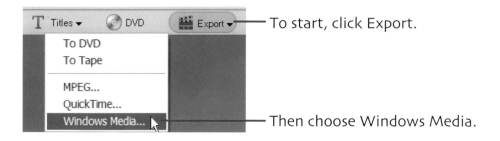 To start, click Export.

Then choose Windows Media.

Premiere Elements displays the encoding parameters here.

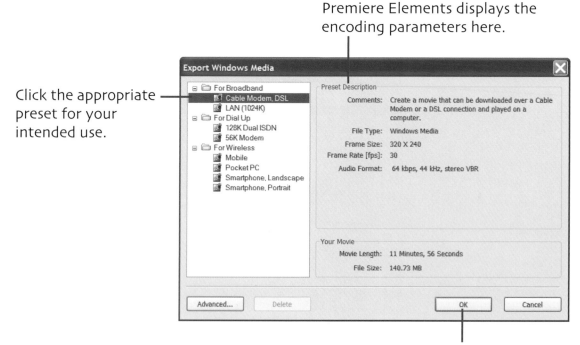

Click the appropriate preset for your intended use.

Click OK to start encoding.

export a dv file

Sometimes you'll want to produce a file you can import into another program, say another DVD authoring program that may offer features that Premiere Elements doesn't. In these instances, the best alternative is to export an AVI file in DV format, which is the highest possible quality file that Premiere Elements can produce. When exporting a DV file, you have to work through several windows of encoding parameters to ensure proper output. We'll start with the general parameters, and work through Video, Keyframe and Rendering, and Audio.

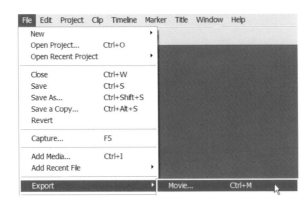

To start, click File > Export > Movie.

Choose the target folder.

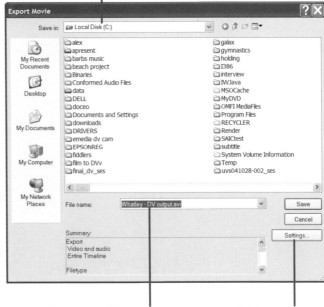

Select the file name.   Click Settings.

export a dv file (cont.)

Choose Microsoft DV AVI for File Type.

Choose either Entire Timeline (shown) or Work Area Bar for Range.

Click General.

Choose both audio and video.

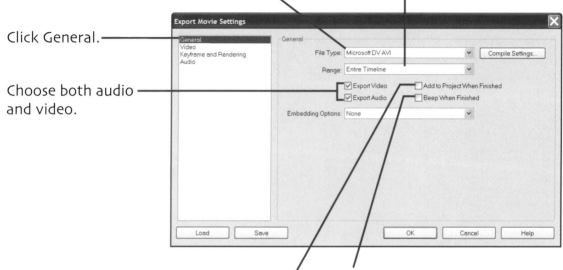

Click this checkbox to add the file to the project once it's produced.

Click this checkbox for Premiere Elements to beep when the file is finished.

Choose DV(NTSC), or click the drop down box and choose DV (PAL) if required.

Click Video.

Leave all other options as shown.

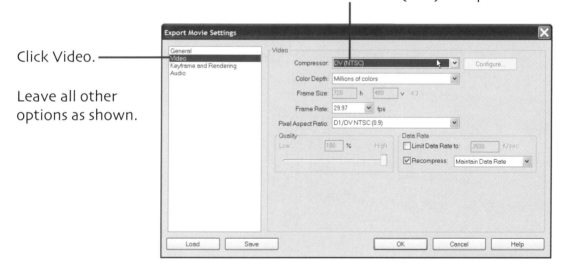

that's a wrap

Click Keyframe and Rendering.

Conform all other options to those shown on this screen.

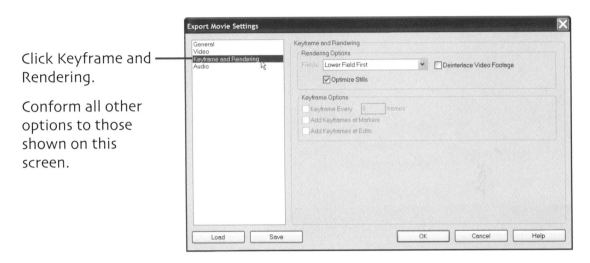

Click Audio.

Conform options to those shown on this screen.

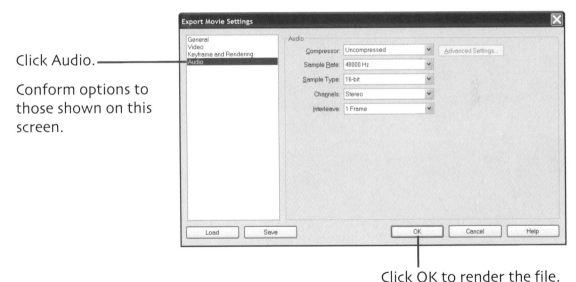

Click OK to render the file.

export a video frame

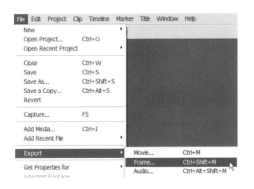

Frequently, you'll want to export frames from your video to email to friends and family.

Start by choosing File > Export > Frame from Premiere Elements main menu.

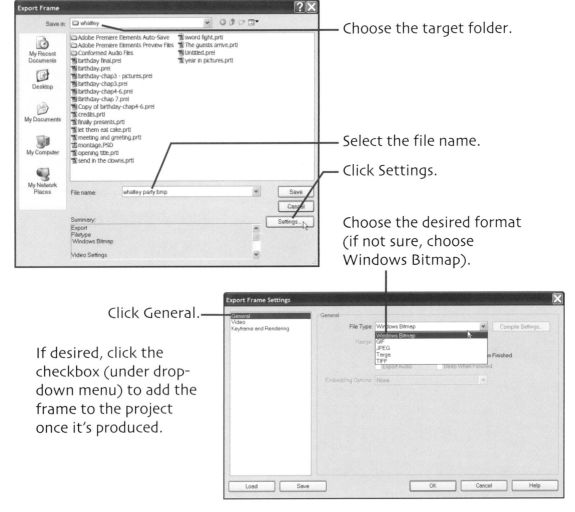

Choose the target folder.

Select the file name.

Click Settings.

Choose the desired format (if not sure, choose Windows Bitmap).

Click General.

If desired, click the checkbox (under drop-down menu) to add the frame to the project once it's produced.

that's a wrap

Click Video. ——————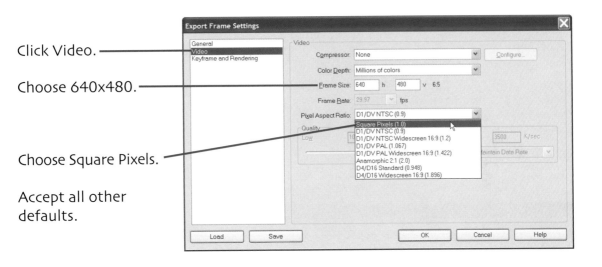

Choose 640x480. ——————

Choose Square Pixels. ——————

Accept all other
defaults.

Click the Deinterlace checkbox.

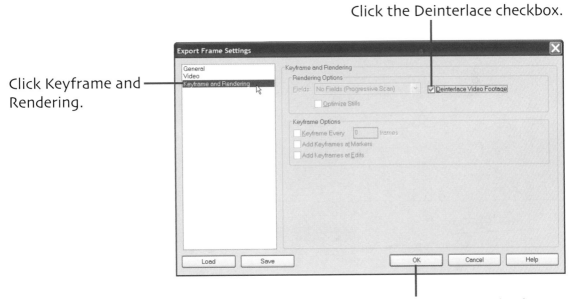

Click Keyframe and ——————
Rendering.

Click OK to produce the frame.

export an audio file

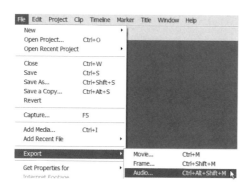

To export an audio file from Premiere Elements, click File > Export > Audio.

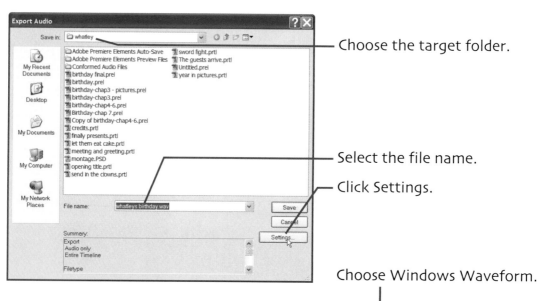

Choose the target folder.

Select the file name.

Click Settings.

Choose Windows Waveform.

Click General.

Choose either Entire Timeline (shown) or Work Area Bar for Range.

Choose other options as desired.

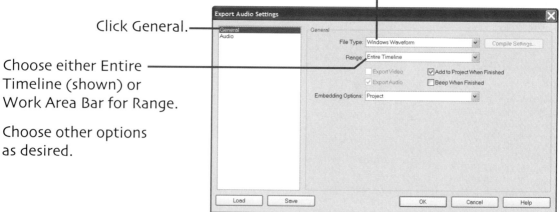

that's a wrap

Click Audio.────────

Conform other options to those shown on the screen.

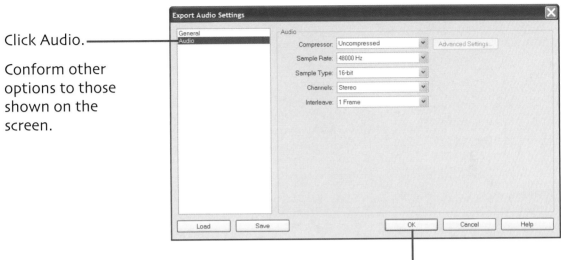

Click OK to produce the audio file.

extra bits

export to tape p. 114

- Premiere Elements may not recognize your camcorder if you set it up while the program is running. If the Export > To Tape menu choice is grayed out, exit and then restart Premiere Elements with the Camcorder connected and in VTR/VCR mode.

- If you're interested in learning more about how to dub your movies from DV to VHS tape, check out Microsoft Windows Movie Maker 2: Visual QuickStart Guide, also published by Peachpit Press, where this process is described in detail.

create an mpeg file p. 116

- Premiere Elements can create video files compatible with Video CD and SuperVideoCD projects, but can't directly produce these types of discs. You'll need a separate authoring program to create Video CDs or SuperVideoCDs.

- If you click the Advanced button in any of Premiere Elements' Export screens, you can access very comprehensive encoding controls. Proceed with caution unless you're an advanced user—since selecting the wrong parameters could produce a file inappropriate for its intended purpose.

export a video frame p. 122

- Video frames exported by Premiere Elements are all fairly low resolution so if used to print pictures larger than 5X7, pixelation may become noticeable.

index

index

index

index

index

index

index

index